Biographies

IN AMERICAN FOREIGN POLICY

Joseph A. Fry, University of Nevada, Las Vegas
Series Editor

The Biographies in American Foreign Policy Series employs the enduring medium of biography to examine the major episodes and themes in the history of U.S. foreign relations. By viewing policy formation and implementation from the perspective of influential participants, the series seeks to humanize and make more accessible those decisions and events that sometimes appear abstract or distant. Particular attention is devoted to those aspects of the subject's background, personality, and intellect that most influenced his or her approach to U.S. foreign policy, and each individual's role is placed in a context that takes into account domestic affairs, national interests and policies, and international and strategic considerations.

The series is directed primarily at undergraduate and graduate courses in U.S. foreign relations, but it is hoped that the genre and format may also prove attractive to the interested general reader. With these objectives in mind, the length of the volumes has been kept manageable, the documentation has been restricted to direct quotes and particularly controversial assertions, and the bibliographic essays have been tailored to provide historiographical assessment without tedium.

Producing books of high scholarly merit to appeal to a wide range of readers is an ambitious undertaking, and an excellent group of authors has agreed to participate. Some have compiled extensive scholarly records while others are just beginning promising careers, but all are distinguished by their comprehensive knowledge of U.S. foreign relations, their cooperative spirit, and their enthusiasm for the project. It has been a distinct pleasure to have been given the opportunity to work with these scholars as well as with Richard Hopper and his staff at Scholarly Resources.

Volumes Published

Lawrence S. Kaplan, *Thomas Jefferson: Westward the Course of Empire* (1999). Cloth ISBN 0-8420-2629-0   Paper ISBN 0-8420-2630-4

Richard H. Immerman, *John Foster Dulles: Piety, Pragmatism, and Power in U.S. Foreign Policy* (1999). Cloth ISBN 0-8420-2600-2 Paper ISBN 0-8420-2601-0

Thomas W. Zeiler, *Dean Rusk: Defending the American Mission Abroad* (2000). Cloth ISBN 0-8420-2685-1   Paper ISBN 0-8420-2686-X

Edward P. Crapol, *James G. Blaine: Architect of Empire* (2000). Cloth ISBN 0-8420-2604-5   Paper ISBN 0-8420-2605-3

David F. Schmitz, *Henry L. Stimson: The First Wise Man* (2001). Cloth ISBN 0-8420-2631-2   Paper ISBN 0-8420-2632-0

Thomas M. Leonard, *James K. Polk: A Clear and Unquestionable Destiny* (2001). Cloth ISBN 0-8420-2646-0   Paper ISBN 0-8420-2647-9

James E. Lewis Jr., *John Quincy Adams: Policymaker for the Union* (2001). Cloth ISBN 0-8420-2622-3   Paper ISBN 0-8420-2623-1

Catherine Forslund, *Anna Chennault: Informal Diplomacy and Asian Relations* (2002). Cloth ISBN 0-8420-2832-3   Paper ISBN 0-8420-2833-1

Lawrence S. Kaplan, *Alexander Hamilton: Ambivalent Anglophile* (2002). Cloth ISBN 0-8420-2877-3   Paper ISBN 0-8420-2878-1

Andrew J. DeRoche, *Andrew Young: Civil Rights Ambassador* (2003). Cloth ISBN 0-8420-2956-7   Paper ISBN 0-8420-2957-5

Jeffrey J. Matthews, *Alanson B. Houghton: Ambassador of the New Era* (2004). Cloth ISBN 0-8420-5050-7   Paper ISBN 0-8420-5051-5

ALANSON B. HOUGHTON

ALANSON B. HOUGHTON

Ambassador of the New Era

JEFFREY J. MATTHEWS

IN AMERICAN FOREIGN POLICY

Number 11

SR BOOKS

SR BOOKS
Lanham • Boulder • New York • Toronto • Oxford

Published by SR Books
An imprint of Rowman & Littlefield Publishers, Inc.
A wholly owned subsidiary of The Rowman & Littlefield Publishing Group, Inc.
4501 Forbes Boulevard, Suite 200
Lanham, MD 20706

PO Box 317
Oxford
OX2 9RU, UK

British Library Cataloguing in Publication Information Available

Library of Congress Cataloging-in-Publication Data

Matthews, Jeffrey J., 1965–
    Alanson B. Houghton : ambassador of the new era / Jeffrey J.
Matthews.
        p. cm. — (Biographies in American foreign policy ; no. 11)
    Includes bibliographic references (p.) and index.
    ISBN 0-8420-5050-7 (cloth : alk. paper) — ISBN 0-8420-5051-5
(pbk. : alk. paper)
    1. Houghton, Alanson Bigelow, 1863–1941. 2. United States—
Foreign relations—1921–1923. 3. United States—Foreign relations—
1923–1929. 4. Ambassadors—United States—Biography.
I. Title. II. Series.
E748.H74 M38 2004
327.73′009′042—dc22
                                                    2003023429

Printed in the United States of America

♾ ™ The paper used in this publication meets the minimum requirements of American
National Standard for Information Sciences—Permanence of Paper for Printed Library
Materials, ANSI/NISO Z39.48-1992.

To my family, especially my loving father,

Lieutenant Colonel Cleve E. Matthews

About the Author

Jeffrey J. Matthews is a historian and associate professor of cross-disciplinary studies in the School of Business and Leadership at the University of Puget Sound. He is the winner of the 2003 Thomas A. Davis Teaching Excellence Award and the author of "Yankee Enterprise: The Houghtons of Massachusetts and the Rise and Fall of 'Corning Incorporated,' 1851–1871," *Essays in Economic and Business History* 20 (Spring 2002); "Industrialist Turned Diplomat: The 1926 Houghton Controversy and the Limits of U.S. Policy toward Europe," *Mid-America: An Historical Review* 83 (Winter 2001); and "To Defeat a Maverick: The Goldwater Candidacy Revisited, 1963–1964," *Presidential Studies Quarterly* 27 (Fall 1997).

Contents

Preface/Acknowledgments

Walter LaFeber, the eminent Cornell historian, once told a reporter from the *Chronicle of Higher Education* that the key to communicating history effectively is to "tell a good story."* I have attempted to heed that advice in writing this diplomatic biography of Alanson B. Houghton. The ambassador was born in the midst of the American Civil War and died during World War II. In the span of those eight decades, the United States emerged as the world's most dominant military and economic power. The Houghton family of upstate New York contributed to America's ascension through its ownership and management of the prominent Corning Glass Works (now Corning Incorporated), a specialty glass company that manufactured an array of industrial and consumer products. Alanson Houghton became president of the family firm in 1910, and under his direction the company became a leader in industrial science and achieved unprecedented financial success.

America's intervention in the First World War proved a boon for Corning Glass Works and transformed Alanson's life. At age fifty-five, Houghton committed fully to public service, and in 1918 and 1920 he was elected to the U.S. Congress. In 1922, President Warren G. Harding asked Houghton to resign his congressional seat and serve as America's first postwar ambassador to Germany. By 1925, Houghton was the most influential ambassador in Europe, if not the world. This book is the story of his diplomatic career, placed in the context of American foreign policy during the 1920s. Houghton was by all accounts an attentive, loving husband and father, but the purpose of this biography is to explore his considerable diplomatic and political activity in the decade after the Great War. Because he entered public service late in life and because this is the first Houghton biography, the book includes a lengthy back-

*Jeff Sharlet, "Why Diplomatic Historians May Be the Victims of American Triumphalism," *Chronicle of Higher Education*, September 24, 1999.

ground chapter that chronicles Houghton's life before he entered the diplomatic realm.

For many Americans, biography is the most satisfying way of learning history, and I am indebted to Scholarly Resources (SR) for including my book in its successful series, Biographies in American Foreign Policy. I especially want to thank Richard Hopper, SR vice president and general manager, and Andy Fry, the series editor, who learned of this project years ago and thought it worthwhile. Andy is a true friend and the ideal editor: critical, suggestive, patient, and supportive. His superb biographies of Henry Sanford and John Tyler Morgan are models for aspiring scholars. Many thanks are also due to Michelle M. Slavin, Toni Moyer, Mary Capouya, and Sharon Costill, who are special members of the SR team. Professor Willard Rollings was a source of inspiration, providing sustained encouragement when I was transitioning from a commercial banking career to academia. Equally valuable has been the unwavering support of Dr. George Herring, the Alumni Professor of History at the University of Kentucky. He first encouraged me to investigate U.S.–European relations during the interwar period. I have benefited from "the Chief's" wisdom and kindness for many years. He and his wife, Dottie, are family. Professors James Albisetti, Mark Summers, and David Hamilton also aided this project in its early stages. Professors Walter LaFeber, Eric Christianson, Robert Topmiller, and Messrs. William M. Franklin and Nathan Campbell were uniquely supportive, and I shall never forget their special contributions. Much of the manuscript also benefited from careful readings and critical commentaries by Professor Nancy Unger of Santa Clara University and Professor Harry Laver of Southeastern Louisiana University. Each did a yeoman's job, and I cannot thank them enough.

My interest in Ambassador Houghton sprang from a reading of the extant literature on American foreign relations in the 1920s. Some historians had noted the envoy's pivotal role in U.S.–German relations. I contacted each of them—Frank Costigliola, Manfred Berg, Kenneth Paul Jones, Sander A. Diamond, and Hermann Rupieper—and asked whether the ambassador's activities merited further study, and perhaps even a biography. All five responded quickly and encouraged me to proceed.

The private collection of Houghton family papers archived at the Corning Incorporated headquarters provides the documentary cornerstone for this project. Two of Alanson's grandsons, James R. Houghton, the current chief executive officer of Corning Incorporated, and Congressman Amo Houghton, a former CEO, granted me unrestricted access to these family records and never asked to see drafts of the manuscript. On several occasions, Congressman Houghton shared remembrances of his grandfather, and he arranged my interview with Andrew Elder, Alanson's young footman during the 1930s. Mr. Elder, recently deceased, was a man of great dignity and clear memory. It was a pleasure to know him. In brief, this biography could not have been completed without the Houghton family's openness and interest, or the munificent support of several Corning employees, especially Michelle Cotton, the unflappable supervisor of the Department of Archives and Records Management.

Also crucial was the financial aid granted by the Herbert Hoover Presidential Library–Museum, the University of Kentucky, and the University of Puget Sound. Funds from the Department of History at Kentucky underwrote several trips to the National Archives in College Park, Maryland, the National Archives and the Library of Congress in Washington, DC, and a summer-long research trip to the German Foreign Ministry in Bonn and the British Public Record Office near London. My stay in Europe was made especially pleasant by the warm hospitality and *das kaltes Bier* extended by the Nordgauer, Haydock, Plotz, and Matthews families. Also significant has been the moral support given to me by my beautiful children, Kathryn and Emily, my parents, my brothers, Earl and Andy, my grandmother, Margaret Matthews Lampe, and Hank and Betty Walters. During the past few years, many amigos, including Tony, Ed, Tom, Mark, Rob, Russ, Dave, Dan, and Scott, have provided valuable encouragement and graciously expressed (or feigned) interest in this project. Steven, Joe, Brad, Tom, and Joey have encouraged me to "dream on" for more than twenty years. Professor Michael Jones and my mother, Margareta Matthews, helped me brush up on my German and clarified various translations.

I also want to thank my good friends and many students at the University of Puget Sound, including members of the Enrichment Committee, which is so ably led by Dr. John Finney. They are simply the best colleagues one could have. Keith, Paula, Alva, Tom, John, Lynda, and Les were all there when I needed them most. Newcomers Kathi and Travis have become fast friends. Charles Courtney, a former State Department official and a scholar in residence, read several draft chapters and shared his keen perspective. I would like to thank Dean Terry Cooney for his vision and consistent support. All my life I have been blessed with an inordinate number of loyal compadres: thank you for making my life so enjoyable. Finally, I want to express my undying appreciation and immense affection for my wife, Renee, who has sacrificed so much for me. A master teacher and dedicated parent, she is undoubtedly the most loving and caring person I have ever met.

Chronology

1863

October 10   Alanson Bigelow Houghton is born in Cambridge, Massachusetts

1865

April 9   Robert E. Lee surrenders to Ulysses S. Grant, ending the American Civil War

1886

June 25   Houghton graduates from Harvard and soon undertakes postgraduate studies in Europe

1889

September   Houghton begins his career at Corning Glass Works as a shipping clerk

1891

June 25   Houghton marries Adelaide Louise Wellington of Corning, New York

1897

April   Houghton is made vice president of sales at Corning Glass Works

1898

April 20   The United States declares war on Spain
December 10   The United States and Spain sign the Treaty of Paris

1900

November 6   President William McKinley wins reelection

1901

September 14   McKinley dies after an assassination attempt. Theodore Roosevelt becomes president

1904

November 8   Roosevelt is elected president in his own right

1908

November 3   William Howard Taft is elected president

1910

January   Houghton is made president of Corning Glass Works

1912

November 5   Woodrow Wilson is elected president

1914

August 1   Germany declares war on Russia; the First World War begins

1917

April 6   The United States declares war on Germany

November 15   Lenin and the Bolsheviks seize power in Russia

1918

January 8   President Wilson announces his "Fourteen Points"

November 5   Houghton is elected to the U.S. House of Representatives

November 11   Germany signs an armistice with the United States and the Allied Powers

1919

January 18   The Paris Peace Conference opens, without German officials
               Houghton becomes Chairman of the Board, Corning Glass Works

June 28   The Paris Peace Conference concludes with the signing of the Versailles Treaty

1920

March 19   The U.S. Senate refuses to ratify the Versailles Treaty

November 2   Houghton is reelected to the House of Representatives
               Warren G. Harding is elected president

1921

August 25	The United States and Germany sign the Peace Treaty of Berlin
November 12	The Washington Naval Conference convenes

1922

February 6	The Washington Conference ends with the Four Power Treaty on the Pacific Islands, the Five Power Naval Treaty, and the Nine Power Treaty on China
February 8	One U.S. dollar is worth 199 German marks
February 9	Congress establishes the World War Foreign Debt Commission
February 10	Houghton is appointed ambassador to Germany
March 30	Houghton delivers his "Peace" speech at the Metropolitan Club
April 16	Germany and Soviet Russia sign the Treaty of Rapallo
August 10	The United States and Germany sign a war claims agreement
October 28	Mussolini and the Fascists assume power in Italy
December 28	One U.S. dollar is worth 7,588 German marks
December 29	Secretary of State Charles Evans Hughes delivers a policy address to the American Historical Association

1923

January 11	France begins its occupation of Germany's Ruhr
August 2	Harding dies unexpectedly. Calvin Coolidge becomes president the next day
August 7	One U.S. dollar is worth 3,300,000 German marks
September 26	German passive resistance ends
November 30	One U.S. dollar is worth 4,200,000,000 German marks

1924

April 24	The Dawes Plan is published

August 16	The London Reparations Conference ends
November 4	Coolidge is elected president
November 8	Hitler launches his ill-fated "Beer-Hall Putsch" against the German government

1925

February 21	Houghton leaves Berlin, ending his three-year ambassadorship
	Houghton is appointed ambassador to the Court of Saint James's in London
April 9	The Dawes Plan is issued
April 26	Field Marshal Paul von Hindenburg is elected president of Germany
May	Houghton arrives in London
December 1	Germany, Great Britain, France, Italy, and Belgium sign the Locarno Treaties

1926

January 27	The U.S. Senate adopts a resolution, with strict reservations, that would allow the United States to join the World Court
March 17	The "Houghton Controversy" begins
May 10	U.S. Marines land in Nicaragua to quell a revolt
May 18	The League of Nations Preparatory Disarmament Commission convenes
September 10	Germany joins the League of Nations
December 10	The 1925 Nobel Peace Prize is awarded to Charles G. Dawes and J. Austen Chamberlain, and the 1926 Nobel Peace Prize is awarded to Aristide Briand and Gustav Stresemann

1927

January	The United States sends its Asiatic fleet to China
May 21	Charles Lindbergh flies the *Spirit of St. Louis* solo to Paris
June 20	The Geneva "Coolidge" Naval Conference convenes
August 2	Coolidge announces his intention not to run for reelection
August 4	The Geneva Naval Conference fails

1928

June 15	Herbert Hoover is named the Republican presidential nominee
August 27	The United States, France, and fourteen other nations sign the Pact of Paris, also known as the Kellogg–Briand Pact
September 28	Houghton is named the Republican U.S. Senate nominee from New York
November 6	Houghton is narrowly defeated, while Hoover is elected president

1929

January 15	The U.S. Senate (85 to 1) ratifies the Kellogg–Briand Pact
March 28	Houghton leaves the U.S. embassy in London to enter retirement
June 7	The Young Plan is announced
October 29	Prices on the New York Stock Exchange collapse

1930

April 22	The London Naval Treaty is signed
May 17	The Young Plan is initiated
June 17	Hoover signs the Smoot-Hawley Tariff Act
November 27	Secretary of State Frank B. Kellogg wins the 1929 Nobel Peace Prize

1931

June 20	Hoover proposes a one-year moratorium on all intergovernmental debts and reparations
September 18	The Japanese destroy part of the South Manchurian railroad
September 21	Great Britain abandons the gold standard

1932

January 2	The Japanese Army takes control of Chinchow in Manchuria
January 7	The Stimson Doctrine refuses to recognize Japan's conquest of Manchuria
February 2	The doomed World Disarmament Conference begins in Geneva
July 9	The Lausanne Conference ends. Major European governments agree to cancel all

| | debts owed by Germany if the United States will cancel Europe's war debts |
| November 5 | Franklin D. Roosevelt is elected president |

1933

January 30	Adolf Hitler becomes chancellor of Germany
March 27	Japan quits the League of Nations
October 14	Germany quits the Geneva Disarmament Conference and announces its intention to resign from the League of Nations

1934

April 13	The U.S. Congress forbids loans to governments in default on payments to the United States
August 2	Hindenburg dies
December 29	Japan announces that it will withdraw from previous naval disarmament treaties by December 1936

1935

June 18	The Anglo-German Naval Treaty is announced
August 31	President Roosevelt signs the first Neutrality Act
October 3	Italy invades Ethiopia
December 9	The Second London Naval Conference convenes

1936

February 29	The Second Neutrality Act is passed
March 7	German forces enter the demilitarized Rhineland
July 18	The Spanish Civil War begins

1937

July 7	The Sino-Japanese War begins
October 5	President Roosevelt delivers his "Quarantine" speech
December 11	Italy withdraws from the League of Nations

1938

| January 10 | The Ludlow war referendum resolution is buried in committee |

	March 13	With the Anschluss, Austria is absorbed into the Third Reich
	September 30	The Munich Pact cedes Czechoslovakia's Sudetenland to Germany
	November 14	The U.S. ambassador to Germany is recalled for consultation
	December 6	British Foreign Minister Anthony Eden resigns to protest the Munich Pact policy of appeasement
1939		
	March 14	Germany invades Czechoslovakia
	March 31	Great Britain, followed by France, guarantees Poland's security
	April 1	The United States recognizes Spain's Fascist government
	April 7	Italy invades Albania
	April 14	Germany revokes its nonaggression pact with Poland and terminates the Anglo-German Naval Treaty
	August 23	Germany and Soviet Russia sign a nonaggression pact
	September 1	Germany invades Poland; the Second World War begins
	September 3	Great Britain and France declare war on Germany
	September 17	Soviet Russia invades Poland
	November 4	Roosevelt signs a new Neutrality Act repealing the general embargo to belligerents
	November 30	Soviet Russia invades Finland
1940		
	April 9	Germany invades Norway and Denmark
	May 10	Germany invades Luxembourg, the Netherlands, and Belgium Winston Churchill becomes prime minister in Great Britain
	June 5	Germany invades France, which surrenders on June 22
	July 10	German planes attack England, beginning the "Battle of Britain"
	September 3	The U.S.–British "Destroyers for Bases" deal is announced

| November 5 | Roosevelt is reelected again |
| December 29 | Roosevelt calls on the United States to become "an arsenal for democracy" |

1941

January 8	Roosevelt submits a $10.8 billion defense budget
March 11	Roosevelt signs the Lend–Lease Act
June 14	Roosevelt freezes German and Italian assets in the United States; seven weeks later he freezes all Japanese assets
June 22	Germany invades Soviet Russia
June 24	Japan occupies southern Indo-China
July 26	The United States announces a complete embargo of trade with Japan
August 14	Roosevelt and Churchill issue the Atlantic Charter
September 16	Houghton dies suddenly at his summer home in South Dartmouth, Massachusetts
December 7	Japan attacks Pearl Harbor

1

The Dawn of a New Era

Coming in the aftermath of the first global war, the decade of the 1920s was a pivotal period in world history. The Great War had wreaked havoc on the international scene. More than fourteen million people died and another twenty million were wounded. The war, and the inflation it inspired, disrupted manufacturing, agriculture, and international capital and trade flows. The conflict consumed some $400 billion and devastated thousands of towns and entire farm regions. The war toppled the Old World empires of Russia, Germany, Austria–Hungary, and Ottoman-Turkey and left in its wake a contentious and untried European political system that pitted the victors against the vanquished. Thus, the 1920s witnessed the world's desperate search for a new era of peace, stability, and prosperity.

The United States, under the leadership of Democratic president Woodrow Wilson, had entered the war belatedly on behalf of France, Great Britain, and their allies and had proved a decisive force in defeating Germany and the Central Powers. After the Armistice, Wilson sought to create a new international system founded partly on the principle of a "peace without victors" and his desire to rehabilitate Germany and enhance French security. To restore the European economies, he pursued a moderate reparations settlement with Germany and a relatively free flow of international trade and investment. To maintain peace and deter aggression, he promoted collective security through a new international organization, the League of Nations, and a specific Anglo–American pledge to protect France from a resurgent Germany. At the Paris Peace Conference, however, the American president was forced to compromise his much-heralded

1

Fourteen Points platform when the Allies demanded that Germany pay substantial economic, territorial, and military penalties for the destruction wrought by the war. Still, Wilson trusted that the post-war order would be managed effectively by an American-led League of Nations, which he considered the heart of the 1919 Treaty of Versailles.

The Wilsonian vision proposed a major shift in American foreign policy, which had traditionally avoided binding political and military commitments abroad. Perhaps not surprisingly, the president's program suffered a severe setback when the new Republican majority in the U.S. Senate refused to ratify the Versailles treaty without amendments limiting American obligations. Although criticism of the treaty was widespread, with some charging that it betrayed Wilson's own progressive ideals, most opponents railed against the unprecedented commitment to collective security via the League. In the end, the president, who believed that he had adequately safeguarded America's freedom of action, refused to amend the treaty and failed to rally sufficient public support to sway the Senate reservationists.

The November 1920 elections returned the Republicans to the White House and strengthened their majorities in both houses of Congress. With the Senate's consent, President Warren G. Harding concluded separate peace treaties with the Central Powers and secured for the United States all of the entitlements of the Versailles compact, which had been ratified by the Allies, without any of the related obligations. Although Harding and his Republican successor, Calvin Coolidge, shared Wilson's objective of building a peaceful and prosperous postwar order, they differed fundamentally on means and priorities. The Republicans often promoted international cooperation and conciliation, but, unlike Wilson, they were unwilling to countenance foreign political commitments and military guarantees. They adhered instead to the foreign policy tradition of unilateral action and aversion to "entanglements" abroad. They refused, for example, to pursue membership in the new League or to guarantee French security. The Republican administrations were much more dedicated to domestic economic priorities such as providing farmers and manufacturers with tariff protection and reducing federal debts, taxes, and spending. The dogged pursuit of these nationalist objectives seriously constrained America's ability to bolster global stability and economic prosperity.

Over the decades, historians have differed widely in their characterizations of Republican foreign policy in the 1920s. In the immediate aftermath of the Second World War, conventional wisdom indicted interwar policymakers for being naïve and isolationist. The Republicans were roundly criticized for evading the practical military and political responsibilities that were commensurate with the nation's substantial postwar power. By the 1960s, however, a group of revisionist scholars began to reject "the legend" of American naïveté and isolationism. They argued instead that the Republicans of the 1920s acted adroitly on plans for an informal and business-led economic empire. From these two competing schools of thought, there has arisen a predominate post-revisionist synthesis that characterizes Republican foreign policy as "independent internationalism." This persuasive interpretation asserts that the United States was extensively engaged in postwar world affairs but vigorously opposed binding international political and military commitments, save arms limitation agreements.[1]

Undeniably during the 1920s, America played an active and influential role on the world stage, with its private citizens typically at the forefront. Economic expansion was unprecedented. In the ten years after the war, American trade more than doubled to $10.2 billion, and in 1929, U.S. goods accounted for 16 percent of world exports. Americans also exported more capital than any other nation. Led by firms such as Ford, RCA, Eastman Kodak, Standard Oil, Du Pont, Firestone, United Fruit, and International Harvester, aggregate U.S. direct foreign investments increased from $3.9 billion in 1919 to $7.6 billion in 1929. Indirect investments, including bonds and other securities, totaled more than $3.0 billion in Europe alone. Along with their products and capital, U.S. citizens also exported their culture through increased tourism and the purveyance of American art, science, technology, and manufacturing processes. Hollywood films enjoyed market shares in excess of 70 percent in Britain, France, Canada, and throughout South America. U.S. cultural internationalism was also evident in the major postwar drives for world peace and humanitarian assistance. The Woodrow Wilson Foundation, the Carnegie Endowment, the League of Nations Non-Partisan Association, and the Women's International League for Peace and Freedom were only a few of the hundreds of organizations composing America's vibrant and disparate peace movement. Groups active in global philanthropy and humanitarian relief efforts included the Red Cross, the Federal Council of Churches, the Rockefeller Foundation, the American Friends Service Committee, and an umbrella association, the American Federated Russian Famine Relief Committee. A testament to this expansion of commerce and culture was a visible anti-American backlash that led to publications such as Robert Aron and A. Dandieu's *Le cancer américain*, which appeared in Paris in 1931.

While generally in agreement with the fundamental precepts of the postrevisionist scholarship, which accentuates the activities of private citizens, this study demonstrates that America's official representatives abroad also played an important part in U.S. foreign relations of the 1920s. Moreover, focusing on U.S.–European diplomacy, the argument posits that the now-popular term "independent internationalism" is an inadequate and misleading characterization of formal U.S. foreign policy. In the American lexicon, the word "independent" often connotes admirable and positive characteristics, but given that U.S. policy failed to protect national interests by its inability to construct a stable postwar order, the adjective is inappropriate. Historians might more accurately emphasize the restricted and circumscribed nature of the mainstream Republican internationalism practiced by the Harding and Coolidge administrations. It was in fact a *conservative* and frequently reactionary form of internationalism that left the administrations vulnerable to the sweep of global developments and to constant political attacks by more progressive-minded critics in the Republican and Democratic ranks.[2]

This biography examines America's conservative internationalism from the perspective of Ambassador Alanson B. Houghton, who, in the 1920s, became not only its leading diplomat abroad but also the chief policy critic within the Harding and Coolidge administrations. Although he was a prominent international figure of the interwar period, few remember Houghton today. Unlike his less influential peers, he did not encourage a contemporary biographer, nor did he publish his memoirs. As the American ambassador to Germany and to Great Britain, he did maintain a lengthy diary, and when this became known, several publishers clamored for the publication rights. But he did not take the matter seriously until the late 1930s, when he hired an editor who conducted interviews with Houghton and other members of the Republican administrations. Alanson Houghton died in 1941 just as the editing had entered its final stages. His family attempted to have the diary published during World War II, only to be rebuffed because his views were deemed too critical of American foreign policy and too sympathetic to Germany and its first democratic government. The typed manuscript, over 1,000 pages in length, and the ambassador's voluminous private papers have remained under the Houghton family's wary control ever since.[3]

The inaccessibility of Houghton's papers has made it difficult for historians to assess fully his role in the formulation and conduct of U.S. foreign policy. There is no doubt that he was a central figure in Republican diplomacy. In October 1928, a decade after the Armistice, Frank H. Simonds, a respected journalist of international affairs, penned a suggestive editorial in the *New York Herald Tribune*. No American, he declared, "has contributed more alike to the service of his own country and to the larger task of [postwar] reconstruction than Mr. Alanson B. Houghton. What he did in the dark and difficult years which followed our resumption of diplomatic relations with Germany will probably never be generally known, but certainly no American since the Civil War has deserved better of his country. And certainly he has been the outstanding figure in our diplomatic service since the war."[4]

Yet few scholars have reviewed Houghton's entire manuscript collection, which was not organized by Corning archivists until the 1980s. Consequently, most diplomatic histories of the interwar era ignore Houghton or relegate him to the margins. When he does appear, the focus is almost exclusively on his Berlin experience, neglecting his four years in London. German historians, who were the first to write extensively on U.S.–German relations in the 1920s, were also the first to recognize the ambassador's considerable influence. Like their American counterparts, they did not utilize his private papers. There have been some notable exceptions, and the work of these scholars offered both inspiration and a starting point for this biography, which benefited from unrestricted access to Houghton's diary and personal files.[5]

Inspired by the First World War, Houghton, a millionaire industrialist, became an increasingly important figure in the Republican party, which dominated American politics throughout the 1920s. More specifically, he became associated with the select group of men who made and implemented U.S. foreign policy. After a thirty-year career at his family's Corning Glass Works, he was swept into politics by the wave of patriotism and sense of duty that washed over the country. In 1918 and 1920, New York elected him to Congress, where he served on the prestigious House Foreign Affairs Committee and the powerful Ways and Means Committee. In 1922, President Harding appointed him as the nation's first postwar ambassador to Berlin, where he served successfully for three years and established himself as the most prescient and influential member of the U.S. diplomatic corps. In 1925, after playing a significant role in Coolidge's presidential election, Houghton was awarded the blue ribbon post of the Foreign Service, the ambassadorship to Great Britain. His diplomatic accomplishments justify previous intimations that he acted as the "grandfather" or "stepfather" to three of the most important diplomatic achievements of the 1920s—the Dawes Plan, the Locarno Treaties, and the Kellogg–Briand Pact. By the time of his retirement in 1929, many contemporaries, including some wontedly hostile to Republicans, hailed Houghton as the most effective diplomat in living memory and expressed regret that he had not been appointed secretary of state.[6]

Houghton's approach to public service and international relations derived from his privileged upbringing and business experience. He and his family subscribed to a philosophy of social responsibility, which postulated that the most powerful and wealthy in society were obligated to improve the general welfare. Inspired by his parents and his education at St. Paul's School and Harvard, Houghton served as a steward and underwriter of local charities, churches, hospitals, and schools. The First World War expanded his social commitment to the national and international commonweals. His schooling, which included several years of postgraduate travel and study abroad, contributed to his cosmopolitan outlook. Moreover, as a business executive, he understood the significance of foreign trade and investment, and he appreciated the growing integration of the world's economies, politics, and cultures. When the United States emerged from the war as a predominant power, rivaled only by Britain, Houghton reasoned that the nation had inherited new and wide-ranging obligations in international affairs. It had become incumbent upon Americans, the ambassador believed, to foster stability, harmony, and prosperity, especially in Western Europe and the Western Hemisphere, where he thought the nation's primary interests lay.

Houghton's foreign policy perspective meshed hardheaded realism with optimistic idealism, and his strategy often mirrored his business practices of taking the initiative, abandoning traditional methods, and making immediate sacrifices for long-term gains. The ambassador, for example, became a staunch advocate of the U.S. military occupation of postwar Germany, because it ameliorated tense relations between Allied forces and German civilians and because it symbolized America's leadership in the New Era. He also supported the application of political and economic pressure on Berlin, London, and Paris to bring about compromise and cooperation. Moreover, he acquiesced to foreign raw-material monopolies such as the producers of crude rubber and advocated moderate war-claims settlements and an intra-European free trade system—all to revitalize the world economy and promote international stability and goodwill. Houghton's approach to peace and prosperity was most evident in his determined plan to have the United States forgive $10 billion in European war debts (equivalent to approximately $109 billion in 2003). In return for canceling these loans, he wanted the major powers, including Japan, to commit to comprehensive arms control. He also sought to reduce Germany's reparations, to execute a nonaggression pact, and to make future war declarations subject to popular referendums.[7]

Because of differences over what constituted "vital" American interests, Houghton's policy prescriptions often ran afoul of the Harding and Coolidge administrations' conservative internationalism. All agreed, however, that Latin America, especially the Caribbean and Central America, directly affected national security and prosperity. Latin America's geographic proximity, lucrative markets, and Panama Canal all served to justify U.S. hegemony in the Western Hemisphere. Houghton and the Republican leadership also agreed on policy in Asia, where, in contrast to Latin America, U.S. interests and influence were minor. In the Asian–Pacific theater, the Republicans were willing to defend American colonies, including the Philippines, and to work for international cooperation and the Open Door, but U.S. geopolitical commitments were largely restricted to diplomatic consultations and arms control agreements. Where Houghton and the administrations differed was over Western Europe.

There was little disagreement over the broad objective of promoting stability, security, and prosperity in Europe. Houghton and the administrations also agreed that an industrially revived and disarmed Germany was key not only to European rehabilitation, but also to the welfare of the world economy and the development of foreign markets. Furthermore, the Harding and Coolidge administrations often recognized, but did not necessarily implement, the measures needed to revive Europe, such as stabilizing international currencies, remitting war debts, reducing reparations and tariffs, and promoting capital investment. At least three key assumptions, however, constrained Republican European policy: that the United States should refrain from military–political commitments such as alliances or League of Nations membership; that Europe should assume the primary burdens and responsibilities for its own post-war reconstruction; and that America could prosper even without European recovery. As historian Melvyn Leffler explains, "Although American officials often recognized what measures were necessary to restore European stability, their desire and ability to take commensurate action were circumscribed by internal economic priorities, strategic considerations, and political factors." A healthy, revitalized, and secure Europe, in other words, was deemed valuable to the United States, but it was not yet considered *essential* to the nation's well-being. Here Houghton and the Republican administrations parted ways.[8]

The ultimate subordination of European reconstruction to domestic political and economic priorities caused Houghton actively to criticize Republican foreign policy. He too opposed entangling alliances and entry into the League. The former he considered unnecessary, even detrimental to national safety, and the latter a political impossibility given a sharply divided U.S. Senate. But Houghton did not believe that Europe, particularly Western Europe, should be left to shoulder the heavy burdens of postwar recovery. He disputed the idea that long-term American prosperity was possible independent of European stability and economic growth. As a result, Houghton proved more willing than the Republican administrations to use American economic power as an overt diplomatic tool for promoting political compromises in international relations. The ambassador understood that effective diplomacy needed to be backed by a willingness to use either economic pressure or military force. Throughout his diplomatic career, he argued that the United States, as a new and dominant world power, possessed heightened international obligations, thus remarking in 1922:

> The American people must understand their responsibility and their opportunity. God has given us the power to render a vast service to humanity. No such opportunity ever has come to any nation in two thousand years. The world has become an economic unit. The United States must recognize this and shape her policies in accord with this new fact in her history. The idea of isolation must be dismissed. The sentiment and the sense of responsibility for building a better world civilization must be cultivated.[9]

Houghton believed that lasting prosperity and security depended upon close political, diplomatic, and economic cooperation among the United States, Great Britain, and Germany, and to a lesser extent France and Japan. He did not believe that Soviet Russia would emerge as a major power until the 1940s. The Big Five countries were key because of their industrial and financial might, both actual and potential. America and Britain were predominant and would remain so for the foreseeable future. Germany, he thought, would assuredly return to its prewar economic prowess, thereby making its military revival inevitable. In France, despite a large standing and reserve army, the ambassador perceived a measure of relative and ongoing weakness due to the country's limited financial and industrial capabilities. In contrast, Japan, although a second-tier regional power, was on a steady upward trajectory. A few historians and some of the ambassador's contemporaries, many living in France, have accused Houghton of being pro-German. He was; but propelled largely by matters of realpolitik, he was equally pro-British, and there is no evidence that he placed German or British concerns above American interests.

Houghton's conviction that U.S. vital interests were inextricably linked to Germany and Britain set him apart from the Republican foreign policy establishment, which would not fully accept such thinking until after the Second World War. The ambassador's insight stemmed partly from his considerable knowledge of German society. He had studied the nation's language, history, and political economy as an undergraduate at Harvard and as a graduate student at the University of Berlin. Moreover, as an executive at Corning Glass Works, he had competed and cooperated with German firms for decades. In brief, he respected and admired German science, industry, education, and arts. Nevertheless, he, like most Americans, possessed scant sympathy for the Wilhelmian government, and during the Great War he willingly converted his company's manufactures to matériel for the Allied and American war machines. After the Armistice, he supported French and British demands for German territorial concessions and substantial reparations. Germany's revival as a great power, however, he never doubted. Consequently, Houghton worried that even a justifiably harsh punishment, particularly one thrust upon its new democratic government, would prove counterproductive to postwar reconstruction, the success of which lay ultimately, he thought, in the hands of officials in London, Washington, and Berlin. Houghton's calculated and activist diplomacy often drew praise from conservatives and progressives of both political parties, suggesting that more aggressive and thoughtful leadership from the Harding and Coolidge administrations was possible. Taken a step further, less conservative Republican leaders could have changed for the better the course of interwar history and made less probable the rise of Adolf Hitler and the outbreak of World War II.

From 1922 to 1929, Houghton labored with European and American leaders to build a foundation for peace and prosperity among the major powers. His exceptional experience provides a unique and valuable perspective on American foreign relations after the First World War. It is hoped that readers of this first Houghton biography will concur with journalist James B. Morrow, who, after interviewing the ambassador, concluded: "Here, then, is a man worth writing about and worth reading about." He was the ambassador of the New Era.[10]

Notes

1. The catchphrase "independent internationalism" first appeared in Joan Hoff-Wilson, *American Business and Foreign Policy* (Lexington, KY, 1971), and it is now used in the leading textbook surveys of U.S. foreign relations. See also Howard Jones, *Crucible of Power: A History of Foreign Relations from 1897* (Wilmington, DE, 2001), 112; Thomas G. Paterson et al., *American Foreign Relations: A History since 1895*, 5th ed. (Boston, 2000), 113; and Walter LaFeber, *The American Age: United States Foreign Policy at Home and Abroad since 1750* (New York, 1989), 318. Even Robert D. Schulzinger's *U.S. Diplomacy since 1900*, 5th ed. (New York, 2002), emphasizes America's "independent internationalism" and "independent foreign policy" despite his titling the 1920s chapter "The Triumph of Conservative Internationalism," 125–45.

2. The international activities of private U.S. citizens are given special attention by scholars adhering to a corporatist (business–government cooperation) interpretation of the 1920s. Two classic works are Michael J. Hogan's *Informal Entente: The Private Structure of the Cooperation in Anglo-American Economic Diplomacy, 1918–1928* (Columbia, MO, 1977, 1991); and Emily S. Rosenberg, *Spreading the American Dream: American Economic and Cultural Expansion, 1890–1945* (New York, 1982). Also representative are Rosenberg's *Financial Missionaries to the World: The Politics and Culture of Dollar Diplomacy, 1900–1930* (Cambridge, MA, 1999); and Frank Ninkovich's survey, *The Wilsonian Century: U.S. Foreign Policy since 1900* (Chicago, 1999). The scholarly emphasis on America's unofficial businessmen–diplomats has come at the cost of underappreciation of the role of official government representatives. For example, Houghton, who was an actual businessman–ambassador, is never even mentioned in Rosenberg's important books.

3. Although the Houghton family controls access, the Alanson B. Houghton Papers collection is maintained by archivists at Corning Incorporated in Corning, New York (hereafter cited as Houghton Papers).

4. *New York Herald Tribune*, October 25, 1928.

5. The most "notable exceptions" are Frank Costigliola, Manfred Berg, Hermann J. Rupieper, Kenneth P. Jones, and Sander A. Diamond. See my Preface/Acknowledgments and Bibliographical Essay in this volume.

6. Manfred Jonas, *The United States and Germany: A Diplomatic History* (Ithaca, NY, 1984), 169–70, 181–82; Kenneth Paul Jones, "Alanson B. Houghton and the Ruhr Crisis: The Diplomacy of Power and Morality," in *U.S. Diplomats in Europe, 1919–1941*, ed. Kenneth Paul Jones (Santa Barbara, CA, 1981), 24–39; Hermann J. Rupieper, *The Cuno Government and Reparations, 1922–23: Politics and Economics* (The Hague, 1979), 71–72; Frank Costigliola, "The United States and the Reconstruction of Germany in the 1920s," *Business History Review* 50 (Winter 1976): 477–502; Stephen A. Schuker, *The End of French Predominance in Europe: The Financial Crisis of 1924 and the Adoption of the Dawes Plan* (Chapel Hill, NC, 1976), 24; F. G. Stambrook, " 'Resourceful in Expedients'—Some Examples of Ambassadorial Policy Making in the Inter-War Period," Canadian Historical Association's *Historical Papers* (1973): 301–20.

7. All currency valuations were calculated as of 2003, using the Federal Reserve of Minneapolis Website, "What Is a dollar worth?" at *www.minneapolisfed.org/research/data/us/calc/.*

8. Melvyn P. Leffler, "American Policy Making and European Stability, 1921–1933," *Pacific Historical Review* 46 (May 1977): 207–28. No scholar has demonstrated a better understanding of interwar Republican foreign policy. See the Bibliographical Essay.

9. John B. Ascham, "Ambassador Houghton's Message to Methodism," *Western Christian Advocate* (September 13, 1922): 2, in Houghton Papers.

10. James B. Morrow, "A Business Man Ambassador," *Nation's Business* 10 (June 1922): 18–19.

2

Scholar, Industrialist, Public Servant

1863–1922

Characterized by ceaseless activity and successful
accomplishment along many lines of endeavor, the
career of Alanson B. Houghton . . . is one of striking
interest. It is the story of a man who has been a leader
in thought and action, a leader of men—the story of
a life devoted to the up-building of a great business,
to the service of his fellow man, and to the state and
nation.
—*Corning Evening Leader*, August 28, 1918

At 11:45 A.M. on March 17, 1922, the factory horn at
the Corning Glass Works blew four loud blasts. Coming at an unusual time, the noise startled the firm's fifty-
eight-year-old chairman, Alanson Bigelow Houghton,
who was working in his second-story office. Within mo-
ments, two veteran employees appeared at his door. Grin-
ning widely, one asked, "We don't know exactly what to
call you, Mr. Ambassador?" Houghton smiled and said,
"Call me Alan, just as you have since we were boys." The
men laughed and escorted Houghton outside to the court-
yard, where they were greeted by the Corning Glass
Works Band and seven hundred cheering factory workers. The employees had gathered to celebrate Houghton's
recent appointment as the first U.S. ambassador to Germany after World War I. Several men pulled Houghton
aboard a large flatbed truck draped in red, white, and
blue bunting. They presented him with a burgundy sou-
venir album and a massive, heavy silk American flag. The
book contained the names of all those assembled and an

inscription expressing profound reverence for their beloved chief. Overcome by the moment, Houghton's throat tightened, making it difficult for him to speak. When the words finally broke through, he thanked the crowd for the most moving experience of his life. He expressed his allegiance to the people of his hometown, Corning, New York, and his hope that while abroad, he might accomplish "some real service to this tortured old world." After a stirring rendition of "The Star-Spangled Banner," the ambassador stepped off the makeshift platform into the throng of spirited admirers. A Corning newspaper described the scene as one of the most impressive events in the town's history.[1]

In the New Era of the 1920s, many Americans held corporate executives such as Houghton in high regard. The First World War had prompted unprecedented public service among the nation's business elite. Scores of bankers, lawyers, and industrialists had converted their firms to government service, entered politics, enlisted in the military, or joined wartime agencies as dollar-a-year-men. They had played an integral role in winning the war, and their managerial skill and economic expertise were needed for postwar reconstruction, both domestic and international.

The war proved to be the major turning point in Houghton's life. He had spent thirty years as a prominent industrialist and community leader. In 1918 he mounted an unexpected and victorious campaign for the U.S. Congress. In the House of Representatives, he promoted a businesslike legislative agenda that emphasized governmental efficiency and effectiveness. He advocated revised tariff, tax, and transportation laws as well as the reorganization of the military and of the budget and appropriations process. Republican leaders recognized that the millionaire was no ordinary congressman, and he became an increasingly important figure in the party.

Following his landslide reelection in 1920, Houghton's preoccupation with domestic reforms gradually gave way to a foreign policy agenda, which aimed to reverse a postwar resurgence of political isolationism and economic nationalism. In early 1922 he agreed to relinquish his congressional seat to become the nation's ambassador to Germany. In the international realm, as in the business and political spheres earlier, he championed new and progressive policies to meet evolving conditions. Above all, he believed that the United States had emerged from war as a predominant military and economic power, and thus had acquired new responsibilities for fostering world peace and prosperity. He would spend seven years as a public servant living abroad, all the while attempting to convince Americans that, in the postwar era, their future was intertwined with Europe's and that they must abandon their traditional isolationist attitude toward Old World politics and begin to exert international leadership. While in the diplomatic corps, he gained membership in the exclusive club—later dubbed the American Establishment—that formulated and implemented U.S. foreign policy. He emerged as the nation's, if not the world's, most influential ambassador of the 1920s.

Houghton's Anglo-Saxon ancestry and his privileged East Coast upbringing typified that of other members of the American foreign policy elite. The oldest of four siblings to survive infancy, he was born in Cambridge, Massachusetts, on October 10, 1863. As Protestants, the first Houghtons had come to the New World from England more than two centuries earlier. The family settled forty miles west of Boston in the Lancaster Valley. Over succeeding generations, they proved able farmers and respected community leaders. Alanson's paternal grandfather, Amory Houghton, was a pioneer of American capitalism. As a boy in 1828, he abandoned the family fields for a carpenter's apprenticeship in the bustling suburb of Cambridge. His story of Yankee enterprise progressed almost mythically from farm boy to skilled craftsman, to wharf merchant, to corporate investor, and, finally, to industrial manufacturer. In 1851 he organized the Union Glass Company of Somerville, Massachusetts, the first of many forerunners to the Fortune 500 firm, Corning Incorporated.

The glass business was a family affair, and Amory Houghton's protégé was his eldest son, Amory Jr., Alanson's father. During the Civil War the Houghtons sold Union Glass for a small fortune and moved to New York, where they invested unwisely in the Brooklyn glass industry. In 1868, after losing considerable money, the family was uprooted again for a fresh start in Corning, a small town in western New York. With the help of local boosters, they built the Corning Flint Glass Works. This new company had to struggle from the outset. Indeed, it fell into bankruptcy in 1870, essentially sending grandfather Houghton into retirement. Within two years, however, Amory Jr. and his younger brother Charles had managed to reacquire the firm on credit and organized its gradual revival.

Alanson's parents, Amory Jr. and Ellen Anne Bigelow, had married before the Civil War while still living in Massachusetts. Although the Cambridge–Somerville Houghtons were an industrious clan, the "old money" Boston Bigelows believed that their precious Ellen had married below her station. Perhaps in a bid for reconciliation, the newlyweds named their first son after his maternal grandfather Alanson Bigelow, a partner in the prosperous jewelry house of Bigelow Brothers & Kennard. The young Houghtons enjoyed a successful marriage, and more children followed.

The Houghton brothers (from left to right): Charles F., Alfred, and Amory Jr. *Courtesy of the Houghton Family and Corning Incorporated*

Both parents influenced Alanson's personality and behavior. His father was a commanding figure, with a large, stocky frame and deep voice. A stern man of few words, his introspective and reflective nature lent itself to mastering the intricacies of nineteenth-century glassmaking. But drive and determination were the critical family qualities handed down from generation to generation. Business affairs had hardened Amory's personality, but his occasional dry sense of humor did not go unappreciated by friends and family. And, though a staunch teetotaler, he found ample time to pursue the personal vices of fast carriage horses and competitive billiards. For warmth and affection, Alanson turned to his mother. The diminutive Ellen exuded charm and compassion. She was a dutiful wife and a generous parent who found emotional and physical release in reading, sewing, organ music, and social work. Husband and wife, both children of privilege, dreamed of their first son returning to Cambridge to attend Harvard College.

The small Corning community provided happy childhoods for many Houghton youths. The town revolved around the expanding glass factory and always seemed abuzz with activity. Large barges and noisy tugs navigated the Chemung River. Railroad traffic was fast, furious, and frequent. Parades were not uncommon, and those of traveling circuses, especially P. T. Barnum's, were the most popular. Without motion pictures, radio, or television, Corning's children were left to their own devices—swimming, tree climbing, and baseball in summer, and sledding, skating, and sleighing in winter. When not playing with his younger brother Arthur, Alanson, it appears, preferred to explore the great outdoors and read books.

As the glassworks prospered, so did the Houghton lifestyle. In 1878, when Alanson was fifteen, the family literally moved up in Corning by purchasing, for $10,000, the hillside Patterson estate, a sizable neo-Gothic stone house with gated grounds that encompassed an entire city block. The sprawling property included stables for a coach and horses, and in the mansion a billiards parlor for Amory Jr. and a music room for Ellen. The family's obvious wealth inspired a generation of local entrepreneurs, including IBM founder Thomas J. Watson Sr., and the steady profits from the glassworks guaranteed Alanson's higher education. Given the limited quality of his public education in Corning, his parents sent him to a reputable preparatory school to better his chances for Harvard.

In the fall of 1880, Alanson initiated a family tradition by entering St. Paul's School, a $500-per-year boys' academy just west of Concord, New Hampshire. Established in 1856, the school's rustic and isolated locale appealed to many old-stock families of the wealthy urban class who dispatched their sons by rail from Baltimore, Philadelphia, Boston, and, especially, New York City. By the onset of the Civil War, the school had garnered a national reputation, and America's new industrial elite began to send their children to St. Paul's, "not because it was an idyllic country school, but because its mixture of discipline, high educational standards, and energetic Christianity offered a pathway to worldly success." Alanson's schoolmates included sons of great men and great men in the making such as William Randolph Hearst, Harry A. and James R. Garfield (whose father was the serving American president), and J. P. "Jack" Morgan Jr. and his cousin Junius. Perhaps the most prominent member of Houghton's "fourth form" (quasi-junior) class was John Jacob Astor Jr., the heir to the family fortune who would later serve in the Spanish-American War, build New

York City's Astoria Hotel (later the Waldorf-Astoria), and go down with the *Titanic*.[2]

For many students, especially those who had abandoned the comforts of home for the first time, the St. Paul's experience was exceedingly difficult. The discipline and regimen were rigorous and New Hampshire's bleak, freezing winters psychologically depressing. The demanding curriculum of Latin, Greek, Mathematics, English, and History required constant study. Church worship, or "camp meeting," as William Hearst put it, was compulsory, once per day and thrice on the Sabbath. The boys were confined to campus all but one day per month, and gift packages from home were forbidden. Moreover, the school instructed parents not to provide their sons with pocket money lest it encourage materialism and other sinful habits. If these circumstances were not difficult enough, Alanson, nearly seventeen, suffered the humiliation of being placed a year behind his peers, a consequence of his deficient Corning education.[3]

Houghton struggled academically his first year and did not join any of St. Paul's sports teams, clubs, or associations. Still, he demonstrated the familiar Houghton tenacity and persevered. Others were less resolute. The Californian Hearst, for example, had coaxed his mother into rescuing him from dreary New Hampshire. Alanson's second and final year at St. Paul's was happier. Now more secure, he delved into his studies and extracurricular activities. He became a member of the Missionary Society, the leading student organization. His literary flair surfaced when he captured first prize in a school essay contest. He became assistant editor of *Horae Scholasticae*, the school newspaper, and he contributed poetry under various pen names. Unlike his inaugural year, he earned "First Testimonial" honors for grades near the top of his class and a much-coveted award for Best English Composition for "The Place of Daniel Webster in American History."

The highpoint of Houghton's education at St. Paul's came on the last day of spring examinations in 1882, when, as the school's "Library Orator," he delivered to parents, faculty, and students an evening lecture on the state of "English Fiction." The well-crafted address drew from Shakespeare, Shelley, Scott, and Burns. The speech revealed the emergence of a progressive philosophy central to understanding Alanson's forthcoming careers in industry, politics, and diplomacy. He believed that mankind was engaged in a "continuous struggle for improvement," and that imagination and innovation were the primary means to achievement. He concluded that the "most successful man in any department of life is he who can throw himself amidst future events, and plan how to meet them." Young Alanson rode the wave of his St. Paul's success ninety miles southeast to Harvard Yard.[4]

The move to Massachusetts was a homecoming of sorts. The Houghtons had left Somerville for New York almost twenty years earlier, shortly after Alanson's birth. The young man returned as a confident and flowering poet and writer, and he could not have wished for a better field for cultivation. Cambridge hosted not only the nation's first and most eminent college, but thanks to its prominent faculty, famed citizens, and prosperous publishing trade, the city had also become a literary capital. At the apex stood the Longfellow house on Brattle Street, to which Hawthorne, Emerson, and the like made frequent pilgrimages.

Houghton arrived at Harvard when higher learning in America was undergoing a major transformation. Before the Civil War, college educators focused on Mathematics, Greek, and Latin as the best means for instilling mental discipline in students. After the war, most of the historic colleges either became liberal arts schools or developed as modern universities replete with course electives, specialized departments, research seminars, scientific laboratories, and graduate training. Harvard had embarked on the latter path under the stewardship of President Charles Eliot. Unfortunately for Houghton, in 1882 the school still prescribed courses for freshmen. Along with 250 classmates, he slogged through Latin, Greek, Classical Lectures, Algebra, German, Mathematics, Chemistry, and Physics. As students were often seated alphabetically, many lectures found Houghton near the boisterous William Hearst, who after leaving St. Paul's had continued his studies with private tutors in California. Initially, Alanson delivered less than stellar performances in most subjects, but his course work progressed. He found time to satisfy his inclination for writing by joining the staff of Harvard's primary student daily, the *Herald*. In many ways, he appeared more bound for a newspaper career than Hearst. The next year, when the *Herald* merged with its competitor to form the *Herald-Crimson*, Houghton was made managing editor.

Alanson was hardly a wallflower when it came to Harvard life. He joined a bevy of clubs, both new and established, including those for philosophy, history, art, finance, and chess. He gained membership in the whimsically named Hasty Pudding Club, the Institute of 1770 for orators, and the literary O.K. Society. From these associations emerged an impressive clique that included Houghton,

George Santayana, Thomas P. Sanborn, William W. Baldwin, and George R. Carpenter. They often escaped to Boston for fine food, theater, and female companionship. These young men were also prolific writers, and none was busier than the glassmaker's son who quipped to his father, "My pen is at times much like a woman's tongue—it runs away with me."[5]

From his first semester, Houghton contributed features and poems to the student newspapers, and later to the literary magazine *Advocate* and the witty *Harvard Lampoon*. His work found an appreciative audience among several Boston critics who reproduced his pieces in city newspapers. He benefited from his relations with Harvard's outstanding faculty. In its superb Philosophy Department, he and his friends were challenged and inspired by the brilliant and competing minds of William James and Josiah Royce. Even more influential was English professor Barrett Wendell, one of the most influential teachers of the late nineteenth century. Above all, Wendell pressed his students to develop independent and creative ideas. In Houghton and his circle of friends, the professor found prized pupils whom he brought into his home to meet the literary men of Boston.

Encouraged by such dedicated faculty, Houghton organized his coterie and founded the long-lived magazine *Harvard Monthly*. The first issue, selling for 25 cents, rolled off the presses in October 1885. The journal included essays, poems, book reviews, and wide-ranging editorials. Houghton served as editor-in-chief, and his own contributions confirmed his abilities as a poet and author. An avid reader of contemporary reformers Henry George and Karl Marx, his prose was often brooding. A friend recalled that the plight of "human suffering dominated [Houghton's] judgments" while at Harvard. Santayana, who would become an eminent philosopher, considered some of Houghton's work "scornful and revolutionary," with "a good deal of verbal facility and technical ingenuity." The *Harvard Monthly*, thanks in no small part to Houghton's energetic leadership, was a resounding success. On the magazine's second anniversary, the *Boston Daily Advertiser* recounted its brief history and proclaimed that the sheet was vastly superior to any other college journal, that the literature was "absolutely and inherently good," and that some articles had even garnered favorable comment from abroad.[6]

The *Monthly*'s success mirrored Houghton's achievements in the classroom. Once beyond the prescribed courses of his freshman year, his marks improved noticeably. One of his History papers, "Can the United States Guarantee Neutrality of the Canal between the Atlantic and the Pacific?" was presented at a meeting of the American Historical Association. By graduation in June 1886, he had earned "Dissertation Honors" magna cum laude with special mention in English Composition and Political Economy (Economics). Elected Class Poet, he penned an extensive graduation piece warning of the inevitability of change and the need to meet future challenges. He read the poem at Commencement, sharing the stage with geologist John Wesley Powell and naturalist Joseph Leidy, both of whom received honorary degrees, and keynote speaker Charles Francis Adams Jr., then president of the Union Pacific Railroad. In all, Houghton's four years at Cambridge had contrasted sharply with the low road traveled by classmate Hearst, whose apathy and antics had brought about his expulsion.

After graduation, President Eliot offered Houghton an instructorship, presumably on the condition that he pursue a doctorate. His classmates expected that he would take "some soft editorship on the *Atlantic Monthly*" or withdraw to Emerson's Concord to "write pensive verses." But Houghton and some friends, including Santayana, elected for travel and postgraduate study in Europe, especially in Germany because of its progressive universities. Transatlantic travel had increased rapidly after the Civil War, and graduate students were often at the forefront. Houghton's two years abroad afforded him a worldly sophistication and served as unwitting preparation for his future career as a diplomat. He spent roughly half his time living in Germany, one-quarter in France, and the balance touring Italy, Russia, Austria–Hungary, Norway, Sweden, and Great Britain. As with many Americans venturing overseas, the experience helped to shape his worldview and contributed to his "internationalist" and activist foreign policy perspective.[7]

When Houghton and Santayana reached Germany's University of Göttingen in midsummer 1886, they were retracing the pilgrimage of many influential Americans, including Benjamin Franklin, John Lothrop Motley, Edward Everett, George Bancroft, John Pierpont Morgan, Elihu Root, and Henry Wadsworth Longfellow. But Göttingen, renowned for its excellence in medicine and science, was only a temporary stop. The Harvard men were more interested in philosophy and political economy as taught at the University of Berlin. They roamed freely in Berlin, taking in a broad, often at random, selection of open lectures. Houghton studied German history under Professor Heinrich von Treitschke, a vehement nationalist who had recently succeeded the legendary Leopold von Ranke

Alanson B. Houghton at Harvard. *Courtesy of the Houghton Family and Corning Incorporated*

as historiographer of Prussia. He found more satisfaction with Berlin's famous economists, including Gustav von Schmoller, a pioneer in economic history, and Adolf Wagner, an advocate of the new inductive approach to problems of political economy.

Houghton studied in Berlin for several semesters and, unlike Santayana, he enjoyed it. He buried himself in academic work, and time passed quickly. From Germany, he traveled throughout Central Europe and eventually moved to Paris where he studied Sociology at the Sorbonne. Little is known of his experience in France, but while abroad, he concentrated less on poetry and more on economic and political analyses, a trend that had started in Cambridge. With the possible exception of Professor Wendell, no faculty member at Harvard influenced Houghton's maturing intellect more than Charles F. Dunbar, a banking and currency specialist and former editor of the *Boston Daily Advertiser*. His popular Economics lectures represented Harvard's first attempt to connect the theories of John Stuart Mill and other classical economists to the issues of modern industrial society. As a teacher and mentor, he helped to develop Houghton's self-confidence and critical thinking.

While in Europe, Houghton completed a lengthy study of Italian monetary policy begun under Dunbar. The topic seemed a natural given his success in courses such as "The Economic History of Europe and America since 1763" and "Investigations and Discussion of Practical Economic Questions." His manuscript focused on Italy's financial development since unification in 1861, especially the conditions surrounding its suspension and resumption of specie payments, an occurrence not unfamiliar to Americans. At twenty-five, Houghton demonstrated a grasp of international finance as well as a respect for political expediency. Drawing upon Italian, French, and German sources, his analysis was well grounded in modern European history. The sober financial examination, tightly crafted, contrasted sharply with his moody Harvard prose. Dunbar approved the work, which was published in two installments of the *Quarterly Journal of Economics*.[8]

Houghton's study of political economy somehow led to a friendship with the multifaceted James Bryce, the English historian and Oxford law professor who served in Parliament for twenty-seven years prior to his becoming ambassador to the United States in 1907. From the Harvard graduate Bryce received material for his *American Commonwealth*, one of the most authoritative surveys of U.S. society. Houghton's contribution amounted to a comparative review of governmental regulation in the British and American economies. A Harvard class report described his efforts as "a set of tables and notes on 'Laissez-faire.' " Macmillan & Company published a pamphlet of Alanson's work along with Bryce's manuscript. A Houghton family friend later remarked that Alanson had helped the professor "for the first time fully understand the question of [America's] Federal–State relationships." Despite such assured exaggeration, Bryce appreciated Houghton's "valuable aid."[9]

In the summer of 1888, Houghton persuaded his father to join him for a whirlwind tour. Alanson's delightful journal of the trip reflects the grandeur of the Old World and the breadth of his cosmopolitan education. In Paris they visited Notre Dame, the Chamber of Deputies, the Louvre, the Trocadero tower, and the Latin Quarter, where Alanson had lived and studied. Next, they went by train through Germany and cruised along the Nordic coast, encountering several American warships. They inspected countless castles, museums, and churches and spent considerable time at various international expositions. After Stockholm came St. Petersburg, and then Moscow, where they toured the palace suites occupied by Napoleon, marveled at "the monstrous boots" of Peter the Great, and inspected the Moscow Glass Factory. After a week in Russia, the pair turned east for England and Ireland, their final destinations. After two months of travel they "bade adieu . . . to the 'effete despotisms of the old world' " and sailed for New York.[10]

Alanson returned to Corning with his father for a respite from academia although he promised a public lecture related to his studies. More than a few eyebrows must have been raised when word circulated that Amory Houghton's son would be expounding on "The Socialism of Karl Marx." In fact, a large crowd gathered at the Baptist Church to hear him. His careful exposition on "the weightiest social question" was met with rapt attention. What impressed many in the audience was the speaker's impartiality, his "calmness of tone and temper," and the "entire absence of bias, clap-trap, 'spread-eagleism and the like.' " The balanced speech received thunderous applause, and the *Corning Leader* remarked that the thought-inspiring talk signaled Houghton's "rich and promising" future.[11]

Alanson left his hometown for Europe in early 1889 to continue his postgraduate studies in Italy. This expedition, however, was cut short when word arrived that his father had taken ill. He returned to Corning, and agreed to shelve his academic ambitions for a few months and to work in the family business. The "few months" ultimately stretched into thirty years. By the time Amory recovered, he had persuaded his son to remain at the glassworks. It is likely that the father viewed his son's extensive and expensive education as a capital investment from which he expected a financial return. Younger brother Arthur had already entered the plant after graduating from St. Paul's School. Like his brother, Alanson learned the glass business from the ground up; the apprenticeship was hardly superficial. His father demanded that he work alongside the office staff and factory crews in ten-hour shifts, six days per week. He started as a shipping clerk earning $1.25 per day. Although he demonstrated an early penchant for marketing and sales, he was not made an officer of the company for five years.

By the mid-1890s, Alanson had completely settled down in Corning. There were occasional trips abroad, to Europe, North Africa, and the West Indies, but these were largely recreational excursions. At the factory, his uncle Charles had taken him under his wing in the sales department. Alanson's executive talent was demonstrated in contract negotiations in which he was beginning to take a leading role, and at thirty-one he was made Second Vice President. He married his beloved, Adelaide Louise Wellington, a childhood friend and the daughter of a prominent Corning banker. Their wedding in 1891 was a spectacular affair with guests arriving from all over the country. The press lavished praise on the up-and-coming Houghton. The *New York Times* described him as "a well known Harvard man" who had founded the *Harvard Monthly* and assisted with Bryce's *American Commonwealth*. A local paper perceived "a young man of great brilliancy," one of the "most forcible writers" in western New York. The couple built a comfortable house at 4 East 5th Street, where they lived for several decades and raised five children: Amory, Quincy, Matilda, Eleanor, and Elizabeth.[12]

All, however, was not well. A series of tragedies struck the Houghton family after Alanson's wedding. In 1892 his uncle Alfred, who suffered from recurring bouts of depression, committed suicide in Corning. Two years later, Alfred's wife passed away, leaving three young daughters parentless (one of the children was the future mother of actress Katharine Houghton Hepburn). The girls lived with various relatives, and Amory managed their inheritances stingily. In 1897, Amory's other brother, Charles, began to suffer strange phobias, including fear of water and horse-drawn carriages. After disappearing one evening, he was found by his nephews Alanson and Arthur lying in a factory storage shed, dead from a self-inflicted gunshot wound. Charles's death was a seminal event in Alanson's life. The job of overseeing corporate sales and marketing would now fall entirely upon the younger Houghton.

As Amory's health deteriorated during the first decade of the twentieth century, Alanson and Arthur emerged as the controlling executives at Corning Glass Works. Alanson officially became president in 1910. The brothers were the beneficiaries of their family's storied business experience. They inherited a prosperous enterprise and an appreciation for the crucial linkage between the dynamic marketplace and the necessity for product and process innovation. Their father had revived the glassworks in the 1870s through a low-volume, high-margin strategy. Rather than compete on scale, he decided to focus production on specialty goods such as medical and

chemical ware, lantern globes, and railroad signal lenses. To improve product features, the company also initiated pioneering development collaborations with clients, industrial engineers, and
university physicists. The firm's rising reputation for creativity and
superior craftsmanship led to an invaluable relationship with Thomas Edison, and during the 1880s and 1890s, Corning Glass established itself as the nation's largest manufacturer of light-bulb
casings.

In building one of the nation's premier glassworks, the Houghton family contributed to America's Gilded Age ascendancy as a
great industrial power. The firm's concentration on specialty goods
enabled it to forge lucrative bonds with the railroad and electrical
interests, two pillars of the Second Industrial Revolution. The decades after Appomattox were a period of phenomenal economic
expansion. Propelled by small and large enterprises, U.S. manufacturing output began to surpass Great Britain's. This rapid industrial growth coincided with a scramble for empire among the
world's major powers. European nations were conquering the Af-
rican continent and, along with Japan, carving out spheres of influence in Asia. In 1898 the United States asserted itself overseas
by launching a war against Spain, which concluded with the annexation of Hawaii and the Spanish colonies of Guam, Puerto Rico,
Cuba, and the Philippines.

These late-nineteenth century shifts in world power provided
a dramatic backdrop for the generational leadership changes at
Corning Glass Works. As a senior corporate executive, Alanson
proved a shrewd negotiator, an innovator, a risk-taker, and, above
all, a visionary. These were all talents he later applied to the diplomatic service. His formidable skills as a negotiator had surfaced
early. According to one company official, he was "quick to grasp,
analyze, and solve" complex problems and able "to avoid the dangerous pitfalls surrounding them." He played a critical role in trust
agreement negotiations that established price schedules and production quotas with competitors Libbey Glass Works and the Phoe-
nix Glass. He also negotiated a series of long-term sales contracts
with the nation's dominant electrical corporations, General Electric and Westinghouse Lamp. Together, these profitable agreements
helped to secure for Corning Glass an estimated 40 percent of the
national market for light bulbs and related tubing. During these
complicated contract talks, Houghton demonstrated considerable
skill in resolving conflicts while still protecting his company's
interests.[13]

As a corporate strategist, Houghton seemed at times without peers in the glass industry. His vision of Corning Glass Works as a world leader in specialized products demanded constant innovation and significant risk-taking. His determination to produce the best railroad and marine signal glass, for example, inspired the firm to establish a unique optical laboratory in 1904. After only a year, the lab discovered optimal color schemes for trackside warning lights, a finding that soon persuaded the Railroad Signal Associa-

Corning Glass Works. *Courtesy of the Houghton Family and Corning Incorporated*

tion to adopt Corning's specifications as national standards. Almost overnight, one employee wrote, the glassworks became "the Mecca" for American railroad engineers. Similarly, Houghton's demand that his plant produce a more durable industrial glass led the company to expand the optical lab into a more comprehensive research and development facility managed by university-trained scientists. By 1910, the commercial production of heat-resistant, shatterproof lantern globes was in full swing, and only a few years later, Corning began shipping its first line of Pyrex ware.[14]

In addition to leading complex contract negotiations and streamlining product innovation, Houghton was also determined to develop new manufacturing technology. He understood the competitive necessity of improving efficiency and standardization, especially in regard to lightbulbs—the company's most profitable product. When other Corning officials, including his father, objected to investing large sums in a proposed mechanization scheme, Alanson and his brother financed the engineering project from their own personal accounts. After much experimentation, the brothers in 1913 finally delivered to the glassworks their first semiautomatic bulb-making machine, which manufactured an astonishing 420 lightbulbs per hour, thus enabling the firm to produce several million bulbs that year. After 1916, annual bulb production would exceed 100 million.

No person was more responsible for institutionalizing Corning's now famous commitment to corporate science and engineering than Alanson Houghton. By 1913, the company had established one of the nation's earliest corporate research laboratories, pioneered revolutionary product lines, and developed mass manufacturing technology. Thanks to Houghton's progressive leadership, it was especially well positioned to meet the unprecedented business challenges of World War I. Although the company was just beginning to market its wares abroad when the war broke out, it had important connections to Europe. England, Austria–Hungary, and Germany supplied valuable raw materials such as refined potash, red lead, and rich clay. Corning had also initiated the exchange of confidential formulas and production technology with leading European glass companies. The firm adapted to wartime disruptions through a combination of materials substitution and innovative product development. Moreover, it greatly expanded its factory to capitalize on the sudden decline of European exports and the rise of British and U.S. government contracts. War-related production eventually occupied 85 percent of factory capacity. Revenue grew from under $1 million in 1900 to more than $12 million in 1920, with pretax profits exceeding $2 million (roughly equivalent to $18.4 million in 2003).

The demands of the war not only enhanced company performance but also changed forever the career of its forward-looking president. As Houghton's corporate responsibilities increased over the years so did his commitment to community service. As a young man, he had joined the local volunteer fire department and served as the unofficial town scholar, conducting free public lectures on matters of political economy. After his father's death in 1909, Alanson's public obligations increased substantially. His parents had been active, generous benefactors. Amory Jr. had dominated Corning's communal affairs, and as the city's largest employer, he had accepted a high level of social responsibility much as the Boston Brahmins had. Besides paternalistic concern for his employees, the two focal points of Amory's public service were Christ Church (Episcopal) and the Board of Education. Alanson's mother pioneered several social agencies, including the Corning Hospital and

Alanson B. Houghton. *Courtesy of the Houghton Family and Corning Incorporated*

the Corning Conservatory of Music. Of equal importance was her commitment to the Social Service Society, which investigated local health and social problems and spearheaded enforcement of child-labor laws.

Following Amory Jr.'s death, Alanson assisted his mother in managing these charitable affairs, and he and his siblings established a $25,000 endowment for the Corning Hospital. He replaced his father as a vestryman at Christ Church and as a member (and later president) of the Corning school board. Over time, his commitment to the causes of religion and education assumed a regional and national character. By 1918, he had become a trustee of Hobart College (Geneva, New York) and St. Stephen's College (now Bard College), the president of the Board of Religious Education for the Episcopal Diocese of Western New York, and a regular delegate to the Church's national conventions. Among his contributions to the latter was his leadership on the Business Methods Committee, which completely reorganized the Church's financial system.

America's entry into the First World War further transformed Houghton's commitment to public service. To nobody's surprise, he played a decisive role in the management of Corning's successive Liberty Loan drives. With patriotic fever running high and the Glass Works decorated with flags and bunting, the workers pledged their allegiance to President Woodrow Wilson. Houghton ordered the company to invest $50,000 in war bonds. When word spread that financial speculators were acquiring government bonds at a discount, he issued a terse statement to his 2,500 employees, warning them about loan sharks and reminding them of their duty to carry their bonds through to maturity. Recognizing that war-induced inflation was strapping family budgets, he offered, as a last resort, to repurchase employee bonds at par value. Houghton also recognized the confusion and inefficiency of various competing relief drives, so he helped consolidate and streamline the efforts of the YMCA, the Knights of Columbus, the Red Cross, and other agencies under a "War Chest" umbrella organization.

Despite his success in fundraising and his deft management of the glassworks' wartime production, Houghton still believed that his contributions to the overall war effort were inadequate, especially in light of the hundreds of Corning young men shipping out for combat. His own son, Amory, a student at Harvard, was determined to serve. If he was going to give his son to the country, he could not refuse to give himself. In February 1918 he announced his candidacy for the U.S. Congress.

Since the founding of the Republic, the Houghton family's political loyalties shifted easily from the Federalists to the Whigs, and then to the Republican party. The only break from the Republican ranks appears to have come during the 1884 presidential election when the Houghtons, like many other "good government" Mugwumps, bolted from the allegedly corrupt James Blaine in favor of civil service reformer and Democrat Grover Cleveland. On certain occasions, Houghton family members had dabbled in politics. The senior Amory served as town councilman in Cambridge and, during the Civil War, as a district alderman. In 1878, Charles was elected to the New York State Assembly. His brother, Amory Jr., served as a Republican presidential elector for James A. Garfield in 1880 and later ran unsuccessfully as a "dry" (temperance) candidate for the Corning Excise Board.

Alanson's first political appointment came in 1900 when Governor Theodore Roosevelt selected him as a trustee of the Willard State Asylum. He also served as a presidential elector in 1904, supporting Roosevelt, and four years later he backed TR's hand-picked successor, William H. Taft. As a delegate to the Republican National Convention in 1912, Houghton, like Elihu Root, Henry L. Stimson, and other New York luminaries, felt obliged to support the incumbent Taft over the resurgent Roosevelt. In 1916 he served again as a Republican presidential elector, supporting New York's reform governor Charles Evans Hughes. Still, Houghton's decision to run for Congress two years later shocked many friends. They exclaimed that he "wasn't the vote-hunting type," that his urbane demeanor, style, and obvious wealth would put off voters. But Republican officials, including his brother-in-law, State Senator William J. Tully, had prodded him to take the plunge. "I always declined to go into politics," Houghton recalled, "but when the war came, everything that I had been doing didn't seem to matter." Corning's largest newspaper applauded the about-face, stating that "the conditions we face today call for hard-headed business judgment, rather than theories voiced in oratorical flights."[15]

Although a dedicated Republican, Houghton presented himself to voters as a nonpartisan community leader. His campaign emphasized his calm temperament, good moral character, active citizenship, broad education, and business experience. He pledged to support President Wilson's prosecution of the war, to facilitate local crop sales to the federal government, and to vote for constitutional amendments establishing Prohibition and women's suffrage. He characterized the nation's problems as essentially economic ones that required pragmatic, businesslike solutions. In foreign affairs, he promised the promotion of U.S. farm products abroad, the expansion of the merchant marine, and the maintenance of a powerful navy to defend national interests. Houghton informed voters that after the war America must be prepared to "take its place among nations as a world power—THE WORLD POWER." On election day, he won all five counties and every major population center in his congressional district. He carried the largest plurality of any politician in Corning's history. By the time he took the oath of office on Capitol Hill in 1919, the Armistice had been signed and Congress's energies turned toward postwar reconstruction in Europe.[16]

The four years of carnage had caused more than thirty million casualties and a further reconfiguration of the international balance of power. The Russian, Hapsburg, Ottoman, and German empires were shattered. Inflation, taxation, and debt wracked the modern and once-prosperous economies of Great Britain, Germany, and France. Of the Atlantic powers, only the United States thrived during the war. Isolated from the battlefront, American manufacturing boomed, and its real and relative global strength increased dramatically. When measured in terms of industrial energy consumption, the nation's manufacturers outpaced Britain's by more than three to one, Germany's by four to one, and France's by ten to one. Moreover, the United States emerged from the war as a leading creditor and exporter. How the country would exercise this predominant power remained to be seen.

America's wartime economy had been managed by a Democratic president and supported by a Democratic Congress. However, the 1918 midterm elections, which brought Houghton into public office, marked a changing of the guard. After ten years as the minority party, the Republicans recaptured control of both houses of Congress, a position they would hold for more than a decade. A primary cause of the Democratic party's demise was the revolt of Far and Middle West farming communities whose voters were angered by discriminatory federal price controls that granted preferential treatment to Southern cotton. Having thrown off Democratic rule, the House Republicans chose not to revert to the autocratic leadership of Joseph G. "Uncle Joe" Cannon (R-IL), who had reigned as Speaker during the Roosevelt–Taft era. Instead, they elected the deferential and phlegmatic Frederick H. Gillett (R-MA), who guided reforms aimed at decentralizing power within the Grand Old Party. More important, the Republican revival caused a major shift in the relationship between the legislative and executive branches, with Congress reasserting its prerogatives after twenty years of expanding presidential power.

During his two terms, Representative Houghton proved less concerned with the division of federal authority and more interested in creating an effective and efficient national government. As a business executive, he had developed market strategies and operational procedures to adjust to ever-changing conditions. He approached government policy in similar fashion. Just as the war had forced Washington to assume new responsibilities in managing the economy (such as seizing control of the railroads), he believed postwar conditions demanded further policy adjustments. To ensure peacetime prosperity, he advocated revised tax, tariff, and transportation laws. To promote government efficiency, he supported the reorganization of the army and the overhaul of the budget and appropriations process.

By the time the 66th Congress convened on May 19, 1919, the Armistice was already six months old, and the demobilization of war industry and military personnel had begun in earnest. In Washington, domestic priorities frequently superseded international ones. The Republicans moved swiftly on several key pieces of progressive legislation, passing, with large majorities, amendments supporting women's suffrage and the prohibition of alcohol. Houghton fulfilled popular campaign pledges by backing both measures. Thereafter, managing the nation's difficult conversion to a peacetime economy consumed the most congressional time and energy.

Houghton and his colleagues responded to postwar challenges in several ways that affected trade and transportation. To assist farmers at a time of declining commodity prices, they passed the Fordney Emergency Tariff, which was vetoed by Wilson. Through the Merchant Marine (Jones) Act and the Esch–Cummins Transportation Act, Congress moved to curtail federal control over the shipping and railroad industries. Neither law sought to remove all government influence. These acts granted the Interstate Commerce Commission and the Shipping Board new authority to stabilize, rationalize, and enhance these key means of commercial traffic. For example, the Transportation Act was to improve management–worker relations by creating a nine-member Railway Labor Board to help govern industry wage scales and working conditions. The committee included three representatives each from labor, management, and the public. Although he had successfully opposed labor unionization at Corning Glass Works, Houghton supported giving rail workers a prominent voice on the board. When archconservatives in Congress opposed the idea, the glassmaker responded curtly, "I am satisfied that [it] is right, and that settles it with me."[17]

Houghton and many of his colleagues were equally concerned with improving efficiency within the government. They targeted both the military and the federal budget system for reorganization. In 1920 the Republican Congress passed the National Defense Act, which has been described as "one of the most constructive pieces of military legislation ever adopted in the United States." The act recognized the country's inherent dependence on civilian soldiers by establishing the Army of the United States with three permanent components—the Regular Army, the National Guard, and the Organized Reserves. In addition, it streamlined promotion procedures, increased maximum troop strength (threefold over prewar levels), and added several "modern" branches to the Army's organizational structure—the Air Service, the Finance Department, and the Chemical Warfare Service.[18]

There had been support for reforming the confused federal appropriations process since the Taft administration, and the dire funding problems that arose during the war reinvigorated such inclinations. Many Americans sympathized with a Massachusetts congressman who in 1918 snarled, "The President is asking our business men to economize and become more efficient while we continue to be the most inefficient and expensive barnacle that ever attached itself to the ship of state." To meet the challenge, the 66th Congress, with Houghton's enthusiastic approval, adopted the Accounting Act of 1920. The law sought to centralize the budgeting process in the Executive Branch by creating a Bureau of the Budget (forerunner to the Office of Management and Budget). It also proposed a General Accounting Office (GAO) to act as a congressional watchdog on fiscal matters. President Wilson sanctioned the Republicans' Defense Act but vetoed the budget bill on the grounds that he would require discretionary authority to remove the comptroller general of the GAO. In all, Wilson vetoed or "pocketed" twenty-eight bills sent to him by the new Congress, and the Republicans, with only a slight majority in the Senate and a fifty-seat advantage in the House, usually failed to override him.[19]

In this fractious political atmosphere, Houghton earned a reputation as a hard-working, fair-minded, and congenial legislator. Shortly after his arrival in Washington, he had informed House majority leader Frank W. Mondell (R-WY) that he did not expect special treatment in Congress because of his position in industry or his financial contributions to the party. He added, however, that he had already grown tired of long-winded speeches and wanted a demanding, if not influential, assignment. "I don't care what it is," he recalled saying, "nor how hard or humble the duty, just so it will keep me busy. I am not looking for anything spectacular, just an opportunity to be useful." In a political era when the seniority system predominated and congressional freshmen were usually posted to relatively weak and unpopular committees, Houghton was appointed to the prestigious Committee on Foreign Affairs. His unusual authority was further demonstrated late in the first session when his New York colleagues selected him as the state's representative on the Republican National Congressional Committee, which in turn appointed him to its Executive Committee. Although only "a first term man," a newspaper reported in 1919, Houghton's early efforts "on the floor of the House and as a member of the Foreign Affairs Committee [had] already stamped him as a leader in his party."[20]

Houghton's committee work reflected his overall record of supporting legislation to stabilize the economy and rationalize governmental affairs. His approach was evident during hearings on the annual appropriations for the Diplomatic and Consular Services. He believed that foreign trade remained critical to the domestic economy and that an expanded and more professional State Department was needed to help manage the country's position in the postwar world. When Wilson's secretary of state, Robert Lansing, and other State Department officials lobbied the Foreign Affairs Committee for an unexpectedly high level of funding, Houghton responded sympathetically. He demanded, however, that the department be more detailed and systematic in formulating its funding request. He warned that if such a large federal expenditure were not better justified, the Congress, which was guided by the prevailing mood for "economy" in domestic affairs and "isolation" in global affairs, would slash the appropriations bill. He offered the following advice to Wilbur J. Carr, director of the Consular Service:

> Is it not true that the first thing we all seek to realize is this tremendous [public] demand for economy? You go home and hear nothing else. If now we come in with a bill that makes a substantial increase over anything incurred during the war, what will happen? Foreign trade has increased enormously, the requirements of the foreign service have increased enormously, and we

have had to build a larger organization. Everybody knows that.
But we have got to go into detail to justify the increase.

There are a great number of men downstairs [in Congress]
and throughout the country who say "Let us get America out of
this thing. Why should we be spending all this money doing this,
that, and the other thing, all over the world. Let us get back." We
find that [isolationist] feeling almost everywhere. . . . [The Congress needs] a rational explanation of why it is necessary to ex-
pend this money now. . . . The trouble I am afraid of . . . is that
unless we show a sound basis at the outset . . . you may run into
an arbitrary cut. That is the thing to be afraid of.[21]

Houghton's willingness to bypass the intense partisanship of
the era was not lost on his western New York constituency. His
office received hundreds, if not thousands, of letters from Democrats and Republicans alike. Some were innocuous and easily answered. Most were heartfelt communications from war veterans or
their families requesting financial assistance. Houghton expended
considerable energy on working with the various federal bureaus
to process the applications of his constituents. New York voters
and Republican leaders rewarded the congressman's responsive-
ness and his dedication to efficient, businesslike government.

Houghton's reelection in 1920 seemed guaranteed. On the national scene, the "Wilson coalition" had disintegrated. Many stalwart progressives deserted the president after the war, feeling
betrayed by his compromises at Versailles and his support of government attacks on dissenters at home. Moreover, key voting con-
stituencies, including Irish-Americans, were hostile to Wilson's
League of Nations, a circumstance that did not bode well for Democrats, given the president's call for a "solemn referendum" in favor
of the world body. The Democrats' disarray was apparent in
Houghton's congressional district, where the party had considerable difficulty in fielding a candidate.[22]

Houghton assumed nothing. He canvassed the district and
launched a biting attack on the Democratic party's mismanagement
of the wartime economy. He railed against reckless spending, cit-
ing federal orders for 21 million shoes despite the fewer than
4 million men in service, and requisitions for 25 million harnesses
for the government's 300,000 horses and mules. On the positive
side, he pointed to the progressive legislation of the 66th Congress,
including women's suffrage, Prohibition, military realignment, and
industrial reorganization. If reelected with a Republican administration, he promised prolonged prosperity stimulated by tariff and

tax reform. Editorials in the regional press lauded his practicality and record of nonpartisanship. The *Oswego Times* praised "the purely business way in which Mr. Houghton has approached and performed his duties in Washington. The practical sense of the glass manufacturer has been a distinct asset." On election day, Houghton captured 70 percent of the votes, carrying every city and county in New York's 37th District. "He is the first man I ever heard speak," one Democrat noted, "who could get the goodwill and THE VOTES of the other party and make them think they were doing their duty to their country and themselves."[23]

The magnitude of the Republican party's victory in 1920 was overwhelming. Warren G. Harding and his running mate Calvin Coolidge defeated Democrats James Cox and Franklin D. Roosevelt by 277 electoral votes. The party gained a 20-seat advantage in the Senate and a whopping 170-seat majority in the lower chamber. Even Democratic fixtures in the House, such as Tennessee's Cordell Hull, lost reelection bids.

Harding wasted little time in taking advantage of the lopsided victory. With much of the country mired in a postwar recession, he called the 67th Congress into special session. When new House committee assignments were made, party leaders rewarded Houghton for his congressional work and his smashing reelection victory. Despite his minimal seniority, he was elevated from the Foreign Affairs to the Ways and Means Committee, probably the most powerful and desirable body in the House due to its broad jurisdiction over federal taxation and other financial matters. The committee included some of the most influential members of Congress: Joseph W. Fordney (R-MI, committee chair); Nicholas Longworth (R-OH, future majority leader); Willis C. Hawley (R-OR); John Q. Tilson (R-CT, future majority leader); Claude Kitchin (D-NC, minority leader); and John Nance "Cactus Jack" Garner (D-TX, future minority leader).

Republican lawmakers moved swiftly to provide Harding with a legislative program to stabilize the economy and promote efficiency, including bills vetoed by his predecessor. In May 1921 the president signed an emergency tariff law that raised duties on foreign foodstuffs, embargoed explosives and dyes, and included general antidumping provisions. Two weeks later, Harding drastically reformed the appropriations process by approving the Budget and Accounting Act, a landmark in progressive governance. He quickly appointed Charles G. Dawes, an Illinois banker and public utilities consolidator, as the nation's first Budget Director. Many significant laws followed, including the Sweet Act to establish the Veterans Bureau, the Highway Act to improve roadways, the Sheppard–Towner Act to assist mothers and children, and various farm relief measures.

Houghton supported these initiatives and, through his position on Ways and Means, worked to reinvigorate the national economy. He agreed in principle with the president and Treasury Secretary Andrew Mellon that a reduction in wartime tax schedules was necessary to stimulate growth. But the House committee considered the administration's planned cuts too drastic and partially offset reductions in personal income taxes with increases in corporate taxes. In late 1921, Harding signed the Revenue Act, which reduced the highest income tax bracket from 65 to 50 percent and increased the corporate rate from 10 to 12.5 percent. In the meantime, Houghton and his fellow GOP committeemen also devised a new tariff policy to guarantee agriculture and industry protection from cheap imports that stemmed from the postwar depreciation of foreign currencies. The tariff bill was consistent with the high duties and antidumping provisions of the existing emergency law, but the new bill also allowed the president, in his conduct of foreign policy, to adjust rates up or down by as much as 50 percent. The controversial legislation passed quickly in the House but bogged down in the Senate. By the time the Fordney–McCumber Tariff finally became law in September 1922, Houghton had resigned his congressional seat to become America's first postwar ambassador to Germany.

Houghton's departure from Congress stemmed from his dissatisfaction with the tedious process of lawmaking. As the executive of a large corporation, he was accustomed to taking charge of his professional affairs and overcoming the challenges of the marketplace. By comparison, his daily work in Congress seemed dreary. Only one year after arriving in the nation's capital, the novelty and excitement of congressional life began to fade. While never losing his zeal for national service, he questioned the relative influence of an individual congressman. "When I came to Washington as a member of Congress," he recounted, "I was never so bored in my life. . . . I had been in the habit of telling people what to do. . . . I was way beyond . . . the stage in a person's development where a Congressman's routine would have interest."[24]

Regardless of his dislike for the political regimen, Houghton had much to show for his three-year stint in Washington. Patriotism more than political ambition had compelled him to public service, but it was his ability to draw upon decades of managerial expertise that helped him put "the nation's business" on a more effective and efficient basis. His dedication and diligence in the House won him the respect of colleagues and constituents on both sides of the aisle. He formed lasting and politically important friendships. His landslide reelection in 1920 stamped him as one of western New York's most popular political figures, while his leadership on the Republican National Congressional Committee and elevation to the House Ways and Means Committee demonstrated his growing influence within the majority party. As a legislator, Houghton supported a moderate progressive agenda, which championed social legislation related to women's suffrage and Prohibition and demanded internal governmental reforms such as streamlining the military and overhauling the federal appropriations process. Houghton ultimately aligned himself with Old Guard Republicans on measures promoting tariff protection and private property rights, but his backing of key transportation and tariff bills arose in part on their designation of expert or "scientific" advisory committees. He believed that objective, quasi-governmental bodies such as the Interstate Commerce Commission and the Shipping, Tariff, and Railway Labor Boards could help bring stability and prosperity to the postwar economy.

When he decided to leave Congress for the diplomatic corps, Houghton was forced to broaden his outlook as a public servant. Nevertheless, his business approach to problem solving, which had inspired his conduct in Washington, also governed his views on international relations. Even before the 1920 elections, Houghton had informed his closest Washington confidant, John Dwight, that if the Republicans captured the White House, he would petition the new administration for a European ambassadorship, perhaps Spain. Dwight, a well-connected Republican insider who had served as House majority whip in the Cannon era, advised Houghton not to settle for a "second-rate post" like Madrid, but rather to "take Berlin."[25]

Houghton's nomination for the ambassadorship to Germany came in a circuitous and fortunate fashion. He was not chosen, as many historians have contended, because of his business acumen and an ability to solve pressing international economic problems. On the contrary, his selection was rooted in pure political patronage. In the four-way fight over the 1920 Republican presidential nomination, he had supported the moderate candidate, Frank Lowden, a popular reform governor from Illinois and a personal friend of Dwight's. As governor, Lowden had demonstrated a measure of independence and a willingness to work with progressives. During the war, he had become more closely associated with former president Theodore Roosevelt. All of this did not sit well with Republican reactionaries, but Houghton admired the governor and respected his commitment to efficient and effective governance. When Lowden failed to amass enough delegates at the divisive Republican convention, he and his followers agreed to back the Old Guard's conservative candidate, Senator Harding. After winning the nomination, an appreciative Harding asked Lowden and Dwight what they wanted as compensation for their pivotal support. Working in tandem with New York's congressional delegation, the duo lobbied for Houghton's diplomatic appointment.

Only weeks after Harding's inauguration, journalists began to link the Corning glassmaker with the German ambassadorship. New York Senators James W. Wadsworth Jr. and William M. Calder met privately with the president and his secretary of state, Charles Evans Hughes, to urge the appointment. Most press reports expressed little surprise over Houghton's "probable" nomination, given the "high regard" for him in political circles demonstrated by his "unusually good" committee assignments. While the president considered Houghton an excellent choice, there was little he could do until America's technical state of war with Germany was terminated and normal diplomatic relations were restored. On July 2, 1921, Harding signed a congressional resolution, vetoed by Wilson during the League controversy, which repealed America's declaration of war. Eight weeks later, the Peace Treaty of Berlin was executed, and by November, both governments had ratified it, opening the door for the formal exchange of envoys. By that late date, several competitors had emerged for the Berlin post, including former ambassador to Germany David Jayne Hill, but Houghton and his supporters had received secret assurances from Harding. On January 18, 1922, the White House announced that Houghton's name would be sent to the Senate for confirmation. Henry Cabot Lodge, the chairman of the Foreign Relations Committee, moved quickly and forwarded a favorable nomination report to the full Senate. Houghton was confirmed on February 10 without objection. Editorials in the United States and Germany supported the appointment. The *Washington Star* noted how Houghton's political experience, familiarity with Europe, and especially his business expertise would enable him to "master the dislocations of the war" and provide the Harding administration with insightful advice "as to the best methods and means for setting them right again."[26]

The delay in his appointment allowed Houghton time to contemplate his approach to international affairs. Thirty-five years had elapsed since he first crossed the Atlantic for postgraduate studies at Göttingen, Berlin, and Paris. During that time, America and Germany had risen to challenge Great Britain's industrial and naval supremacy. As a student and admirer of European culture and history, he had returned to Britain and the continent on several occasions before the war, even as late as August 1914, when he was temporarily stranded in London. There is little doubt that his university and travel experiences in Europe shaped his global outlook toward a more active world role for the United States. His professional career at Corning Glass Works, which included key relationships with European firms, further cemented his worldview. In business, he came to understand the integration of the global economy through raw material and capital exchanges, trade competition, and technology transfers. Most important, he came to appreciate America's changing position within the international system.

As a congressman, Houghton publicly expressed certain apprehensions relative to these changes. He feared that America would return to "the national tradition" of isolating itself from international political problems without realizing that its emergence as a foremost industrial and financial power also brought new leadership obligations regarding world peace and prosperity. For those suffering from disillusionment over the war's results, Houghton sought to clarify America's motive for fighting in it. It was not altruism, he proclaimed, but rather a calculated action necessary to defend the country's "vital interests," especially the freedom to navigate the seas. America's new, dominant position in the postwar era, he believed, had enlarged the nation's security interests and thus required the implementation of a new and more active foreign policy.[27]

Houghton, in brief, wanted the United States to assume a leadership role in world affairs. He vigorously supported the Harding administration's convening of the Washington Conference in November 1921. With the Versailles Treaty stipulating the terms of Germany's postwar disarmament, the conference's primary objective was to prevent an arms race among the naval powers: the United States, Great Britain, and Japan. Political leaders in all three

countries believed that unbridled military spending would perpetuate international instability and jeopardize economic recovery. In
his finest hour as secretary of state, Hughes shepherded the conference toward three multilateral treaties that substantially reduced,
through tonnage limitations, the number of large capital ships allowed in fleets. The United States, Britain, Japan, France, and Italy
agreed to a capital ship ratio of 5:5:3:1.75:1.75, respectively. Japan
accepted a position of inferiority to America and Britain on the condition that the powers limit the construction of new fortifications
in the Pacific. Moreover, all nations remained free to build smaller
crafts such as cruisers and submarines. The treaties also created a
structure for future Great Power cooperation over China and issues of Pacific security, and they essentially terminated the two-
decades-old Anglo-Japanese military alliance. Houghton reveled
in America's leadership at the Washington Conference.

   In terms of the peace settlement in Europe, he urged Americans to back the Allied demands on Germany for disarmament and
reparations as well as to support the partial dismemberment of the
Central Powers and the legitimacy of independent buffer states such
as Poland, Yugoslavia, and Czechoslovakia. But Houghton worried
that the victors might inflict an overly harsh punishment on the
newly democratic Germany, thereby threatening the likelihood of
a lasting peace. Just after his election to Congress, he accurately
prophesied that "the Germanic people are altogether too numerous, too virile, too industrious, too competent to remain permanently crushed. . . . Sooner or later we know [they] will rise and
assume a place among the great nations. And sooner or later, if
some means to prevent it are not found, the old game of dividing
into armed camps will be begun again and war will follow."[28]

   Houghton's prescription for preventing such a calamity was
the expansion of America's world influence, especially in Western
Europe. This outlook should be understood in part as his extension of the elite class's social responsibility from the domestic to
the international realm. "I am eager," Houghton announced, "to
see a [wealthy] America rise to a moral duty and to a moral leadership." During the latter part of the war, he had declared in favor of
America's participation in a new international organization such
as the League to Enforce Peace, which was being championed by
former president Taft. As historian Thomas Knock states, the "conservative internationalist" proponents of Taft's league supported
boards of arbitration and conciliation in certain disputes and also
believed to some extent "that the United States should pursue in-

ternational stability through the power of deterrence inherent in collective security, yet reserve to itself the right to improve its capacity to undertake independent coercive action against the forces of disorder that threatened the national interest." Houghton had no illusions that warfare could be eliminated, but he felt certain that after the devastation of the Great War, America must strive to "render war more difficult."[29]

Houghton's enthusiasm for any collective security arrangement was deflated by the tumultuous battle over the League of Nations in 1919–1920. In his congressional reelection campaign, he criticized the Treaty of Versailles for bearing "little resemblance to a 'peace without victory,' " and, he added, "it certainly differed materially from the so-called '14 points' which Mr. Wilson had enumerated as the basis of peace." He attacked the League on partisan and philosophical grounds, echoing the criticisms of both progressives and conservatives in the Senate. He argued that the treaty had been designed less as a mechanism for promoting world peace and more as a means to perpetuate the dominant political and territorial position of the Allied Powers. He believed that by joining Wilson's League, American war-making powers would be transferred from Congress to the executive. Moreover, he feared that the League Council might force the United States to abandon the Monroe Doctrine, and that the country would ultimately lose control over its immigration policy. After the Senate rejected League membership in March 1920, Houghton resolved that world leadership by the United States would have to be exercised outside any formal international organization, except the Permanent Court of International Justice, known as the World Court. The Harding administration adopted the same position.[30]

Before departing for Berlin, Houghton gave press interviews and delivered several addresses that offered a view of his foreign policy outlook. Those familiar with his active leadership at Corning Glass Works and in Congress recognized his forward-looking approach. In a dinner speech at Delmonico's in New York, he spoke of the increasing importance of European stability and commerce to American prosperity. He emphasized the futility of his nation's traditional isolationist sentiments. "I am one of a generation which grew up in the belief that America was self-contained and self-supporting and self-sufficient and that we could get along . . . well without the rest of the world," but "Americans might as well make up their minds to the fact that this nation's welfare 'is inextricably bound up with the welfare of the world.' "[31]

He expanded on this theme several weeks later in a much-publicized speech at the exclusive Metropolitan Club. Before the problems of postwar reconstruction could be solved, he argued, the people of America and Europe needed to move beyond traditional and wartime thinking. He called upon the victors and vanquished to develop a new "mental attitude" based on objectivity, fairness, and mutual respect. If people clung too closely to regressive issues such as war guilt, then world progress would be thwarted by a renewal of the deadly conflagration. Yes, Germany had lost the war, and must therefore "foot the bill," but the charge should not exceed reason. The process of reconciliation must be a practical one. Houghton underscored the special role for the United States. In this New Era, the nation had a central task, a "conscious duty," to help rebuild European civilization. The country, he declared, could no longer remain aloof from the Old World; "we Americans must do our part" and do it "now."[32]

Though short on specific recommendations, Houghton's message attracted attention across the country and in Europe. America's ambassador in London, George Harvey, concluded that its conciliatory tone had been generally well received in Britain but not in France, where the population was less forgiving of its wartime enemies. Germany embraced the sentiment fully, and several newspapers hailed Houghton as America's new "Peace Ambassador." Reaction at home was decidedly mixed. The newly formed American Legion denounced the address, and the *New York Tribune* lamented that the ambassador's approach to Europe "will scarcely make a great hit." There were also rumblings at the State Department. Secretary Hughes sent a message cautioning Houghton on the limits of "Ambassadorial license" when making pronouncements on U.S. foreign policy.[33]

Yet many newspaper editors came to Houghton's defense, arguing that his worldview was grounded in common sense, especially in light of his upcoming "difficult and thankless post." The *New York Times* applauded his explication of the integrated world economy and extrapolated that he viewed current tariff policy "only as a stepping stone to freer trade." The glassmaker "will be missed from Congress," the newspaper continued, but "there is a man's job to be done in Berlin." Despite the minor controversy, Houghton himself believed that he stood on solid political and diplomatic ground. The day before the speech, he had consulted privately with Harding at the White House. There, he received approval to emphasize "the hundred years of friendship and good will" between

America and Germany and to downplay the "few years of war and bitterness." The president had, in fact, squarely endorsed his spirit of conciliation: "That's a good thought. Say it as often as you can."[34]

Although Houghton was embarking on a new career at the age of fifty-eight, his privileged upbringing and considerable experience in commerce and politics had prepared him well for the intricacies of major power diplomacy. His impressive background and immense wealth made him, in the parlance of the day, "a big man," and this stature emboldened him to think independently and act resolutely. He would become a key instrument of Republican foreign policy in the 1920s. While abroad, however, he discovered that he did not always agree with Republican priorities and tactics, and so he labored tirelessly to adjust the course of American foreign policy.

Notes

1. *Corning Evening Leader*, March 18, 1922; James B. Morrow, "A Business Man Ambassador," *The Nation's Business* 10 (June 22, 1922): 18–19; "A Business Man as Ambassador to Germany," *Current Opinion* 2 (August 1922): 193–95.

2. August Heckscher, *A Brief History of St. Paul's, 1856–1996* (Concord, NH, 1996), 30–37.

3. Ben Procter, *William Randolph Hearst: The Early Years, 1863–1910* (New York, 1998), 27–29.

4. *Horae Scholasticae*, 1881–1882, vol. 15, 140–42, St. Paul's School Archives, Ohrstrom Library, Concord, New Hampshire.

5. Houghton to Amory Houghton Jr., December 1, 1885, Houghton Papers.

6. George Santayana, *Persons and Places* (New York, 1963), 200–201; *Boston Daily Advertiser* clipping (not dated) found in scrapbook "Verses," Houghton Papers.

7. *Boston Record*, June 26, 1911.

8. Houghton, "Italian Finances from 1860–1884," *Quarterly Journal of Economics* (January 1889 and April 1889): 233–58, 373–402.

9. James Bryce, *The American Commonwealth* (London, 1888), vii; Alanson B. Houghton, *Seven Tables: Illustrating in Some Points the Extent of Governmental Interference in Great Britain and the United States* (London, 1888); "1886 Class Report #2," Harvard University Archives; Anson Phelps Stokes, "(Houghton) Biographical Sketch," Houghton Papers.

10. Houghton, "Journal: A. Houghton Jr. and A. B. Houghton, Trip to Norway, Sweden, and Russia, Summer of 1888," Houghton Papers.

11. "1886 Class Report #2"; *Corning Leader*, October 6, 1887.

12. *Corning Daily Democrat*, June 27, 1891; *New York Times*, June 27, 1891. Houghton's second son, Quincy, died from appendicitis in 1907.

13. George Buell Hollister, "Historical Records of the Corning Glass Works, 1851–1930," typescript, 1951, revised 1960, 12, Corning Incorporated Archives, Corning, New York (hereafter cited as Corning Archives).

14. Ibid., 50–55.

15. Arch Merrill, *Fame in Our Time* (Rochester, NY, 1960), 139–43; Frederick L. Collins, "Abroad with Our Ambassadors," *Woman's Home Companion* 5 (January 1926): 15; *Corning Evening Leader*, February 25 and August 28, 1918.

16. *Corning Evening Leader*, October 26, 1918.

17. "Flashlights of Famous People: Alanson B. Houghton," *Springfield* (MA) *Evening Union*, March 9, 1925.

18. U.S. Army, *American Military History* (Washington, DC, 1989), 405–12. The National Defense Act allowed for an army of 300,000 soldiers. Congress reduced troop strength to 125,000 in 1922.

19. Paul D. Hasbrouck, *Party Government in the House of Representatives* (New York, 1927), 15.

20. "How to Succeed Though Rich," undated clipping from *Saturday Evening Post*, Houghton Papers; *Corning Evening Leader*, September 30, 1919.

21. House Committee on Foreign Affairs, *Hearings on Diplomatic and Consular Appropriations Bill*, 66th Cong., 2d sess. (Washington, DC, 1920), 60–98.

22. David Burner, *The Politics of Provincialism: The Democratic Party in Transition* (New York, 1967, 1986), 59–72; Thomas J. Knock, *To End All Wars: Woodrow Wilson and the Quest for a New World Order* (New York, 1992), 256–69.

23. Clipping from the *Oswego* (NY) *Times*, October (?), 1920, Houghton Papers.

24. Notes from Jonathan Mitchell interview with Alanson B. Houghton (hereafter cited as Mitchell interview), June 4, 1941, Houghton Papers.

25. Ibid.

26. *Corning Evening Leader*, April 18 and May 14, 1921; *New York Tribune*, May 14, 1921; *Washington Star*, February 9 and March 28, 1922.

27. *Corning Evening Leader*, October 26 and December 24, 1918.

28. Ibid., December 23, 1918.

29. Ibid., October 26 and December 24, 1918, and June 1, 1920; Knock, *To End All Wars*, 55–58.

30. Untitled and undated campaign speech, Houghton Papers.

31. *New York Times*, February 22, 1922.

32. Houghton, "Metropolitan Club" (speech), March 30, 1922, Houghton Papers; Morrow, "A Business Man Ambassador," 18–19.

33. "Ties with Germany Renewed," *Literary Digest* 73 (April 15, 1922): 14; Hughes to Houghton, April 1, 1922, Houghton Papers; Sander A. Diamond, "Ein Amerikaner in Berlin: Aus den Papieren des Botschafters Alanson B. Houghton, 1922–1925," *Vierteljahrshefte Für Zeitgeschichte* 27 (July 1979): 431–508.

34. *New York Times*, February 23, March 29, April 1 and 3, 1922; Alanson B. Houghton Diary (hereafter cited as ABH Diary), April 8, 1922, Houghton Papers; Houghton, "Speech to Consuls," August 7, 1922, Houghton Papers.

3

Confronting Conservative Internationalism

1922–1923

> The American people must understand their responsibility and their opportunity. God has given us the power to render a vast service to humanity. No such opportunity ever has come to any nation in two thousand years. The world has become an economic unit. The United States must recognize this and shape her policies in accord with this new fact in her history. The idea of isolation must be dismissed. The sentiment and the sense of responsibility for building a better world civilization must be cultivated.
> —Alanson B. Houghton, 1922

Houghton recognized that his ambassadorial appointment had come during a transitional period in the history of U.S. foreign relations. The eight-year Wilson presidency had represented a culmination in America's rise as a global power. Never had the nation's military been so formidable and so fully deployed. Never had the government been so involved in European political affairs. And never had U.S. trade, investment, and culture been so prominent on the world stage.

Influenced by these developments, there evolved, after the Great War, three competing brands of American internationalism. The Democratic Wilsonian approach, perhaps best described as collective progressivism, underscored the worldwide spread of U.S. economic and geopolitical interests. Through membership in the League of Nations and the Permanent Court of International Justice (the World Court), Wilsonians sought to construct a

postwar order based on international commitments for political cooperation and compromise, collective security and large-scale disarmament, and the freer flow of trade and investment.

The Republican party's ascendancy, which began in 1918, effectively bypassed Wilson's program by invoking the American
tradition of unilateral action in world affairs. Moreover, the Republicans, while in favor of expanding trade and investment, were
also inclined to grant tariff protection to American farmers and
businessmen. The Republicans for the most part supported the
Wilsonian policy of disarmament, but other international issues
often divided the party into two foreign-policy camps. Mainstream
Republicans, represented by the Harding and Coolidge administrations, perceived America's vital interests traditionally, limiting
them essentially to the Western Hemisphere. For these conservatives, the highest priorities were maintaining regional U.S. hegemony and safeguarding the domestic economy. On the other side,
progressive Republicans, including senators Robert "Fighting Bob"
La Follette (WI), William E. Borah (ID), and George Norris (NE),
advocated an internationalist approach distinct from conventional
Republicanism. These so-called radicals not only objected vehemently to Wilson's commitment to collective action but also opposed the pro-big business orientation of Harding and Coolidge.
"Peace progressives" such as Borah sought postwar stability
through a strident, moral foreign policy of anti-imperialism (political and economic) and antimilitarism (even in Latin America),
which their many detractors simplistically labeled as isolationist.

With Harding and then Coolidge occupying the White House,
and Republican conservatives and unilateral progressives dominating Congress, there was little chance in the 1920s of the United
States joining the League of Nations or committing to a military
alliance system. Even participation in the World Court proved un-
workable. Throughout the decade, American economic and cultural
power continued to surge around the globe, but general disillusionment with the Versailles Treaty combined with the Republican
ascent had a restraining effect on U.S. political and military involvement overseas, especially regarding Europe.

In foreign affairs, as in his business and political careers, Ambassador Houghton championed activist policies designed to meet
the challenges of evolving circumstances. During his seven years
as a diplomat, he offered the Republican administrations a provocative policy alternative that sought to promote political engagement
in Europe by blending the three varieties of American internation-

alism. The ambassador thought that his nation's emergence as a predominant power required Washington to assume an active and responsible role in international affairs even if not a League member. He considered the 1921–1922 Washington Conference, which produced naval arms control and a framework for stability in the Pacific, an exemplar for American leadership in the postwar era. Houghton wanted the Harding administration to apply itself equally to the complex reconstruction problems confronting Europe. The economic and political revitalization of Western Europe was especially important, and Houghton believed that peace and prosperity among the major powers were ultimately dependent on close cooperation among the United States, Great Britain, and Germany. He recognized that the critical postwar issues of war debts, reparations, inflation, trade, investment, and security were tightly interwoven and required innovative solutions. In several ways, his pursuit of progress on these fronts proved analogous to his far-sighted corporate initiatives, which years earlier had transformed Corning Glass Works into a modern, internationally renowned enterprise.

During his first year and a half in Berlin, Houghton built an impressive intelligence network that included confidants in the highest echelons of German politics and business. In that span, he tackled the controversy of the U.S. military occupation of Germany, the important economic issue of U.S.–German war claims, and the policy of his country's nonrecognition of Soviet Russia. He also reported vividly on Germany's descent into what historian Gerald Feldman describes as "the Great Disorder," which severely undermined the viability of the new Weimar Republic and bolstered the popularity of extremist ideologies. The Harding administration valued the ambassador's commentaries on and forecasts of European affairs. It resisted his policy prescriptions, however, and came to resent his accusations that the United States, by dint of its inactivity, was failing to fulfill its obligations as a world power. Houghton's early experience in Berlin reveals the administration's determination to remain aloof from European political problems and suggests its fateful consequences. Moreover, it illustrates the ambassador's determined attempts to adjust the course of America's conservative internationalism in the New Era.

On his way to Germany, Houghton undertook several fact-finding missions. In early April 1922 he visited London to glean from the American ambassador insights into British foreign policy. He learned of the mounting tensions between Britain and France over Allied policy, particularly in regard to German reparations. Several days later, he crossed the Channel for Paris. There, he arranged briefings with America's unofficial representatives on the Allied Reparations Committee, Roland W. Boyden and James A. Logan. From Paris, Houghton traveled to the German Rhineland town of Coblenz to inspect the Allied and U.S. military occupation.

The presence of American soldiers in Europe had become an increasingly controversial issue in the United States. Eager to cut military expenditures and avoid entanglement in European politics, Congress discerned little justification for continuing the army's deployment. President Harding also favored recalling the troops, but he had been persuaded during the winter to maintain temporarily a contingent of some 5,600 soldiers to mollify French security fears. Immediately after the Washington Conference, he reduced the American presence to just 2,000 men. By late March, the War Department had announced plans to terminate the occupation. Apparently, Secretary Hughes had been excluded from this decision, but he soon convinced Harding not to withdraw the troops. He needed them for leverage in his difficult negotiations with the Allies over recouping from Germany some $240 million in American occupation costs.

Houghton arrived at Coblenz on April 18 and was fully aware of the mounting pressure to recall American forces. Ambivalent himself, the ambassador investigated the issue, and his policy recommendation proved pivotal. He consulted first with General Henry T. Allen, commander of American Forces in Germany (AFG). Allen had become the fiercest proponent for continuing the U.S. deployment. Having lost much of his sympathy for France because of its provocative and domineering occupation policy, he believed that the AFG served as a harmonizing political influence for both the Allies and the Germans. Houghton also arranged private interviews with senior French, British, and Belgian officials. All supported the retention of American soldiers because of the volatile relations between French forces and the local German population. French High Commissioner Paul Tirard even assured the ambassador that France had no intention of inflaming its relations with Germany by making the Rhineland "another Alsace Lorraine."[1]

In considering the issue, Houghton understood why most Americans opposed a prolonged occupation. The notion of the U.S. military being entrenched in the Old World, especially in a time of peace, ran contrary to the nation's traditional foreign policy. Nobody relished the prospect of American soldiers being dragged into a conflict between French troops and German civilians. On the other hand, Allen and the Allied commissioners convinced him that the AFG was playing a crucial stabilizing role. To recommend the recall of the troops ran counter to the Republican objective of restoring world order and also to the ambassador's personal goal of heightening America's involvement in Europe. Therefore, he advocated compromise.

His report arrived at the State Department on April 25. He underscored his interviews not with Allen, but with the Allies. The army's withdrawal, he averred, would immediately increase friction between France and Germany and indefinitely postpone European recovery. Houghton stressed that it was not the size of the deployment that mattered the most. A significant reduction in the 2,000-man force was feasible, especially since a smaller contingent minimized the dangers of military engagement. The mere gesture of America's ongoing involvement, he argued, would exert a calming influence.

Hughes was elated by the ambassador's dispatch and rushed it to the White House. Harding reacted quickly. Referring to Houghton's cable, he instructed Hughes to comply "with the manifest general wish for the retention of a military force there. . . . My own judgment is that we might reasonably reduce our numbers to approximately one thousand men." Hughes, still using the troops as a negotiating tool, notified the press that the AFG would not be withdrawn entirely because the Allies and Germany appreciated its "very wholesome" influence. The president's decision pleased Houghton. The army's presence fostered stability and provided at least a semblance of American political leadership in the Old World. Over the next several months, the envoy labored diligently to educate his many visitors from America, especially members of Congress, on the positive influence exercised by Allen and the AFG.[2]

Houghton finally reached the American embassy in Berlin on April 20 and wasted little time in making his diplomatic rounds. Although Chancellor Joseph Wirth and Foreign Minister Walther Rathenau were away at the Genoa economic conference, the new envoy called immediately on Secretary of State Ernst von Simson, Undersecretary Edgar Haniel, and Division Director for American Relations Dr. Karl von Schubert. Two days later, Houghton presented his credentials to Friedrich Ebert, Germany's first democratic president. After formal exchanges, the ambassador emphasized his personal commitment to restoring friendly relations between the

United States and Germany, and in return, President Ebert promised full cooperation. Houghton then sought out other members of Berlin's diplomatic community. He was most disappointed by the unconciliatory attitude of the French ambassador, Charles Laurent, who expressed little desire to improve his country's relations with Germany. More promising was the blunt British ambassador, Edgar Vincent D'Abernon. Houghton had been informed that his British counterpart opposed French stridency and had significant influence with the German government. What he liked immediately about D'Abernon—and planned to emulate—was his independent thinking. What he liked least—and planned to avoid—was his cautious attitude toward initiating change. D'Abernon believed "that time alone can work the situation out," Houghton noted. "He will be caught sooner or later when events actually take place."[3]

Houghton's first official assignment was to negotiate a bilateral agreement to settle American financial claims against Germany. The war damages were estimated at between $300 and $400 million (roughly equivalent to $3.2 and $4.4 billion in 2003). Although Secretary Hughes later claimed credit for the final pact, the ambassador actually played the decisive role in its formulation and outcome. Houghton recognized that the claims issue presented another early opportunity to impress upon Washington and the American public the goodwill and cooperative nature of Germany's democratic government. Before leaving the United States, he had informed officials at the State Department of his plan to have Berlin accept a lopsided claims commission with two American judges but only one German. Such a patently unfair design was unprecedented, and Hughes expressed healthy skepticism regarding Germany's willingness to accept an inequitable proposal. Houghton believed that such gestures by Berlin were essential to building political support for American involvement in European affairs.

He sprang his proposal on the Foreign Office while Wirth and Rathenau were still away. He even suggested that the Germans formally propose the one-sided commission to the United States. When Undersecretary Haniel objected to the scheme, the ambassador explained the positive effect it would have on attitudes in Congress and on U.S.–German relations. Houghton also rallied support for his plan among influential Germans, including Carl Bergmann, Germany's chief reparations negotiator, Friedrich Rosen, Wirth's first foreign minister, and senior executives at Deutsche Bank. When Rathenau finally met with Houghton on June 1, he expressed sincere appreciation for the ambassador's larger objectives and agreed to consider the plan. The next day, Houghton lobbied Chancellor Wirth, whose government had been formed a year earlier dedicated to *Erfüllungspolitik*, the policy of fulfilling obligations to the Allies. After meeting Wirth, Houghton received a counterproposal from Rathenau that essentially accepted his claims-commission plan. The ambassador reviewed the note with his staff and forwarded the text to Hughes with a statement that the Germans had demonstrated a serious commitment to improving their foreign relations. He hoped that Washington would reciprocate.

While waiting for the administration's reply, Houghton met frequently with Germany's foreign minister. The pair quickly became kindred spirits, leaving the British ambassador in awe of Rathenau's "peculiar confidence" in Houghton's leadership. Undoubtedly, the duo's similar backgrounds played an important part in their entente. Before the war, Rathenau had been president of his family's business, the Allgemeine Elektrizitäts-Gesellschaft, one of Germany's largest electrical companies. Indeed, Houghton stated that the flowering relationship rested on their approach to world problems as businessmen seeking rational and durable solutions, not as diplomatists jockeying for unilateral advantage. Comparing business to diplomacy, the ambassador wrote to his son that foreign policy negotiations were "very much the same thing as talking business questions, with the exception perhaps that the business people are somewhat keener." He also cheered Germany's early cooperation on his claims proposal and jeered at Washington's comparatively slow response.[4]

When Washington finally accepted the "German" plan in late June, Houghton delivered a draft agreement to the Foreign Office. After a cursory review, Undersecretary Haniel unexpectedly objected to certain aspects of the pact. Visibly upset, the ambassador asserted that the accord had already been finalized and that it should go before the German cabinet. That evening, Rathenau arrived at the American embassy for a long conference with Houghton and his guest, James Logan, of the Reparations Committee. The ambassador gained Rathenau's assurance that the claims agreement would be accepted. Houghton believed that he had managed a diplomatic coup. But the ambassador's satisfaction was crushed the next morning by the force of Germany's deadly political realities. News arrived that right-wing extremists had assassinated Rathenau just ten hours after he had left the embassy.

Houghton was horrified. He and the foreign minister had grown close, personally and professionally. "Rathenau and I were sewing ourselves up in the same quilt," he wrote to his political mentor, John Dwight, "and my position here was being made wonderfully strong. Now it is all knocked to pieces." The murder reverberated throughout Europe and threatened to destabilize the German government. Without Rathenau, the Foreign Office, in Houghton's view, was a bedrock of reaction, where the secretaries could not see past the mere "letter of the contract" to appreciate the larger purpose of his initiatives. The thought of giving the United States the trump card on the bilateral claims commission, he wrote, "is so utterly novel in international dealings [that it] staggers them and makes them timid."[5]

Foreign Office officials did, in fact, submit to Houghton an amended claims agreement, which, among other items, stated that the Reichstag needed to ratify all settlements. The envoy, in turn, warned them about a new bill introduced in Congress proposing a war claims commission that excluded German participation entirely. He instructed Undersecretary Haniel that Berlin faced a clear choice between a judicious committee with German representation or an all-American committee susceptible to political whims. He gave Berlin three days to choose. On August 1, Chancellor Wirth informed Houghton that his cabinet had approved the original claims agreement in its entirety and that he would personally champion the pact with key members of the Reichstag. Wirth and Houghton executed the agreement on August 10. Immensely pleased with the arrangement, President Harding wanted its details released to the press. He instructed Hughes: "In making the announcement, please *emphasize* the request to us to name [the] umpire. It is so unusual that its significance is worth bringing well to the fore." That night a contented Houghton inscribed in his diary: "So ends the first chapter."[6]

The war-claims agreement was a positive achievement for U.S.–German relations. The episode was symbolic of Washington's relative postwar strength and Berlin's desire for U.S. political and economic assistance. The claims negotiations were also a signal achievement for Houghton as an untested diplomat. His design for an American umpire and his idea that Germany should propose it proved a brilliant stroke. It satisfied a contentious Congress by making Germany appear trusting of American leadership. The pretense of being a German initiative fooled not only most contemporaries but also some future historians, including Hughes's biographers. Important for the ambassador, he had, in a very short time, gained the confidence of German leaders and had demonstrated his worth to the State Department. He received a glowing commendation from Hughes and took satisfaction in knowing that his claims-commission structure served as the model for forthcoming agreements with Hungary and Austria. Above all, the claims negotiations illuminated Houghton's strategy for swaying American opinion toward a more benevolent and active role in Europe's reconstruction.

By the time the claims agreement had been executed, Houghton had completely revamped the American embassy in Berlin. He restored and lavishly furnished the badly dilapidated building. A stingy Congress forced Houghton to pay for the remodeling himself. During his three years at the embassy, he spent an estimated $150,000 from his personal account to cover the capital improvements and most operating expenses. His annual government salary was $17,500. More important, the ambassador's overhaul extended to the management of daily operations. The embassy had reopened in 1919 under U.S. Commissioner to Germany Ellis L. Dresel. Because of his declining health, Dresel rarely left the building during his last months in Berlin, and the embassy staff had been given little direction or supervision. Houghton applied his business acumen to reorganizing the post. He and Warren D. Robbins, the embassy's counselor, coordinated and routinized procedures. Duty assignments for the secretaries were rearranged, and the ambassador instituted weekly staff meetings to further harmonize the work.

Houghton's management of the political and diplomatic affairs at the embassy was far from dictatorial. He encouraged frank and open discussion among his subordinates and confided in them. He had, for example, purposefully asked Robbins and First Secretary Stewart Johnson to help him critique Rathenau's counterproposal to the claims pact. The ambassador's intention was to stimulate among his staff a "broader vision" of American foreign policy, and he hoped that by entrusting them with classified information the embassy would develop as "a more united and homogeneous" concern. Much to his dismay, he soon realized that his secretaries were overly reliant upon the British embassy for intelligence, and as a result, their interpretations and recommendations closely tracked British attitudes. At a special meeting, he reminded his staff that "this is the American Embassy and we are Americans and that the point of view of this Embassy will be determined by [us] and not by the British Ambassador. . . . Our opinion shall originate here rather than up the Wilhelmstrasse."[7]

Alanson B. Houghton with the embassy staff, Berlin. *Courtesy of the Houghton Family and Corning Incorporated*

By midsummer 1922, Houghton's businesslike approach had the embassy running smoothly. He worked conscientiously to cooperate with the U.S. Consular Service, which operated a dozen offices throughout Germany. He included Chief Consul William Coffin in his weekly meetings and supported the idea of a summer convention in Berlin for all of the consuls stationed in Germany. The ambassador emphasized the value of cooperation between the Diplomatic and Consular Services and the foreign-based attachés of the Commerce Department. Serious rivalries had developed among these agencies, but Houghton bridged their ranks within his own jurisdiction. As a congressman, he had supported progressive reforms in the State Department, including entrance exams, merit promotions, and higher salaries. As an ambassador, he sought better managerial efficiency and actively promoted the unification of the consular and diplomatic branches, which occurred in 1924 under the Rogers Act.

Houghton harbored other concerns about State Department procedures. He was especially piqued by the constant shuffling of embassy personnel. By August 1922, he believed that "the wheels" of his finely tuned mission were being lopped off by narrow-minded bureaucrats. When word arrived that the embassy's naval attaché, W. P. Beehler, would be transferred, the ambassador implored Hughes to press the navy for a six-month extension. He insisted that Beehler had "an extraordinary grip" on German affairs. Unlike most of his staff, the naval officer spoke the host language fluently and enjoyed close relations with both German democrats and monarchists. When Beehler's retention proved impossible, Houghton demanded a comparable substitute. Instead, he was sent forty-year-old Commander (and future World War II hero) William F. Halsey Jr., whose understanding of German and the Germans, the ambassador concluded, was "comparatively nil." Within months of his arrival, the embassy staff considered Halsey "a complete washout." Houghton also complained about the transfer of Copley Amory, one of his junior secretaries. His Berlin mission was capable of outstanding work, he asserted, "but what can I do when the Department takes away from me the only man I have who has studied the Russian situation, and places him in Italy, where he can be of little use because he knows no Italian, and sends me in turn a man [Robert M. Scotten] who knows no German. After all, German is the language most used in Germany. Knowledge of Spanish, or even of Guatemalan politics, are not essential to our work here."[8]

Houghton's anger over Amory's transfer stemmed from more than a mere loss of diplomatic efficiency. Germany had established formal diplomatic and economic relations (and secret military agreements) with Soviet Russia in April 1922 under the Treaty of Rapallo, and since then, Berlin had become a center of Communist propaganda and intrigue. The Harding administration continued Wilson's policy of not recognizing the Soviet government because the Communists had repudiated foreign debts, rejected private property rights, and fomented revolution outside of Russia. Republican peace progressives in Congress, led by Idaho's Senator Borah, opposed the U.S. policy and favored immediate recognition. Borah argued that the Soviet state enjoyed widespread support within Russia and was a base of stability for postwar Europe. Having studied Marx and socialism at Harvard and chaired the House subcommittee on Russian affairs, Houghton had become intensely curious about "the Soviet experiment" and made a concerted effort to collect information on Russian political and economic affairs. He questioned the wisdom of America's nonrecognition policy and worked to increase his expertise on the subject.

Houghton entertained an endless parade of visitors attempting to influence his thinking on Russia. He met with rash German conservatives who advocated military intervention and the overthrow of the Communist regime. He also received the less extreme counsel of liberal politicians and prominent industrialists who encouraged American and European investment in Russia to help stabilize the German economy and continental affairs. Lincoln Steffens, the famed muckraker and magazine editor, impressed upon Houghton the precarious health of Soviet Chairman Vladimir Lenin, who, he argued, was more open to dealings with the West than War Commissar Leon Trotsky. Houghton became convinced that, after Lenin's death, a dangerous power struggle would ensue between "moderates" of Lenin's ilk, who supported the market-oriented New Economic Policy, and hard-liners such as Trotsky and Joseph Stalin. Houghton was impressed with the argument that American capital in Russia would promote broader European stability, and he believed that Soviet moderates aimed to protect foreign investments. In the end, however, the ambassador concluded that Lenin's hold on the government was too precarious. While he favored American humanitarian relief in Russia, he recommended to Washington that the United States postpone political or commercial intervention, allowing the Russians to "stew in their own juice for a year or two." Intercession at this juncture would only temporarily prolong the current regime. On July 7, he noted perceptively, "I made a real effort to find some sort of modus vivendi, but I declare I can find none. Russia must get worse before she can get better."[9]

Unknown to the ambassador, Hughes and Commerce Secretary Herbert Hoover planned to send a committee of business experts into Russia to survey economic conditions. While they opposed official recognition, they hoped that Russia's reintegration into the world economy would eventually topple the Communist government. They asked Houghton to meet secretly with Leonid B. Krassin, the Soviet Commissar for Foreign Trade. He was to float the idea of an international investigative committee but actually work for the acceptance of a purely American commission. The ambassador objected to the scheme. First, he argued (contrary to the beliefs of Harding, Hughes, and Hoover) that some form of Communist government was likely to reign indefinitely in Russia. Second, although the Lenin regime might grant concessions to the West, its protection of foreign investment was tenuous at best because Lenin's conservative opponents appeared to be gaining power. Houghton appreciated the temptation to exploit economic opportunities, but he argued that there was no sound basis for intervention until the political situation stabilized. Any immediate action, he added, might weaken Washington's ability to create a favorable climate for long-term American investment. Moreover, any diplomatic initiative would be misinterpreted as a softening of U.S. insistence on debt repayment and private property guarantees.

When the State Department ignored Houghton's protest, he arranged a private luncheon with Krassin at the Esplanade Hotel. Krassin brought Georgi V. Chicherin, the Soviet Commissar for Foreign Affairs. Houghton engaged the commissars on a broad range of issues, even informing them of his view that Marx's strengths lay more in the realm of social philosophy than political economy. When the conversation finally turned to the commission idea, the ambassador displayed his deftness as a diplomat and his capacity to deceive. Knowing that the Russians were bitter about the recent failures of the Genoa and Hague economic conventions, Houghton brought both to the fore to get the Russians to object to a new *international* board of investigation. When he proposed, disingenuously, his desire for such a multinational commission, Krassin dismissed it summarily. Thus, the ground was paved for an American panel. By the end of the meeting, the Russians agreed that the deployment of a committee of American experts, if it avoided political concerns, could be beneficial. The ambassador stressed repeatedly that their meeting had been unofficial, taking place even without the knowledge of the State Department. This ploy gave the Harding administration a means of disavowing responsibility. Krassin and Chicherin agreed to consult Moscow.

Three weeks passed without a response from the Soviets. Hughes began to worry that the Russians were planning to use the ambassador's inquiry to propagate the "false" view that the United States was easing away from nonrecognition. On August 23, in a confidential letter to Houghton, the secretary vindicated the envoy's position on Russian policy. "I am entirely in accord with your view," he wrote, "that it would be inadvisable to take further steps at this time in the direction of an economic inquiry and I have made this recommendation to the President." But the Hughes letter had not reached Berlin when, on August 29, Houghton received a note from Chicherin stating that the Soviets would welcome "with joy" the initiation of trade relations via the visit of a U.S. economic commission. He added a condition, however, that the United States reciprocate by allowing a Russian delegation to investigate the American market.[10]

Houghton must have been relieved when instructions finally arrived not to proceed with the commission plan. To avoid any potential embarrassment, the State Department issued a concise press statement disclosing that Houghton had contacted Soviet authorities to determine their attitude about an American economic committee. The ambassador could not help but criticize the administration's hurried determination to intervene in Russia: the commission proposal "only resulted in convincing the Soviets that the attitude of the United States is changing toward them." The United States would not open formal diplomatic relations with Soviet Russia until 1933.[11]

Houghton preferred that the Harding administration concentrate less on the Marxist regime in Moscow, and more on the fledgling democratic government in Berlin. Russia, he thought, would not develop as a strategically important industrial power for at least a generation. Germany's resurrection, on the other hand, was not only immediately foreseeable, but critical to postwar stability. The confusion stemming from Rathenau's assassination in June had caused suspense in Germany, but the murder actually rallied public support behind the Weimar Republic. The ambassador monitored the political scene closely. Despite his short tenure, he had developed intimate contacts inside the Wirth government and among all the major parties. Through this network, he became privy to behind-the-scenes machinations. In midsummer, he had been informed of the conservative German National People's Party's (DNVP) decision to informally support the Wirth administration, and of the upcoming consolidation of the Independent Socialist Party under the more moderate Social Democratic Party (SPD). These developments, which brought labor and industry behind the government, spoke well, Houghton reported, "for the political sense of the party leaders that in this time of crisis they are willing to subordinate any possible personal advantage . . . to the general safety."[12]

The crisis Houghton referred to was not political but economic, and its development led the ambassador to call for American intervention. Germany's monetary policy, the Great War, and the exacting terms of the Versailles Treaty crippled its postwar economy. The Allies had seized Germany's colonial possessions and divvied up portions of its Central European territory to France, Belgium, Denmark, Czechoslovakia, Poland, and Lithuania. France not only regained ownership of the prized border region, Alsace-Lorraine, which it had lost a half-century earlier in the Franco-Prussian War, but it also received fifteen years of mining privileges in the coal-rich Saar Valley. In total, Germany was forced to relinquish more than one-tenth of its population and one-seventh of its territory.

Moreover, its economy was weakened by the Allied order to pay substantial reparations. In January 1921 the Allied powers had set the bill at 226 billion gold marks plus annuities equal to 12 percent ad valorem of the country's yearly exports, payable through 1963. Many economists thought the indemnity unreasonable and unrealizable, but when Berlin balked at the sum, the Allies expanded their occupation zone along the Rhine River and imposed special tariff duties. Nevertheless, the Allies announced a revised but complicated reparations plan in April 1921 that reduced the sum to 132 billion gold marks (approximately $33 billion in 1921). The figure and the plan's complex schematics represented a compromise between France and Britain, with the latter urging a much smaller financial penalty. Despite German protests that the amount still exceeded their capacity to pay, the Wirth government, fearing further punitive sanctions such as occupation of the industrialized Ruhr Valley, began paying hundreds of millions of marks in cash reparations in addition to payments in kind of coal and timber.

Even worse for Germany, the value of its currency was falling dramatically. When Houghton first arrived at his Berlin post in April, one American dollar was worth approximately 252 marks, by late June, 345 marks, by late July, 670 marks, and by the fourth week of August, 1,301 marks. In other words, the currency lost roughly 80 percent of its value in four months. This devaluation complicated Germany's economic recovery and its ability to make cash payments. The country had financed the war by borrowing instead of taxing and, at the same time, by greatly increasing its money supply to meet rising government expenses. A stubborn reluctance to tax and a willingness to print marks set in motion a decade of hyperinflation that escalated most rapidly after Houghton's arrival. With industrial capacity far below prewar levels and postwar trade constricted by foreign barriers, the Berlin government found it increasingly difficult to accumulate the funds necessary for reparations. In fact, its permissive monetary policy was designed in part to thwart the payment of reparations. Germany's economic difficulties, self-induced or not, threatened to stall the recovery of the Allied nations and the world economy.

The belief that an international loan to the German government might help solve the financial conundrum led to the formation of a bankers' committee in April 1922. Led by J. P. Morgan Jr., the ambassador's classmate at St. Paul's School, the committee met in Paris during May and June to consider the conditions necessary to float a secured loan. In the end, the bankers wanted the Allies to lower Germany's indemnity to ensure that Berlin could make reparations *and* loan payments. French officials vetoed Morgan's plan, demanding that any reductions in reparations be offset by the cancellation of France's war debts to the United States. The Harding administration refused to acknowledge any linkage between war debts and reparations and proffered no diplomatic initiatives.

Houghton wanted desperately to stabilize the mark and strengthen Germany's economy. After negotiating the claims commission pact, he pleaded with Hughes to conclude a comprehensive commercial treaty with Germany to boost its exports and improve its foreign-currency reserves, which would make reparations payments easier. He argued further that a new trade pact granting most-favored-nation status would help Berlin reach similar accords with other trading partners and thereby bolster industrial production and the national currency. When the State Department was slow to respond, Houghton grumbled to a friend about the administration's lack of initiative: "My relations with the Government here are undoubtedly cordial in every way, but it is dreary work dealing with the State Department . . . the people who are in charge seem strangely reluctant to make decisions except of a negative sort."[13]

During the summer of 1922, an anxious Houghton watched the German government struggle to pay reparations. If the Germans were to default, he feared a French military reprisal. Thus, he lobbied for a short-term moratorium on reparations to help stabilize the economy, an idea supported by Great Britain. The ambassador warned Hughes that a total economic collapse in Germany would threaten the very existence of the nascent democracy. He boldly recommended that the United States apply "all possible pressure of a financial sort" on France to ensure a temporary moratorium: "action is now essential on our part. It is dangerous to delay."[14]

But Houghton soon recognized the Harding administration's unwillingness to intervene despite the grave conditions. European Division Chief William R. Castle explained the State Department's position in a confidential letter. The administration was hamstrung, he wrote, by Congress's opposition to interfering in European affairs. As a result, Hughes was locked into an "enforced inactivity" that prevented any action. The secretary of state, according to Castle, recognized that conditions in Germany were deteriorating and that the world was rapidly slipping into a "desperate crisis," but Hughes hoped that an independent, international banking committee would eventually settle the "staggering" reparations problem. If Hughes could, Castle claimed, the secretary would personally tell the Paris and Berlin governments to settle the problem immediately based on Germany's maximum capacity to pay. If the French declined, the secretary would then tell them to "go to h--l." If the Germans refused to compromise, then they "can go bust for all the world cares."[15]

Neither Harding nor his cabinet felt compelled to take an active role in the settlement of Germany's reparations, which proved the most destabilizing international issue of the early 1920s. While administration officials believed that some American interests were at stake in Europe, these interests, largely economic, were not considered of vital importance. Houghton disagreed, contending that America's economic welfare depended on the stability and prosperity of Western Europe. He continued to report on Germany's worsening conditions and the deadlocked negotiations over a moratorium. By late August, with reparations talks stalled and the mark-to-dollar exchange rate approaching 1,350:1, even Undersecretary William Phillips began to reconsider the possibility of American intervention. But Harding and Hughes again squelched the proposition. On August 26 the president informed Phillips, "It is apparent Germany needs help . . . [but] I do not understand what course we might helpfully and consistently pursue." Hughes weighed in four days later, telling his undersecretary, "I do not see that we can make any helpful suggestion."[16]

With negotiations in Europe at a virtual standstill and Washington's policy of nonintervention confirmed, Houghton worried that the reparations problem might prove insoluble. In September, his hopes were buoyed by reports that French and German industrialists had decided to take matters into their own hands by resolving trade disputes. The ambassador learned of these negotiations—later known as the Stinnes-Lubersac Agreement—through private consultations with industrialists Hugo Stinnes, director of the vast Stinnes conglomerate, Kurt Sorge, director of the Krupp works, and Hermann Bücher, executive secretary of the Reich Association of German Industry. Houghton had met with Stinnes on several previous occasions. The most memorable encounter had occurred at the embassy the night before Rathenau's assassination. Stinnes had come to explain the mounting coal crisis threatening German industry and employment. The gathering, which included Rathenau and James Logan, evolved into a long, drawn-out debate over reparations and inflation. Such meetings reflected the ambassador's intimate involvement with Germany's most powerful business and political figures.

The ambassador was impressed with the initiatives of the French and German businessmen and he wired the promising details to the administration in Washington. But in a personal letter to Hughes, he described Germany's ongoing deterioration as a quiet bloodletting. It was possible that the efforts of the industrialists would come too late to save the economy. On the day of his letter, the mark-to-dollar exchange stood at 1,409:1.

In Washington, German Ambassador Otto Wiedfeldt met with Hughes to emphasize the critical state of European economic affairs. He pleaded for U.S. intervention, arguing that America was the only power that could command sufficient confidence and bring about a solution. The secretary acknowledged Europe's difficulties and, while avoiding comment on America's potential role, expressed hope that final reparations would be settled soon by an impartial panel. Later that afternoon, Hughes instructed Ambassador Myron T. Herrick in Paris to encourage J. P. Morgan Jr. to organize a new committee of reparations experts. On October 14, Herrick reported that the European situation was growing more acute and that Morgan, while willing to serve on a new bankers' commission, refused to take the lead in a political matter that demanded government rather than private initiatives.

Hughes also received a dramatic cable from Roland Boyden, the unofficial U.S. observer on the Allied Reparations Committee. He, like Houghton and Herrick, underscored Germany's perilous economic condition, especially the crippling inflation that was leading to the "complete demoralization" of the country. He urged that the United States take "bold and comprehensive action" by demanding that France accept the recommendations of a new experts' committee. Hughes responded with characteristic caution, declaring that "this is not an opportune time for formal statement[s]" by the U.S. government. But finally realizing the necessity of official action to alleviate the situation, he consented grudgingly to a meeting between Herrick and French Prime Minister Raymond Poincaré to discuss the idea of a new international commission.[17]

Although Houghton understood Hughes's preference for resolving Europe's woes by means of a nongovernmental committee, he had not been immediately apprised of Herrick's activities in Paris. There is little doubt that the ambassador would have supported this modest initiative to set reparations at Germany's capacity to pay. But Houghton recognized that Europe's postwar reconstruction problems were not exclusively financial. He understood that Europe's progress was tied to French foreign policy and he was sympathetic to France's dilemma. For Berlin to meet its reparations obligations, it would have to revive the German economy by regaining control of the Rhineland (as collateral for new foreign loans) and have the Allies lift trade restrictions. To ask France to give up "security" and give Germany a free hand was "a difficult thing," Houghton conceded. Throughout 1922, he was mistakenly confident that France's own declining economic position and need for foreign capital would force it to accept a smaller reparations settlement. He believed that the U.S. government should work with France to find a practical solution. For Paris to take unilateral political actions that would prohibit the influx of foreign loans into France and Germany, he claimed, would fly in the face of common sense; it would be analogous to "going out on the end of the limb of a tree and then sawing it off."[18]

Houghton did not believe, however, that all hope and responsibility for postwar reconstruction rested upon France. He recognized that during the last century the world had become increasingly integrated and interdependent and that the United States had evolved as a pivotal economic power. As a result, he believed that America possessed an obligation to secure a more peaceful and prosperous world. Dismayed at the Harding administration's reluctance to take a more active stance in Western Europe, the ambassador began to formulate his own U.S.–led reconstruction plan. He saw the chief problems as economic hardship, moral disillusionment, and inadequate national security, all of which were linked to German reparations and the billions of dollars in outstanding war loans. "The settlement of the reparations question is imperative for the very security of Europe and the progress of every nation," he claimed, and "the question of reparations is inextricably bound up with the question of the repayment of loans made by various allied nations." The solution, therefore, was a quid pro quo among the United States, Germany, and the Allied powers. America could resuscitate Europe's economy, stabilize international currencies, set reparations at a lower level, and bring about a measure of security, all by forgiving the Allied war debts (equivalent to $109 billion in 2003) and making certain political demands. In return for debt forgiveness, Washington should exact from Western Europe a fifty-year, multilateral nonaggression pact, further limitations on armaments, and adherence to the referendum as means for declaring war. All three demands had become popular among American progressives and

the burgeoning postwar peace movement. Such a bargain between
the United States and Europe, the ambassador believed, would promote political stability and goodwill and stimulate international trade
and investment.[19]

Houghton circulated his plan among American colleagues in
Europe and friends in the United States. He received encouragement to proceed despite the fact that war-debt forgiveness was
politically unpopular back home. By October, the ambassador decided to send the proposal to Washington for consideration. "After
a tremendous lot of brooding," he wrote to confidant Dwight, "I
have made up my mind to write the Secretary a letter in regard to
handling the foreign debt. It may be crazy but it seems to me sound.
. . . I shall send you a copy . . . and [if you] get a chance to talk it
over with the President, I think you would be doing him a service.
. . . I know this sounds ambitious, and as I said, perhaps it is a little
crazy, but at any rate I can't get it out of my head, and I may as well
put it to the test."[20]

The ambassador informed Hughes that he had devised a policy
with so much promise to the future of America and the world that
he felt compelled to offer unsolicited counsel. He stressed that because the United States had become a Great Power it had a moral
duty to secure world peace and economic prosperity. "God has been
good to us in America," the envoy claimed. "He has made it possible for us to create and to pile up huge wealth," and unless the
United States intervened, Europe faced two ends: a second world
war and the spread of Bolshevism. Nor were these mutually exclusive paths. Houghton warned that another Great War seemed inevitable unless the nation committed itself to helping Europe
overcome its hardships. "It is alone for the [United States] to decide" which course Europe will take. He concluded by urging
Hughes to discuss the plan with the president. He reminded the
secretary that, to date, the administration had been merely following Congress on foreign policy and that it still had an opportunity
to chart its own course. Should Hughes and Harding decide that it
was politically impractical to present the proposal as official policy,
Houghton asked to offer it personally and unofficially in a Thanksgiving Day speech. He acknowledged that his plan was extremely
ambitious but explained that, when one sees "the forces of civilization in the balance," one must seize the "moral courage" necessary
to provide pathbreaking leadership.[21]

Houghton's means for transforming American policy by directly
intervening in Europe's reconstruction were not unlike two of his

major initiatives at Corning Glass Works. The firm's revolutionary adoption of scientific techniques and mechanized production were largely the result of his innovative leadership, and these endeavors had required not only vision but also a willingness to assume risk. Financial sacrifices, he reasoned, must be incurred to reap future rewards. So, it came naturally to Houghton the diplomat that his "new company"—the United States, which had already amassed huge wealth—should risk part of its fortune to bring about a real and a lasting peace. Houghton signed his letter to Hughes on October 24 and "let it go with prayers."[22]

Meanwhile, with the German currency pegged at 3,568 marks to the dollar, the Allied Reparations Committee and the Wirth government sought to halt the nation's spiraling inflation. In late October and early November, Berlin witnessed a bustle of activity as the Reparations Committee and a separate German-sponsored commission of international economists, including Britain's John Maynard Keynes, converged on the capital to develop a definite plan for economic stabilization. Houghton opened the embassy as a gathering place for their deliberations. Although there were no formal connections between the two committees, there were, according to Roland Boyden, frequent and useful exchanges between the groups thanks to the ambassador, who had created a neutral ground for debates on international problems. In the end, much disagreement over the best path to economic stability remained, but all sides thought that Germany needed to balance its budget, control its foreign currency exchange, and arrange for a sizable international loan. Despite material differences between the commissions and among individual committee members, a majority of the financial experts—and Chancellor Wirth and Houghton—agreed that France's willingness to grant a two-year moratorium on reparations was crucial to Germany's stabilization. Regarding this possibility, pessimism prevailed. Houghton alone seemed optimistic that declining economic circumstances would persuade Paris to accept the judgments of informed experts.

By the time the Reparations Committee left Berlin on November 10, the value of the German currency had plunged further, with one American dollar buying 9,172 marks. The worsening economic crisis created turmoil for German democracy. Houghton, who had been so enamored with the prospect of a broad coalition government, was startled to learn that the SPD, the largest single party, had decided to abandon Wirth over his plans to bring more conservative elements into his coalition. This move severely disappointed the ambassador, who believed that Germany's stability rested upon the political cooperation of labor. In other words, an important opportunity for broad-based leadership had been missed. On November 14, Wirth resigned, leaving the situation greatly confused.

The ambassador kept the State Department apprised of the fluid political scene and accentuated the need for American involvement in the resolution of the reparations problem. Germany's President Friedrich Ebert, he reported, was working tirelessly with party officials to find an acceptable replacement for Wirth. There was considerable speculation that "a wholly new man" would be brought into the government from outside Berlin. Rumors surfaced that a leading candidate was Cologne's mayor, Konrad Adenauer, whom Houghton described as "a man of education and position, possessed of force and initiative," who "measures up pretty well to the situation." The ambassador also grew increasingly interested in southern German politics. Several weeks earlier, with the Wirth regime still intact and before the news of the SPD's decision to withdraw from the government came out, Karl von Wiegand, a Hearst newspaper correspondent, had discussed with the envoy the possibility of a dictatorship by General Erich Ludendorff. The general, who had essentially led Germany during the latter years of the war, had emerged as the presumptive leader of the nation's radical right-wing parties. Houghton at first brushed off the conversation, but by November 8, with Benito Mussolini's seizure of power in Italy, the ambassador became more concerned with Bavaria's volatile political conditions. He dispatched a military attaché to investigate. "Something is certainly brewing in Bavaria," he confided in his diary, "and no one seems to know exactly what it is. Probably it will result in nothing definite, but too much is at stake to permit us to run any danger." A week later, after Wirth's resignation, Germany's political scene changed drastically, and Bavarian events assumed greater importance to the ambassador.[23]

Houghton met with von Wiegand again at the embassy on November 17 and learned more about the "disquieting" intentions of Munich's chief rabble-rouser, Adolf Hitler. The Hearst journalist informed him that Hitler's main program consisted of reaching "some arrangement" with France and establishing a dictatorship in Germany. Von Wiegand warned him that Hitler was capable of initiating a putsch, or coup d'état. Three days later, Berlin was still without a new government, and the ambassador wired Washington that political conditions remained unpredictable. Adding to the uncertainty and representing a "possible future cleavage," he wrote, was the rise of "a very strong . . . Fascisti movement" that exhibited strength not only in Bavaria but in the northern states as well.[24]

On November 21, Houghton elaborated on the tentative state of affairs in a long confidential letter to Hughes. He expressed concern over Germany's indirect proportional voting system, which had led to "parliamentary impotence." The "absurd" unwillingness of the Socialists to support a broad coalition government, he claimed, would weaken the effectiveness of any new administration and bolster the extremist campaigns calling for a dictatorial/ monarchical regime. The ambassador supplied a detailed and alarming description of right-wing developments in the south, and although he identified the National Socialist German Workers' Party (Nazis) with other "Monarchist groups," the report was chillingly perceptive:

> The situation in Bavaria is giving us all some concern. Matters there are rapidly taking on a menacing form. There are four Monarchist groups, all of whom are armed [and] organized. . . . All of them seek and may eventually strike for either a highly centralized and effective government, or for a dictatorship, probably the latter. . . . They are being brought together . . . in a so-called "Fatherlands Union," and if this happens to result in a real union, danger may be apprehended.
>
> The most active of the Monarchist groups is headed by a young Austrian named Hitler who is in control, it is estimated, of thirty thousand armed men, and who, by his vehemence and fanaticism and by his dominating and attractive personality, is rapidly becoming the leader of the whole movement. . . . The model that is being followed by these Monarchist groups is that of the Fascisti in Italy, and . . . [the German Fascists] mean to break down any attempt of the Socialist groups to assert themselves along either political or economic lines.
>
> This Fascisti movement is unquestionably spreading throughout Germany. . . . It offers a method and a means by which conservative people of all shades of political opinion can get together and organize to meet and to repel Socialist aggression. It meets Socialism with its own weapon. It faces loud-voiced and heavy-fisted labor leaders with loud-voiced and heavy-fisted young representatives of other classes. . . . If Monarchy can be kept out of it . . . it is not unlikely to bring within its ranks a large share of the population.

Houghton informed the secretary that he had recently dispatched to Munich a military attaché and that he would monitor the troubling developments.[25]

The ambassador's concern over a right-wing putsch was allayed temporarily on November 22 by the formation of a new government headed by shipping tycoon Wilhelm Cuno. The rise to power of another German businessman greatly pleased the ambassador because he believed that it would enhance the chances for a pragmatic settlement with the Allies. Moreover, he knew and trusted Cuno, who had visited the embassy several times and had organized a reception for Houghton in Hamburg. Earlier in November, when President Ebert offered Cuno the position only of foreign minister, the shipping magnate, who was traveling with his business associate, William Averell Harriman, asked Houghton for his opinion. Houghton advised him to delay making a decision. When Ebert subsequently asked Cuno to become chancellor, Cuno again consulted with the American ambassador. This time, Houghton encouraged him to proceed, but with caution. He emphasized the need for Cuno to have a free hand in selecting a cabinet supportive of his programs. With Ebert's backing, Cuno constructed a right-leaning moderate government that found the Socialists in passive opposition and the Nationalists in a position of benevolent neutrality. The American ambassador remained a trusted Cuno confidant.

The establishment of a new German government refocused attention on economic problems, and again Houghton wanted U.S. leadership. "There is no use for the American administration to talk about [American] prosperity, of course, in a real sense," he wrote to his son, "until Europe again is prosperous. And Europe will become prosperous whenever we are ready to help." Houghton believed that his plan for security and prosperity, beginning with the forgiveness of war debts, would prompt a final settlement of reparations and set a basis for worldwide recuperation. He understood that remitting the war debts in exchange for disarmament and peace agreements was a highly ambitious policy that would encounter much opposition, but he hoped that Harding would at least let him propose and defend the plan unofficially.[26]

The ambassador enlisted many supporters for his initiative, including State Department bureau chief William Castle, who, while visiting Europe in October 1922, backed Houghton's plan in a letter to Hughes. He argued that at this juncture, only American intervention could "keep Europe sane." He conceded that the public would have to be educated on the merits of debt cancellation before Congress could be swayed, but Houghton's plan championed a great cause that could generate considerable political currency for the Republican party. But Castle's wholehearted backing was partially offset by Boyden, who informed Hughes that he had carefully studied Houghton's plan and agreed with his view of Europe's extreme conditions, and that the situation required American intervention. He sympathized with the idea of remitting the debts because the risks were too large for America to sit by "with arms folded while France . . . pushes Germany into bankruptcy," but he merely urged the administration to make a formal statement regarding reparations and calling on the Allies to help stabilize the mark.[27]

Harding and Hughes considered the Houghton plan but decided that there should be no further discussion of it, especially the idea of war-debt remission, which they determined that Congress "alone" controlled. Congress had recently created a War Debt Commission, which included Harding cabinet officials, to negotiate repayment of the war debts with the Europeans. Although the commission and Harding were willing to offer favorable terms based on a "business basis" formula, they refused to contemplate cancellation, as such a policy would essentially shift the financial burden to U.S. taxpayers and thus allegedly threaten domestic economic growth. Most Americans could not envision the political or economic benefits of making such a large sacrifice. There was a smattering of support for cancellation in Congress and in business circles, but few were willing to invest political capital in the controversial issue. When Hughes cabled the administration's negative verdict to the ambassador in mid-November, he also told him that informal exchanges between Washington and Paris had begun regarding a possible experts' settlement of the reparations tangle.[28]

The administration's indirect negotiations with France proved anything but fruitful. Though offering to meet with Morgan, Prime Minister Poincaré was unwilling to agree to the investment banker's condition of a reparations moratorium. As a result, there appeared little chance that a new experts committee would be formed. By month's end, conditions were rapidly sliding toward a crisis as reports surfaced that France planned to seize Germany's coal mines, railroads, and forests in the Ruhr district. Amid these threats, Houghton met with Chancellor Cuno twice to stress the need for a settlement with France. Since Washington had no intention of intervening, the ambassador advised Cuno to meet personally with Poincaré to hash out their differences. With Cuno's blessing, Houghton traveled to Paris on December 2, hoping to prevent an international calamity. Because Harding and Hughes had refused to act, he elected to initiate negotiations between France and Germany.

Houghton had planned a trip to Paris and London for several months. He claimed that he needed a fresh, non-German perspective. Moreover, he needed rest and, from his British tailor, new clothes. When he arrived in Paris, he met immediately with U.S. reparations representative Boyden and American ambassador Herrick. He informed them that Cuno was ready to begin earnest negotiations. Boyden then visited Jean-Jacques Seydoux, a senior French economic adviser, who thought the démarche an important first step. But when Germany's ambassador officially approached the French government, Poincaré acted as if he were uninterested. By then, Houghton had reached London, where he discussed the reparations crisis with U.S. Ambassador Harvey and German Ambassador Friedrich Sthamer. Houghton's travels sparked speculation in the press about a major U.S. diplomatic initiative. When approached by reporters, the ambassador announced that he was merely on vacation to order new suits. He wrote in his diary: "saw several reporters . . . great excitement over the mysterious object of my visit. . . . I told them again trousers. This has the advantage of being partly true, in which respect it differs from most explanations."[29]

Meanwhile, frustrated by Poincaré's inaction, Cuno, prodded by Houghton, ordered Ambassador Wiedfeldt to meet again with Hughes in Washington. The German envoy announced Berlin's willingness to sign a long-term nonaggression pact with France, Britain, Belgium, and Italy, and to embrace the referendum as a means for declaring war. The proposal stemmed from Houghton's original peace plan but skirted the issue of America's war loans to the Allies. A month had passed since Hughes and Harding had rejected the Houghton proposal, and during that time the crisis in Europe had worsened. Because the administration now feared French military action against Germany, Hughes considered the German proposition an important move toward peace that could have a positive and powerful effect on the public at large. He conveyed this attitude to the French ambassador in Washington, who forwarded the scheme to Paris. Houghton wired the State Department to stress the need for France and Germany to begin new talks, and he pointedly reminded Hughes: "All eyes are now centered on Washington."[30]

Poincaré rejected the German proposal and notified Washington that Germany had been declared in "voluntary default" of reparations payments—a signal that France would take military action. Hughes felt boxed into a corner. His tepid European diplomacy had failed completely. Democrats and Republican progressives roundly criticized the administration's inactivity. Senator Borah recommended that the president organize a conference on European economic problems. Under public pressure, Harding and Hughes repeatedly assured the press that they were not "indifferent or aloof," that they were taking "definite steps" and "doing everything possible" to bring about European stability. To silence critics and possibly forestall a French invasion of Germany's industrial heartland, Hughes gave a much publicized policy address to the American Historical Association on December 29. Later claiming to have been inspired by the voice of God, he expressed America's interest in European recovery and called for a voluntary and independent experts' commission to resolve the reparations crisis.[31]

The belated public pronouncement had no effect on the Allies, who met in Paris in early January 1923 to devise a common reparations policy. As a basis for new negotiations, Cuno sent word to the Allied powers that Germany was prepared to pay between 20 and 30 billion gold marks if given a four-year moratorium. His plan, which included a proposal for a nonaggression pact, was summarized in a New Year's Eve speech at Hamburg, after which he telephoned Houghton. The ambassador believed that Cuno had made a sincere and domestically popular offer that could be used as a foundation for earnest negotiations. He admitted to Hughes that Germany could pay more, but at the risk of losing broad political support in the Reichstag. The Allies considered the proposal too modest and did not discuss it at the Paris convention. A complex British proposal, granting Germany a four-year moratorium and fixing reparations at 50 billion marks, was rejected by France, Belgium, and Italy. No compromise was found. On January 9 the Reparations Committee, with Britain in fervid dissent, again declared Germany in default of its timber and coal deliveries, and with this justification, France, Belgium, and Italy expanded the military occupation to the Ruhr Basin.

Washington's immediate reaction to the renewal of hostilities was to recall all American soldiers stationed in Germany. "We are getting our troops out of Europe," announced isolationist Senator Hiram W. Johnson (R-CA). "Let us hope that we are getting ourselves out of European entanglements and European disputes and problems." For his part, Hughes now assured reporters that there had long been a consensus in America to withdraw the troops and that the administration had worked diligently to prevent the Ruhr invasion. He attempted to convince them that U.S. policy was not one of "isolation" but rather "the right kind of co-operation." Cuno, through Houghton, pleaded for the retention of U.S. troops as an ameliorating factor. But Harding had always felt uneasy about the deployment, and Congress had ratcheted up the pressure to bring the men home. Houghton had labored for months to publicize the political role of America's limited military presence and had persuaded friends such as former governor Frank Lowden (R-IL) and Congressman John Tilson (R-CT) to make speeches in support of the deployment. But conditions in Europe had reached a dangerous stage, and the intense fear of entanglement made the recall inevitable. Houghton regretted the move, believing that it would hasten continental instability.[32]

As a military counteroffensive was impractical, the Germans simply refused to cooperate with French occupation forces. The Cuno administration's policy of "passive resistance" included the stoppage of cash reparations payments and coal deliveries to the Allies and the closing of some factories, railroads, and mines. The Ruhr crisis and the German government's liberal financial policy of granting commercial loans and increasing the money supply to meet budget deficits had a catastrophic effect on the national currency. By January 31, 1923, the ratio of the mark to the dollar had fallen to 49,000:1. The French reacted to Germany's intransigence by declaring martial law in the occupied zones, arresting resistant industrialists, and expelling uncooperative civil servants.

Officials at the American embassy in Berlin reacted with alarm as they were briefed by Germany's leading businessmen. Paul Reusch and Fritz Thyssen, who were described as "almost incandescently hot," warned that "a long and desperate struggle to the death" had begun and vowed that reparations would never be paid "at the point of bayonet." Embassy counselor Warren Robbins reported to the State Department that "the whole barrel is loaded with dynamite." Houghton prepared Washington for a protracted struggle. He gave repeated assurances that the Cuno government and the policy of resistance enjoyed vast support throughout Germany and that a new nationalist spirit had swept the country. Looking ahead, the ambassador feared that the disastrous economic consequences of the crisis would ultimately jeopardize Germany's democratic institutions. He laid much of the responsibility for Europe's precarious state squarely upon the United States.[33]

Houghton reasoned that the United States, as a predominant power, had failed to meet its "moral" obligation to promote international peace and prosperity. "Giving good advice and . . . urging financial settlement" in Europe, he lamented, hardly constituted a responsible or far-sighted foreign policy. Indeed, it seemed incredible to the ambassador that, having sacrificed thousands of American lives and billions of dollars in the Great War, the United States would sit idly by while Europe reverted to warlike conditions. Moreover, it seemed supremely ironic that a nation that had just fought a war "to make the world safe for democracy" now tolerated a French assault upon Germany's first democratic government. Worse, America's unwillingness to help settle Europe's postwar problems threatened its own economic security since national prosperity depended upon European prosperity.[34]

Aside from his country's reluctance to assume a leadership role, Houghton also objected to Washington's exclusive focus on reparations. He did not think it wise to paper over French fears and the need for a security treaty. Moreover, he believed a key to establishing postwar security and economic recovery lay in the massive international loans that had arisen from the war. The United States could use the debts as a lever to stimulate the European economies and conclude a security pact. "I can't help thinking," he wrote to Dwight, that the administration "got off on the wrong foot. Mr. Hughes accepted the situation as it was, and . . . confined his efforts to urging financial settlement. The basic problem, however, is not financial. It is moral. And if America had approached it from a large, generous, far-seeing point of view, part at least of the troubles here would have been eliminated, and the remainder of them would have been easier of solution."[35]

Houghton did not shy away from offering his criticisms directly to the administration. On January 29 he complained to Hughes that the United States had failed to seize "the psychological moment . . . we had all been waiting [for]," when the Cuno government with the backing of German industry was willing to accept an impartial reparations committee and enter a security pact with the Allies. By allowing events to reach a crisis stage, he contended, Washington had delivered to the world an ominous lesson that security in Europe could only be attained by brute military force. Houghton made clear the long-term consequences of allowing renewed hostilities and economic calamity. He informed Castle:

> All in all, Europe is in a sorry mess. We ourselves had the power
> at one time to stabilize conditions. . . . We can comfort ourselves
> with the notion that we are going to save part of the sum we

loaned to Europe. We are going to collect some interest. But unless something of a miracle takes place, we may look forward
confidently and happily to a time not far off when another war
will lay prostrate what is left of European civilization. That, I
believe is certain. The irony of the situation intrigues me. Germany had gone under a new leadership. These new men are not
warlike. They are business men . . . willing to accept conditions.
. . . I dare say this strikes your judicial mind as distinctly a pro-
German view. It isn't. It is the simple, old-fashioned truth.[36]

The international implications of the Ruhr crisis and the failure of American foreign policy nearly overwhelmed Houghton. He
became severely depressed and seriously contemplated resignation.
"I hope and pray," he wrote Castle, "that I am wrong" and that the
noninterventionist plans of "the people in Washington are right. A
terrible responsibility rests somewhere." The envoy further questioned his own ability to influence the direction of policy and
thought perhaps he should forsake diplomacy and instead educate
the American public on its new responsibilities in world affairs. "I
do not know how long I shall stay," he wrote Dwight, and "unless
some effective hope of assistance is coming sooner or later from
America, I have no desire to remain after this year. I would rather
come home and work in my own small way to get the actual facts
before our people."[37]

Immediately after the Ruhr invasion, there were no signs of a
change in U.S. foreign policy. The president and Hughes announced
that there was nothing they could do to halt the clash in Europe
and that the United States must "maintain a dignified position" in
"accord with the traditional policies of nonintervention." Twice, in
January and February 1923, the British ambassador in Washington
called on Hughes to determine what conditions would prompt
American involvement. The secretary of state disliked discussing
future possibilities and clung to the position that nothing could be
accomplished until Paris and Berlin agreed to an impartial settlement of reparations. He made frightfully clear his willingness to
let political and economic chaos serve as the driving force to bring
the two sides together. Such a passive and destructive course was
incomprehensible to the American ambassador in Berlin. For the
remainder of his life, Houghton believed that the Ruhr crisis had
sown the seeds of a second world war.[38]

Overcoming his anguish, Houghton embarked on a two-
pronged strategy to help resolve the crisis. First, regarding German policy, he impressed upon Cuno the absolute need to keep

formal lines of communication to Paris. From the eve of the French invasion, he had advised the government not to break formal diplomatic relations under any circumstances because such a move would be disastrous in the long run. The ambassador also had Cuno consider, as a basis for resuming negotiations, a proposal that France withdraw a majority of its soldiers from the Ruhr but leave enough men behind to enforce customs regulations. The ambassador then resumed efforts to draw America into the fray.

In a stream of telegrams and letters to the secretary of state, Houghton underscored the gravity of Franco-German relations and America's responsibilities. He suggested several means of financial and humanitarian intervention. The United States, in cooperation with Britain, could volunteer to mediate the Ruhr conflict and advocate Houghton's idea for a partial French evacuation as a means to opening legitimate discussions about Europe's security and economy. If Paris refused to negotiate, America should aggressively devalue the franc to bring Poincaré to the table. At an absolute minimum, Washington should publicly oppose French militarism and, if necessary, promise food to the occupied German territories. The latter two positions were supported by Republican progressives in the Senate.

In early March, when Houghton became convinced that France had no intention of withdrawing from the Ruhr or adopting the Hughes plan for a new bankers' commission, he pressed the administration to admit the failure of its passive and circumscribed policy and to take swift action against the French currency:

> France . . . is not yet ready to permit a group of international bankers to decide her fate. No, Mr. Secretary, France primarily is not seeking reparations. She is seeking security [through occupation]. . . . The plain truth . . . from Berlin, seems to be that [Americans] having destroyed any balance of power in Europe and left France for the moment all powerful, we have simply let loose a great elemental force which inevitably seeks to satisfy itself. It *is* a force. It can only be dealt with as a force. And unless it is met by armed force in the shape of armies, it must be met by economic force in the shape of threatened ruin. That is the whole story. France must be met by force.
>
> But I believe sincerely if it is to America's interest to save what is left of German capital and German industry, and . . . also German science and German learning and the rest, some positive action is required without too much delay . . . the franc obviously suggests the obvious point of weakness. . . . If it were possible, directly or indirectly, for either or both, Britain and ourselves, to

remove or to overcome the artificial support now given the franc,
the franc would fall. . . . [Then] the sane majority in France would
[compromise]. . . . France alone can furnish the way out.[39]

Houghton's judgment that the United States should take matters into its own hands was again reminiscent of his experience at
Corning Glass Works. Two decades earlier, when he and his brother
had recognized the necessity of automating lightbulb production,
they encountered formidable resistance from company elders who
opposed abandoning traditional methods of manufacture. Convinced that mechanization was vital to the company's survival, the
Houghton brothers took the daring step of financing the expensive
project on their own. Thus, during the Ruhr crisis, when French
leaders demonstrated similar obstinacy, the ambassador believed
that the United States had little choice but to abandon its traditional policy of political isolation from Europe to secure its long-
term interests.

Houghton's pleas for intervention had little support within the
conservative administration. Hughes's determination to avoid involvement in the Ruhr crisis became clear in mid-March 1923 after
he received a secret memorandum from Berlin. The Germans agreed
to accept the Hughes scheme for a committee of reparations experts and to end passive resistance if France would evacuate the
Ruhr. An identical note had been sent to London, where there was
growing sympathy for Germany's plight. Hughes spurned the note,
fearing that it might give the "false" impression that the United
States was contemplating intervention. He advised Houghton that
the Germans should deal directly with France, reminding him that
"confidences of this sort have not been invited by this Government."[40]

Although Houghton met with repeated rebuffs from the State
Department, he found ideological allies at the International Chamber of Commerce (ICC), which convened in Rome during the week
of March 18. A leading member of the American delegation, Fred I.
Kent, an executive with Bankers Trust Company, delivered a well-
received speech that could have easily been drafted by Houghton.
Kent stressed that European rehabilitation and stability were in
America's core interests. Therefore, the United States should consider canceling Allied war debts in return for a reasonable reduction in Germany's reparations. The ICC subsequently passed a
resolution calling for a detailed examination of the war loans, reparations, and currency exchanges. When Kent discovered that both

the French and German delegations were willing to listen to him, he became a self-appointed mediator between Paris and Berlin.

Kent traveled to Paris, where government leaders outlined their demands on Germany and emphasized that Berlin must make the first proposal. In Berlin, Kent discussed the situation with Houghton, who helped to arrange meetings with Cuno and others. As usual, the ambassador encouraged the German government to make every effort to demonstrate its willingness to negotiate a settlement with France. On April 27, he told Ago von Maltzan at the Foreign Office that the next German offer should reiterate support for Hughes's impartial reparations committee, for a Rhineland security treaty, and for joint stock ownership between German and French industrialists. Houghton worked closely with the Cuno government and Kent, who wrote to fellow financier Paul M. Warburg: "The ambassador put himself out in every way to help me in my work and I shall never forget it."[41]

Revisions to the German memorandum were being made just as Houghton prepared for a visit to the United States, his first since arriving in Berlin. On May 1 he wired Washington the latest details of the German plan, which included a pledge of 30 billion marks in reparations and a promise to end passive resistance when the Ruhr was evacuated. But after Houghton departed and before the note was delivered, the Germans pared back the offer, which made its rejection inevitable. Still, many in Britain and Italy were inclined to see the proposal as a starting point and encouraged another proposition from Berlin. A second, more generous German note, pledging large annuities, considerable collateral, and a commitment to support an international reparations committee, was delivered on June 7. It was received warmly by all of the Allies except France, which demanded, among other things, a fixed sum of reparations and an immediate end to passive resistance.

As these diplomatic notes were being exchanged in Europe and relations between France and Britain soured, Houghton returned to America for a badly needed rest. He was joined en route by George Harvey and Cyrus E. Woods, the newly appointed U.S. representative to Japan. During the voyage the three ambassadors debated new approaches to the reparations question. Woods enjoyed Houghton's "splendid honesty and integrity" but reported him to be fatigued and worried, usually "sunk in his chair," burdened by "the responsibilities of the world." His physical appearance and despondency also dismayed officials at the State Department, where

he arrived on May 14. Undersecretary Phillips described the ambassador as "very depressed," and Castle found him "tired and
emotionally all in." Houghton's physical state and conversations
with friends, including Buffalo attorney William J. Donovan (the
future leader of the Office of Strategic Services), led to rumors of
his imminent resignation.[42]

(From left to right): Alanson B. Hougton, George Harvey, and Cyrus E. Woods.
Courtesy of the Houghton Family and Corning Incorporated

The ambassador recognized the threat to his health and received
permission to remain stateside for five weeks. Before retreating to
Corning and later to his summer estate in Massachusetts, he spent
a week in Washington conducting a "mission of enlightenment"
inside and outside the State Department. In extended meetings with
Hughes, Phillips, and Castle, he painted a bleak picture of Europe
and warned that if France did not begin negotiating and if the German economy continued to deteriorate, "war and chaos" should
be expected before year's end. Because of his extreme pessimism
and consistent call for American pressure on France, Hughes, Castle,
and Phillips had in recent months rightly criticized Houghton for
seeing the Ruhr crisis only from Germany's perspective. He did
not fully appreciate the extent of French fears or the intransigence
of many German leaders. Still, Houghton did not hide his contempt
for the administration's reluctance to intercede or his conviction
that the United States was partly responsible for Europe's sorry

state. Hughes and the others explained that the administration had absolutely no desire to be caught in difficult diplomatic negotiations unless it knew from the outset that the discussions would succeed. Such extreme caution seemed irresponsible to Houghton. Regardless of that feeling, he could take some comfort in Hughes's appreciation of his determined efforts. The secretary admitted the gulf between their views, but he remained "very pleased with the Ambassador's transparent honesty and vigor."[43]

Houghton's "mission" also took him to the White House and Capitol Hill. His conference with the president was disheartening. After two years in office, Harding felt beleaguered by the demands of the presidency and was suffering from disabling nervousness and severe depression. The ambassador had hoped to engage him on the pressing issues of Europe, but he found the chief executive uncharacteristically disheveled in appearance and mentally preoccupied. Even his "hair had not been cared for," the envoy recalled, and "his mind was just floating around." Houghton had better success in conveying the gravity of Germany's situation to the chairman of the Senate Foreign Relations Committee, Henry Cabot Lodge, who, after their meeting, described Houghton as a "very intelligent" diplomat. The ambassador met with many other "celebrities" before catching his train to Corning. From there, he wrote back to Dwight that he "had a corking good week" in Washington and "enjoyed every minute of it." But in a confessional letter to Bishop Charles H. Brent, he was less sanguine, stating that he had probably accomplished very little except to emphasize the peril of Europe's situation and the need for U.S. intervention. He closed by saying: "I keep thinking of that man who 2000 years ago walked down the street and passed by his suffering neighbor. That is not my image of America."[44]

Although he was discouraged, Houghton's arguments had had some effect on Hughes. The German note of June 7 appeared to confirm Berlin's sincerity, and, after reviewing it, the secretary casually informed the Belgian and Italian ambassadors in Washington that the administration believed that Germany desired honest negotiations to settle the reparations quagmire. The time seemed ripe to Hughes to attempt another bankers' conference, but he still opposed direct American intervention. He reemphasized to the European envoys that the United States desired no role in Allied negotiations with Germany. Throughout June he repeatedly told journalists that his December recommendation for a new experts' reparations committee never contemplated official U.S. participation because the country had no direct interests in the matter. On June 25, Castle met with Houghton in New York City just before the ambassador returned to Berlin. He reported the glassmaker-turned-diplomat healthy and rested but fixed in his pessimistic outlook on Europe and his disappointment with American policy.

Despite his frustration with the conservative Republican approach to European reconstruction, Houghton could take pride in his early achievements as an ambassador. He had influenced policy by helping to extend, if only temporarily, the army's occupation of the Rhineland. He had championed an unprecedented bilateral agreement for the adjudication of war claims. And while he had initially failed to dissuade the administration from approaching the Soviets, Hughes admitted that the ambassador's position of watchful waiting had proven to be correct. The mere fact that Harding, Hughes, and Hoover had trusted the envoy with the risky covert assignment spoke well of their confidence in him. Another mark of Houghton's success was his acceptance and growing influence inside Germany's top political, industrial, and financial circles. This had come about not only because of his official position but also because of his sympathetic tone, candid nature, and *warmherzige* personality. With a hint of jealously, British Ambassador D'Abernon reported that the American envoy had developed an unusually strong relationship with the Cuno government and that "contact between the American embassy and the larger German industrialists is believed to be extremely close."[45]

There can be little doubt that during the onset of Germany's "Great Disorder," the ambassador did everything in his power to bring about better Allied–German cooperation, to bolster Germany's deteriorating condition, and to induce U.S. intervention. D'Abernon described Houghton and his aspirations quite accurately to his superiors in London: "A glass manufacturer of great wealth . . . [who] has worked very hard to bring America into European affairs, and particularly to strengthen American support of Germany. He is intimate with the German Government particularly with Cuno. In a secondary degree he is, I think, anxious to bring about a close Anglo-American understanding. . . . I find him easy and agreeable to work with . . . the American Embassy remains in close touch with the English."[46]

Houghton's efforts abroad were substantial, and he used his position to promote productive ends. Before the Ruhr crisis, he had worked closely with the Allied Reparations Committee and with the Keynes economic commission to formulate solutions to

Germany's deteriorating financial condition. He provided sound political counsel to the Wirth and Cuno governments and had even persuaded Cuno to adopt his personal plan for a multilateral non-aggression pact, and he had prodded him to open direct negotiations with Poincaré. Houghton also traveled to Paris to activate French diplomacy toward Berlin. After the Ruhr crisis, he spent much of his time trying to stay abreast of Germany's tumultuous political and economic situation. Throughout, he used his clout to push for an open dialogue between the German and French governments and for U.S. involvement. In the coming year, Houghton would be called upon often to exercise his mounting influence not only in European affairs but also in American politics.

Notes

1. ABH Diary, April 18–19, 1922.
2. Harding to Hughes, April 26, 1922, Department of State, *Foreign Relations of the United States, 1922* (Washington, DC, 1934–1949), 2:217 (hereafter cited as *FRUS*, followed by the appropriate year); Department of State, *Press Conferences of U.S. Secretaries of State* (includes presidential press conferences), May 3, 1922 (Wilmington, DE, 1974), microfilm, Series 1, reel 1 (hereafter cited as *Press Conferences*).
3. ABH Diary, May 3, 1922.
4. Edgar Vincent D'Abernon, *The Diary of an Ambassador: Rapallo to Dawes, 1922–1924*, vol. 2 (Garden City, NY, 1930), 51–52; Houghton to Amory Houghton, June 24, 1922, Houghton Papers.
5. Houghton to Dwight, July 15, 1922, and Houghton to Castle, July 29, 1922, Houghton Papers.
6. Harding to Hughes (emphasis in original), received August 10, 1922, *FRUS, 1922*, 2:262; ABH Diary, August 10, 1922.
7. ABH Diary, May 30, 1922.
8. Houghton to Robert C. Pruyn, September 9, 1922, Houghton to Hughes, August 24, 1922, and Houghton to Castle, February 12 and September 15, 1922, Houghton Papers; Warren Robbins to Castle, February 18, 1924, William R. Castle Papers, Hoover Presidential Library and Museum, West Branch, Iowa (hereafter cited as Castle Papers).
9. ABH Diary, June 26, July 5, and July 14, 1922.
10. Hughes to Houghton, August 23, 1922, and Houghton to Hughes (cable), August 29, 1922, Houghton Papers.
11. Houghton to State Department (cable), September 16, 1922, ibid.
12. Houghton to Castle, August 26, 1922, Castle Papers.
13. Houghton to J. S. Sloat, August 28, 1922, Houghton Papers.
14. Houghton to Castle, July 29, 1922, Castle Papers; Houghton to Hughes, July 28, 1922, Houghton Papers.
15. Castle to Houghton, August 4, 1922 (includes Castle memorandum, August 1, 1922), Houghton Papers.
16. Harding to Phillips, August 26, 1922, Warren G. Harding Papers, Ohio Historical Society, microfilm edition, reel 186 (hereafter cited as

Harding Papers); Hughes to Phillips, August 30, 1922, *FRUS, 1922*, 2:160–63.

17. Boyden/Herrick to Hughes, October 14, 1922, and Hughes to Boyden/Herrick, October 17, 1922, *FRUS, 1922*, 2:165–70.

18. ABH Diary, July 29, 1922.

19. Ascham, "Ambassador Houghton's Message to Methodism," 2.

20. Houghton to Dwight, October 12, 1922, Houghton Papers.

21. Houghton to Hughes, October 23, 1922, ibid.

22. ABH Diary, October 24, 1922.

23. Ibid., November 8 and 15, 1922.

24. Ibid., November 17, 1922; Houghton to State Department (cable), November 20, 1922, Houghton Papers.

25. Houghton to Hughes, November 21, 1922, Houghton Papers.

26. Houghton to Amory Houghton, November 9, 1922, ibid.

27. Castle to Hughes, October 24, 1922, Boyden/Houghton to Hughes, November 9, 1922, and Hughes to Houghton, November 14, 1922, *FRUS, 1922*, 2:176–77, 180–81.

28. Hughes to Houghton, November 14, 1922, ibid., 2:181–82.

29. ABH Diary, December 10, 1922.

30. Houghton to Hughes, December 20, 1922, Houghton Papers.

31. *Press Conferences*, December 12–28, 1922; Merlo J. Pusey, *Charles Evans Hughes* (New York, 1951), vol. 2, 581.

32. *New York Times*, January 11–14, 1923; *Press Conferences*, January 11, 1923.

33. ABH Diary, January 25–30, 1923; Houghton to Hughes, January 29, 1923, Houghton Papers; Robbins to Castle, January 30, 1923, Castle Papers.

34. Houghton to Dwight, January 23, 1923, and Houghton to James S. Parker, January 26, 1923, Houghton Papers.

35. Houghton to Dwight, January 23, 1923, ibid.

36. Houghton to Hughes, January 29, 1923, and Houghton to Castle, January 17, 1923, ibid.

37. Houghton to Castle, February 12, 1923, and Houghton to Dwight, February 16, 1923, ibid.

38. *Press Conferences*, January 16–20, 1923.

39. Houghton to Hughes, March 6, 1923, Houghton Papers.

40. Hughes to Houghton (cable), March 16, 1923, ibid.

41. Fred I. Kent to Paul M. Warburg, May 9 and 28, 1923, Fred I. Kent Papers, Mudd Library, Princeton University, Princeton, New Jersey.

42. William R. Castle Diary (hereafter cited as Castle Diary), May 15–16, 1923, Castle Papers; William Phillips Diary, May 14, 1923, Houghton Library, Harvard University, Cambridge, Massachusetts.

43. Castle Diary, May 15–16, 1923, and June 25, 1923; Castle to Robbins, June 15, 1923, Castle Papers.

44. Jonathan Mitchell interview, June 4, 1941; Henry Cabot Lodge to Thomas S. Perry, May 26, 1923, Houghton to Dwight, May 24, 1923, and Houghton to Brent, May 26, 1923, Houghton Papers.

45. D'Abernon to Arthur Balfour, received July 3, 1922, British Foreign Office, Public Records Office, Kew, England (hereafter cited as PRO), FO 371/7536/C9422/725/18.

46. D'Abernon, "Annual Report of Heads of Foreign Missions in Berlin," January 11, 1923, FO 371/8700/C1T11/213/18, PRO.

4

Belated Intervention

1923–1924

I believe we can only regard it with satisfaction that such a great country and such a great people have now shown an interest in the settlement of European questions, and are not following those who once believed that all of American policy could be summed up with the expression "[Avoid] European Troubles."
—Gustav Stresemann, 1924

Houghton thought that the United States had failed in 1922 and early 1923 to meet its postwar obligations as a leading world power. A foreign policy of watchful waiting might be appropriate for U.S.–Soviet relations but not for America's crucial relationship with Western Europe, especially with Germany and Great Britain. Given its disproportionate power, America, he argued, had a major responsibility for bringing key nations together and for actively supporting their welfare. When the reparations crisis and German inflation threatened European stability, he wanted Washington to act vigorously. He understood that international leadership required difficult decisions and, at times, bold action. When France proved willing to destabilize German society, he called on the United States to apply direct political and economic pressure on Paris. Moreover, if postwar security and stabilization meant sacrificing America's massive loans to France and the other Allies, he also favored that.

The conservative nature of U.S. foreign policy in the early 1920s was reflected in Harding and Hughes's refusal to intervene directly in Europe's tumultuous political affairs. And during the second half of 1923, Germany descended further into the Great Disorder that culminated in Adolf Hitler's first attempt to overthrow its fledgling democratic republic. A positive turning point for Europe and American policy finally came in December 1923, when the French government agreed that independent experts should examine Germany's finances and propose a solution to the reparations problem. France's capitulation and issues related to the 1924 U.S. presidential election prompted mainstream Republicans to support direct involvement in Europe. And though technically unofficial, American participation on two new reparations committees was solidly backed by the Harding administration and a majority in Congress.

Although Houghton considered 1922–1923 a dismal period for American policy in Europe, he remained determined to exercise a constructive influence. From his perspective, the formation of the new reparations committees provided the best, and possibly the last, major opportunity for America to exert its power effectively for the benefit of Germany and the broader political economy. Even though U.S. representation was unofficial, meaningful intervention in Europe's political problems had finally arrived, and Houghton seized the opportunity to play a valuable, supportive role. He had already labored for more than a year to bring stability to postwar Europe, and in the process he had won the gratitude and trust of German leaders. He continued to display remarkable personal influence inside Berlin's elite circles, and he drew from his reserve of goodwill to promote a 1924 reparations agreement that became known as the Dawes Plan. As a consequence of his dedication and effectiveness, contemporaries began to hail him as one of the most able diplomats in U.S. history.

Events of 1924 also demonstrated that the ambassador's influence extended beyond European diplomacy. His credibility back home, inside and outside the State Department, increased tremendously, partly because his ominous forecasts of Germany's destabilization were being realized. His name circulated as a possible nominee for New York's governorship, and his political stock rose even higher after Germany ratified the Dawes Plan. Moreover, when foreign policy emerged as a central factor in the 1924 presidential campaign, Coolidge relied on the ambassador to help sway the electorate in his favor. After his election, the president singled out Houghton as one of his most influential campaigners and rewarded his political and diplomatic efforts by making him ambassador to Great Britain. In the end, America's belated leadership in Europe revived the ambassador's spirit for public service and his hope for a more assertive U.S. foreign policy.

During Houghton's absence from Berlin, Germany's political economy declined sharply. Inflation ran rampant. The mark-to-dollar exchange rate declined from 50,000:1 in May 1923 to 200,000:1 in early July. Upon his return, Houghton met immediately with German officials, and he was informed that the government could not continue its limited, artificial support of the currency. By the end of July, the mark had fallen to 1.1 million against the dollar, and a week later it had plunged to 3.3 million. The hyperinflation caused farmers and wholesalers to hoard food. A printers' strike created a scarcity of currency and newspapers. City workers protested in the streets, and coal miners raided farm fields. The results of municipal and trade-union elections signaled increasing support for Left and Right extremists. Unable to lead the Reichstag, the doomed Cuno government ordered the army to defend federal buildings from rioters. Houghton wrote to Hughes of the disastrous conditions and the need for outside intervention: "I feel as if I had come back into the same old building, but found the beams and rafters steadily decaying and the floors increasingly unsound, and that unless steps were speedily taken to repair it, the roof and walls must before long inevitably fall in." On August 12, Cuno resigned.[1]

For his part, Hughes became so depressed by the state of international affairs that he "really wished he was a woman and could cry." The shocking death of President Harding by apoplexy on August 2 rattled the secretary further and disrupted political affairs in Washington. Unlike the secretary of state, Houghton had never been especially close to or fond of the president. He credited Harding for helping lift the country out of the 1920–1921 recession, but he had always decried his passive support for European reconstruction. The envoy did not know what to expect from his successor, Calvin Coolidge, but, as was customary, he proffered his resignation to the new chief executive. When the letter reached Coolidge's desk, the president returned it to Hughes with "no" underscored. After conditions stabilized in the nation's capital, the secretary of state turned his attention back to Europe.[2]

In the past, Hughes had been essentially content to let matters take their course. He thought France's weak economy would impel it to accept a new bankers' commission. But the rapidity of Germany's collapse forced his hand, leading him to promote a strategy consistent with, if not identical to, Houghton's long-held views. On the morning of August 16, Hughes conducted an intriguing interview with the Belgian ambassador, and their discussion has been largely overlooked by historians. He informed the ambassador that the German crisis had created an opportune moment for Brussels (not Washington) to broker a resolution on reparations. If a revolution erupted in Germany, he argued, reparations might never be paid. Hughes suggested that the Allies negotiate secretly with Berlin on three bases: first, agree to set reparations at roughly 45 billion gold marks, subject to Germany's capacity to pay as determined by impartial financial experts; second, agree to substantial disarmament; and third, consent to a multilateral Rhineland security pact. Once the agreements had been reached, Germany was to end passive resistance. France, in turn, would announce the evacuation of the occupied territories and then make public the new accords. As a reward for the agreement, "the American people," Hughes opined, "would be disposed to deal generously with the question of [Allied war] debts." The Belgian must have been shocked by this sudden initiative from the usually tight-lipped Hughes, for he returned to the State Department later that afternoon to verify the secretary's position before cabling his government.[3]

Whether Hughes's unofficial advice would materially affect inter-Allied diplomacy remained uncertain. He encouraged Houghton to continue writing freely on European developments and praised his uniquely perceptive reporting. The ambassador informed Hughes of Germany's escalating food prices and unemployment, and of the new government headed by Gustav Stresemann of the German People's Party (DVP) and backed by the Social Democrats. Prospects were unfortunately dismal. France still refused to negotiate, and Britain refused to interfere with the Ruhr occupation. Houghton characterized the new German government as a regime of surrender. Without British cooperation, Stresemann would be forced to capitulate to most French demands. If he did not, Houghton warned, Germany's democratic experiment would be overrun by a "new kind" of bolshevism that would promise "a better way for the German race." Houghton did not think the Germans would "ever go bolshevist in the Russian sense"; instead, he predicted the rise of a remarkably "efficient and thorough" centralized government brought to power by repudiating war reparations and Western capitalism.[4]

By mid-September, with no hope of diplomatic progress, Stresemann realized the necessity of ending the passive resistance policy.

Houghton so informed the State Department and warned that the unilateral move would be wildly unpopular in Germany. With Hughes away, Acting Secretary of State William Phillips sent the ambassador's vivid telegrams to the White House for consideration. Coolidge remarked that he understood the seriousness of the German situation, but told Phillips that even if Stresemann acted "foolishly" by unilaterally ending the resistance policy, he doubted that it would trigger "the downfall of civilization" as Houghton had insinuated. The president, in fact, proceeded to tell reporters that he was growing optimistic regarding a Franco-German settlement.[5]

Stresemann terminated passive resistance on September 26, and if subsequent events did not initiate the decline of civilization, they did hasten the collapse of the Weimar Republic. The reactionary Bavarian government responded swiftly to Stresemann's decision by declaring a state of emergency, halting gold shipments to the Reichsbank, and suspending its legal commitment to defend the Republic. President Ebert and Stresemann had little choice but to declare a national emergency and grant unprecedented authority to the military, led by General Hans von Seeckt. The Stresemann regime fell on October 3, and Houghton reported that the parliamentary government had essentially collapsed and that societal order depended entirely upon Seeckt's cooperation. Although Stresemann quickly organized a new government, leftist coalitions took control of municipalities in the central German states of Saxony and Thuringia, where unemployment approached 50 percent. The rise of the Left in central Germany threatened a showdown with the conservative German army, the Reichswehr.

The dramatic turn of events alarmed Washington. Suddenly, the extreme pessimism Houghton had espoused for the last nine months appeared justified. Houghton's friend John Dwight, who maintained close contact with the State Department, informed the ambassador of changing American opinion. "Well, at last the bubble has broken in Germany," he wrote, "just what you predicted." He added that William Castle had recently confessed that the ambassador "has been right all the time" and that officials in Washington were "gradually coming around to it and are now facing real facts." Dwight cautioned, however, that Hughes continued to claim powerlessness without congressional authorization. Houghton attempted to influence Congress directly by arranging a dinner meeting at his embassy for Stresemann and the traveling Stephen Porter, the chairman of the House Committee on Foreign Affairs. Their frank conversation centered on America's responsibility to take a

more active role in Europe. Porter found himself alone in defending Washington's "relaps[e] into passivity" after Hughes's much-
publicized but ineffectual speech in December. Stresemann, with
Houghton's concurrence, complained that the United States had
not only an obligation to propose solutions but also the responsibility to work for their adoption. The chancellor argued that a large
American loan was vital to restoring Germany's economy and asked
that the U.S. government make some immediate "gesture," a "mere
statement," indicating it maintained interest in the permanent settlement of reparations.[6]

Whether intentional or not, Coolidge did make a gesture at a
press conference on October 9. When asked whether he planned to
pressure the Allies for an independent reparations commission,
Coolidge replied, no. But he also remarked that the United States
had never rescinded the commission proposal. Four days later,
British Prime Minister Stanley Baldwin asked Hughes to verify
America's willingness to participate in a new reparations committee. The secretary did, using language similar to his uncustomary
advice to the Belgian ambassador two months earlier. He stressed
the imminent danger of economic calamity in Germany and suggested that European cooperation on reparations and arms
control would make Americans receptive to generous war-debt
adjustments.

Any reparations settlement depended on French cooperation,
but Prime Minister Poincaré, ever fearful of Germany's revival, was
unwilling to support an experts' commission without limiting its
authority and scope of inquiry. The Americans and British could
accept the former, but not the latter. In increasingly heated meetings with French Ambassador Jules Jusserand, Hughes consistently
rejected French demands. In explaining the necessity of a free and
impartial commission, he often sounded like Houghton. In short,
he argued that Berlin was willing to pay reparations, but if France
precipitated Germany's total collapse, it risked never receiving
payments. France might gain political security, he claimed, by occupying western Germany, but this could succeed only temporarily
as it would eventually trigger armed German revenge. When the
French refused to budge, the Coolidge administration sought political cover at home. Criticized in recent months for its ineffective
foreign policy by progressives in Congress and in the press, the
president prepared Washington journalists for the worst. On November 6, he stated that the administration had already performed
its "duty" by proposing a solution for a reparations settlement, and,

if France were to reject "our counsel," "we want civilization to understand [that] we tried to do our part." He claimed further that the United States had "no direct interest" in the European embroilment. Three days later, he announced that France's demands had rendered futile the idea of an independent inquiry into Germany's financial condition.[7]

Europe's turmoil led to increased coverage of German affairs in the American press. The *New York Times Magazine* ran an insightful and generally accurate feature on the U.S. ambassador in Berlin. The article centered on Houghton's active efforts to improve European conditions while avoiding personal publicity. Thus, the envoy stood out as "the antithesis of the modern slogan 'it pays to advertise.'" Described as a "curious and interesting phenomenon" among administration officials, Houghton emerged in the piece as a complex and sympathetic figure. As the chairman of Corning Glass Works, he appeared from the outside, according to the *Times*, to personify the iron-fisted corporate executive of American big business. In reality, he was a philosopher of international relations, a student of government, a compassionate humanitarian—at bottom a "soft-hearted idealist." The ambassador was reportedly depressed over conditions in Europe and frustrated by his and America's inability to broker a solution. An unidentified State Department source proclaimed Houghton "the best ambassador we have," and the article concluded that the envoy's intimate but unloquacious approach to foreign relations had set a new standard for diplomatic excellence.[8]

Despite Houghton's intimate and assertive diplomacy, conditions in Germany deteriorated further. Late on November 8, the ambassador had just removed his topcoat after dining at the Italian embassy when a journalist telephoned that Hitler and General Ludendorff, with the apparent support of the Bavarian government, had called for the violent overthrow of the Weimar Republic. The infamous "Beer-Hall Putsch" had begun. The ambassador had warned Washington of problems in Bavaria, a hotbed for monarchist and right-wing paramilitary activity. These groups vehemently opposed both Stresemann's termination of passive resistance and the Communist governments in Saxony and Thuringia. The U.S. consul general in Munich, Robert Murphy, monitored the rise of the Nazi movement. His memoirs praise Houghton as the only senior American official who heeded his reports. Houghton had sent members of his staff to Munich to report on Hitler and Ludendorff's activities, and on several occasions he had summoned Murphy to Berlin. The Bavarians defied the German Defense Ministry by claiming authority over locally stationed Reichswehr troops. And whereas Stresemann and Ebert had willingly used the military against Communist agitators in October, they hesitated before acting on the more perilous Bavarian situation. At 2 A.M. on November 9, a German official called on the embassy to tell Houghton that the government had decided to resist the right-wing putsch with armed force. This proved unnecessary, however, as the Munich police, with the support of the Bavarian government, put down the rebellion before it spread beyond the city.[9]

Although the Nazi uprising had been quelled, Houghton warned the State Department that general conditions were anything but stable. Inflation had spiraled out of control. Unemployment was surging. Riots and shootings were becoming commonplace, and mobs plundered stores around Alexanderplatz. Houghton informed his brother that he was now writing billion-mark checks for household expenses rather than million-mark checks: "I . . . am beginning to look upon old John D. Rockefeller as a mere piker. . . . What a world!" By the time of the Hitler Putsch, the dollar-to-mark exchange rate had reached 1:630 million; a week later, 1:252 billion. Houghton attempted to console Chancellor Stresemann by holding out the prospect of an international reparations conference. But given the collapse of the currency, he knew that the Stresemann administration, despite its honest efforts to save the situation, was finished. It fell at the hands of Left and Right parties on November 23. Depressed and pessimistic, the ambassador wrote to the State Department that "the whole place is hopeless."[10]

European affairs had deteriorated sharply in the months following the Ruhr invasion. Though reluctant to admit it, officials in Washington realized that many of Houghton's predictions had proven accurate. He warned that only U.S. intervention could have prevented the sharp decline. In a private letter to Counselor Warren Robbins of the U.S. embassy in Berlin, William Castle admitted that "the Ambassador's prophecies in the whole matter have unfortunately been generally fulfilled" and that the refusal of the French to negotiate was "an eye-opener to a great many people." The secretary of state confessed his frustration to Houghton directly. "I am much disappointed in the refusal of the French," Hughes wrote confidentially, and "I trust that you will not fail to continue to write me fully." Other Republicans, including Frederick H. Gillett, the Speaker of the House, who had visited Houghton in Berlin, called on the administration to intervene. Gillett even arranged a private meeting with Coolidge to discuss Houghton's original plan to remit the war debts and to demand, in exchange, disarmament pledges and a Rhineland peace agreement.[11]

Alanson B. Houghton leaving the Presidential Palace, Berlin. *Courtesy of the Houghton Family and Corning Incorporated*

When word of a new diplomatic initiative arrived from Paris, consideration of such drastic action seemed superfluous. Faced with France's weakening economy and its diplomatic isolation, Poincaré finally abandoned his hard-line position and encouraged the establishment of an international experts' commission under the auspices of the Allied Reparations Committee. By mid-December, a proposal had emerged for two impartial committees to examine Germany's domestic and foreign finances and to make budget and currency recommendations. Though not explicit, there was an understanding that the committees would also formulate a comprehensive reparations settlement based on Germany's capacity to pay, and that they would encourage foreign investment in Europe. Still wanting to avoid confrontation with Congress and formal commitments to Europe, the Coolidge administration refused to appoint official U.S. representatives to the new commissions. Hughes did manage, however, outside of public purview, to handpick three unofficial American participants: Illinois businessman and Harding's Budget Director, Charles G. Dawes; General Electric executive Owen D. Young; and California banker Harry M. Robinson.

It was crucial to the administration that none of these "volunteers" supported the cancellation of America's war loans. The new reparations committees were to convene in Paris in January 1924.

This sudden progress was matched by a temporary stabilization of conditions in Germany. On November 30 a new minority coalition government was established under Wilhelm Marx, an experienced Catholic Center Party leader. It was the fifth change in governments since Houghton's arrival nineteen months earlier. Stresemann consented to serve as foreign minister, a position he held until his death in 1929. A week after the new government's formation, the Social Democratic Party (SPD), which refused to join the coalition, reluctantly agreed to grant Marx extraordinary governing powers for two months. Houghton informed the State Department that Germany had for the moment returned to a state of "unstable equilibrium" where anything was possible. He, like President Ebert, was extremely disappointed in the SPD's refusal to participate in either the previous Stresemann regime or the new Marx government. Because German political factionalism ran deep, the American envoy questioned whether the Reichstag could ever again be a productive body.[12]

The ambassador was guardedly optimistic about the prospects of the new reparations committee. He feared that Germany or France might impede the investigation and that the committee members would not invest enough time in Germany to obtain first-hand information. He also recognized that acceptance of the experts' recommendations depended on France's continued economic decline, especially the fall of the franc, and on the willingness of the experts to publicize the importance of their efforts. To guarantee that the experts reached "a conclusion . . . of practical value," the ambassador planned to nudge Berlin, and he advised Washington to apply "steady pressure" on Paris. Still, Houghton believed that the United States had failed measurably to meet its obligations as a leading power, and as a result, he remained skeptical about Europe's long-term future. Over the previous year, he had become convinced that the Ruhr occupation and the subsequent upheavals had caused irreparable damage to intracontinental relations. He believed that the Germans would eventually exact revenge. He wrote to Hughes, and to others, that France, encouraged by American timidity, had in 1923 a new "Alsace-Lorraine of her own creation . . . which will serve as a rallying-point for the whole German race, and which, like the old Alsace-Lorraine, will inevitably lead to war."[13]

In early January 1924, Houghton outlined Germany's precarious circumstances. The government's controlled issuance of a new Rentenmark had quelled the hyperinflation and curbed the growth of unemployment. But prices had been fixed at very high levels. Worse, the forced decline in the money supply had led state governments, local municipalities, and large companies to begin issuing their own currency. This would eventually push prices even higher and threaten employment. On the political front, the ambassador noted that everything was "absolutely quiescent." "All eyes are now turned toward Paris," where the American delegation of financial experts had begun to arrive.[14]

Determined to assist the committees in their work, the ambassador immediately solicited from Marx a guarantee of Germany's unfettered cooperation. With the chancellor's pledge in hand, Houghton sought to influence the commissioners directly. Acting on a personal request from Young, he boarded a train for Paris on January 9. As the respective chief executives at Corning Glass Works and General Electric, Houghton and Young had been business associates for more than a decade. Their friendship and mutual admiration allowed for unusually close collaboration.

Young and Dawes had worked out the basis of a possible reparations settlement during their voyage. They sought from Houghton an honest account of the economic and political climate in Europe and his critique of their preliminary ideas. America's unofficial diplomats put the ambassador "through a series of interrogations." Houghton, speaking "freely," urged the committee members to visit Berlin, and he emphasized the need for publicity to sway public opinion, especially in France. He personally pledged the unbridled cooperation of the German government. Dawes wrote in his diary that Houghton was "rendering most useful and constructive service" and that he displayed "a business man's reaction to what is necessary to be done here, and his suggestions and comments command our complete confidence." Young laid out for Houghton the details of his program on January 11. The proposal, in brief, called for the complete restoration and independence of German industry to ensure economic stability and the government's ability to raise taxes, balance its budget, and pay reparations. The German currency would be placed on a gold standard, and a new bank would be organized for the exchange of reparations and loans. Houghton thought the scheme sound. During the next few days, the two men conferred often, rehashing the workings and ramifications of the plan. Before returning to Berlin, Houghton committed his support. When he warned of likely French opposition to restoring German industry, Young disclosed his intention to entice France with a substantial loan.[15]

Houghton's shuttle diplomacy profoundly affected his outlook. The experience rekindled the optimism that had been extinguished by Rathenau's assassination, Washington's recalcitrance, and the Ruhr invasion. He was thoroughly impressed with America's representatives in Paris, especially Young, whom he considered brilliant and a formidable negotiator. The ambassador was also affected by French opinion on two levels. He sensed deep apprehension over the nation's deteriorating economy and gained new appreciation for French fears of a German military reprisal. Despite his sympathy for France, Houghton hoped that its economic weakness might continue for the near term and thus spur full cooperation with the reparations experts. If France rejected their recommendations, he believed a future war with Germany was certain. He knew too well that Right and Left radicalism was on the rise in Germany. "There can be no question as to the sincerity of the French fear of a counterattack by the Germans," he confided in his diary. "They have good reason. There will certainly be a German attack whenever the Germans are able to deliver it, unless by some change . . . the French are moved out of the Ruhr and reduce the military occupation of the Rhineland." A final French influence on the ambassador, one that steeled his determination to be a positive diplomatic force, was his inspection of the grim military cemeteries near Belleau Wood and Château-Thierry. The war-torn countryside and the countless rows of white and black crosses presented "a frightful sight." He found the inhumanity of the scene difficult "to shake off."[16]

To Houghton's satisfaction, both experts' committees came to Berlin in January for a study of German economic affairs. Most commissioners accepted in principle the American-designed framework, although specific problems remained unresolved. Young wanted to ascertain the receptivity of political and industrial leaders to the plan, and over the next two weeks, the ambassador played a central role in helping him to win over German support. The embassy again served as a central terminal for the exchange of ideas and information. Working in tandem, Young and Houghton convinced the Marx government and industrialists such as Hermann Bücher of the Reich Association of German Industry of the merits of the experts' proposals. The ambassador marveled at Young's effectiveness as a negotiator. Stresemann, he claimed, "simply fell into his lap." Industrialist Hugo Stinnes, although a harder "nut to crack," also agreed to back Young's approach after several late-night sessions in Houghton's library.[17]

Not all was work in Berlin. Houghton treated the committee members to fine food, spirits, and entertainment. There were numerous teas, luncheons, and dinners, and on at least one occasion, Dawes took to the embassy piano. One of the more sober and interesting dinner parties may have occurred when Houghton and Young dined with retired Field Marshal General Paul von Hindenburg, but there is no record of their conversation. In the end, the experts' mission to Berlin was a success. Dawes recalled that the ambassador's services had been "invaluable" and that his "judgment was mature and sound. His intimate acquaintance with the leading German statesmen and industrialists and their confidence in him saved us much lost motion—for the Experts' Plan was a diplomatic as well as an economic task, though not generally so regarded."[18]

Although Houghton considered the experts' work in Berlin triumphant, he warned the State Department against any premature celebration. There remained unsettled issues, including disagreements over the establishment of a new "gold bank" and German tax-revenue projections. Still, Houghton hoped the commissions would report by March 1, as prolonged delay might have the undesirable effect of providing time for the franc to stabilize or for the Rentenmark to collapse. Although the new mark had steadied the economy, there continued throughout Germany growing dissatisfaction with the republican government. Houghton met frequently with Stresemann to discuss politics. By mid-March 1924, Chancellor Marx, unable to reconcile the disparate demands of the Socialists and Nationalists, dissolved the Reichstag and called for new elections in May. The increasing political uncertainty caused Houghton to cancel a long-planned American vacation. The elections meant yet another German administration with which to deal.

Much to Houghton's chagrin, he anticipated a center-right regime coming at the expense of the SPD and the German Democratic Party. He predicted for Hughes that the Socialists would be "badly cut to pieces" by the Communist Party (KPD), allowing the conservative Nationalists to emerge as the largest party. The ambassador also noted with trepidation the rising popularity of the radical right-wing *völkisch* (radical) organizations, which he characterized as essentially a Hitler–Ludendorff party. Though on trial for the failed putsch, Hitler and Ludendorff attracted press coverage and bathed in considerable public sympathy. Houghton, who had ordered the American vice consul in Munich to attend the trial, described *völkisch* organizers as "composed largely of the expropriated middle classes and the former officer class." The ambassador informed Hughes that Hitler's self-defense at the trial had "showed him to be a popular orator, skilled at playing upon the emotions of a not specifically intelligent audience." While Houghton considered the whole development "a sorry mess" for Germany, he predicted ominously that such a reactionary political organization would successfully "serve as a dragnet to catch the discontented elements throughout the Republic." He concluded that it was "safe to assume that they will form a very substantial block" in the next Reichstag.[19]

Although Houghton recognized that nothing could prevent electoral gains by either the German Right or the Communists, he hoped that a fair and reasonable report by the experts' committees would have some restraining effect. But the committees' work bogged down, and on March 25 he wrote to the secretary of his frustrations with the current "period of more or less hysterical anticipation." On the following day, Young cabled Berlin to ask Houghton to participate in a final round of consultations.[20]

Houghton bolted for Paris without official approval. Young disclosed in private sessions the details of the commission's draft plan, asking for the ambassador's critique. Houghton supported its essential features but warned of Germany's volatile political situation and offered counsel on how to "escape playing into the hands of the German reactionaries." He recommended changes on two fronts. Regarding taxation, he advised abolishing certain transportation levies and lowering taxes on agriculture while raising them on industry. The latter, he argued, had already benefited from the hyperinflation. The report should also assume Germany's good-faith compliance by excluding references to possible penalties, and the commissioners should state their intention to protect the living standard of Germany's working class. Young was receptive to these suggestions and planned to include them in the final document.[21]

While in Paris, Houghton discovered a sharp breach among some of the financial experts. The British delegation and a group of American technical advisers argued that the reparations schedule worked out by Young and Dawes demanded payments in excess of Germany's ability to pay. Such an aggressive plan, they believed, would hamper European efforts to raise foreign capital. When the ambassador learned that several experts planned to denounce the report publicly, he intervened. Over four days, he met

privately with American advisers Arthur N. Young, Charles Herring, Walter S. Tower, Leonard P. Ayres, and Edwin W. Kemmerer
to hear their complaints and "dissipate some of the gloom." The
advisers griped that they had been treated "like office boys," that
their counsel had been ignored. Houghton expressed sympathy for
their "rational" ideas. But he reminded them that Owen Young's
arrangement was not only an economic plan but also a political
treaty, and that heretofore no meaningful agreement had been
reached. Young's judicial compromises, he declared, enabled a significant diplomatic achievement that was in America's vital interests. He warned them against making their objections public.[22]

Houghton's sojourn in France proved influential. With the exception of Ayres, he persuaded the advisers to suppress their dissatisfaction, and Ayres's lone criticisms had little effect. Moreover,
before leaving, Young showed the ambassador an updated draft
report that incorporated the bulk of his recommendations. As part-
ing advice, the envoy instructed Young on the political value of
simultaneously distributing the final report in all of the leading
capitals. By the time this was done on April 9, Houghton had already begun working for Germany's unconditional acceptance of
the so-called Dawes Plan.

Back in Berlin, the ambassador maintained constant contact
with German officials, especially Stresemann. Acceptance of the
plan was so crucial that Houghton was willing to involve himself
in Germany's domestic politics. "I can't do anything formally, of
course," he wrote to James Logan in Paris. "Informally, however, a
good deal can be accomplished." Using Houghton's language, Marx
drafted a note to the Reparations Committee approving the experts'
report. But the chancellor needed the Reichstag to approve companion legislation, so Houghton prodded the government to promote the plan among German voters before the May 4 elections.
Marx and Stresemann did so, but not without provoking vicious
attacks from Communists and conservatives, who characterized
the Dawes Plan as a *zweiten Versailles Vertrag*, or second Versailles
Treaty.[23]

Houghton was pessimistic over the election outlook for the
Marx government and the centrist parties that supported ratification. The Communists (KPD), the Nationalists (DNVP), and the far
right *völkisch* coalition were all gaining momentum. On election
day, Houghton reported the polling stations jammed and the police out in force. The results surprised few observers. On the Left,
several million socialists voted not for the SPD, which received

6 million votes, but for the KPD, which drew roughly 3.6 million votes. Many others chose the opposite extreme. The *völkisch* coalition, in its first national election, attracted nearly 2 million voters, and the Nationalists added more than a million to their already substantial base. In the end, the middle parties, those positioned between the Communists and Nationalists, lost nearly 8 million votes and their seats in the Reichstag fell from 375 to 254. In other words, those parties publicly advocating the unconditional acceptance of the Dawes Plan represented barely 50 percent of the Reichstag.

Stresemann and Houghton discussed the political possibilities. It would be difficult to organize a new majority coalition government. As an alternative, the foreign minister thought a public referendum on the Dawes Plan would cinch its ratification. Houghton was not so confident and did not think it prudent to wait and see. Instead, on May 8, he met secretly with Dr. Otto Hoetzsch, a Nationalist foreign policy leader. The ambassador threatened Hoetzsch that if his party failed to support the Dawes Plan unconditionally, no American loans would flow to German industry. U.S. bankers, he declared, demanded "sane normal-minded Germans."[24]

Frustrated with the short-sighted machinations of these political parties, the ambassador pondered retirement. He deemed Germany's inability to form a majority coalition government incomprehensible, informing Secretary Hughes: "The capacity of German politicians to do the wrong thing is beyond belief." The Nationalists' demand that war hero Admiral Alfred von Tirpitz be made Germany's new chancellor provided a vivid example. Such a move, Houghton declared, would be a "stupendous blunder."[25]

During May, negotiations between the moderate parties and the DNVP failed miserably. On June 2, with President Ebert's sanction, Marx formed another minority cabinet. The new regime survived a confidence vote in the Reichstag, and with the newfound support of the conservative Bavarian People's Party, momentum shifted in favor of the Dawes Plan. The Reichstag's adjournment granted Marx the time sorely needed to consolidate his position and formulate the legislation for the reparations agreement.

Germany did not have a monopoly on political infighting. In France in May, Radical Socialist Edouard Herriot ousted nationalist hard-liner Raymond Poincaré. Five months earlier, British voters had sacked the Conservatives in favor of Labour's J. Ramsay MacDonald. In America, Coolidge faced challenges within the ranks of the GOP. The accidental president coveted the Republican nomination in 1924, but revelations of the "Harding scandals" created uncertainty, and Coolidge commanded little respect among the party's progressive wing. By February, Houghton had quietly arranged for a delegate's seat at the June Republican convention. He backed former Illinois governor Frank Lowden in 1920, and he might do it again. The ambassador and his political mentor, John Dwight, agreed on the Republican party's central problem: "We have no leadership."[26]

Regardless of the maneuvers, Coolidge operatives secured sufficient delegate commitments by midspring, and Houghton concluded that he could not afford to leave Berlin with the Dawes Plan hanging in the balance. At the convention, Coolidge won the nomination easily, and he hoped the delegates would select a western Progressive as the vice presidential nominee. Coolidge and other mainstream Republicans feared that the Progressives would break ranks to form a third party as they had in 1912. To Coolidge and Houghton's satisfaction, convention delegates selected Frank Lowden, the moderate reformer from Illinois. Lowden, however, abruptly refused the nomination, and businessman Charles Dawes of the reparations experts' committee emerged as the vice presidential nominee. Neither the president nor Houghton was enthusiastic, but nothing more could be done.

Dawes's nomination did nothing to placate Republican progressives, but it heightened the visibility of foreign policy in the election. Coolidge predicted that "the radicals" would again bolt from the party, this time under Senator Robert La Follette (R-WI), who was known to have a substantial following in the Midwest. To offset the La Follette threat, the president accepted the advice of Dwight and others to use the Dawes Plan to attract midwestern German Americans who might otherwise vote for La Follette or the Democratic nominee. Dwight suggested further that Houghton would be a valuable campaigner on the issue, and on June 18, only four days after accepting the presidential nomination, Coolidge ordered the State Department to cable Houghton the following cryptic message: "For a personal conference, the Department desires you at the earliest possible moment to return to the United States."[27]

Within a week, Houghton had boarded the *Leviathan* for the States. In the meantime, Coolidge and Dwight planned to put the ambassador "right into the heart of the campaign." When Houghton arrived in New York on July 1, a crowd of reporters gathered around him. He seized the opportunity to publicize the importance of the

Dawes report not only for Europeans but also for Americans. "The economic stability of the world," he stated, "depends upon the acceptance of the Dawes reparations plan . . . [and it] will bear particularly on the prosperity of the United States." The next day, Houghton participated in several campaign strategy sessions at the White House, where he was staying as the president's guest. Coolidge asked if he were willing to take on a "job" during the fall campaign and exert his influence among "the German element." The ambassador consented without hesitation.[28]

At one dinner meeting that lasted until midnight, the topic shifted to the workings of the reparations plan. Coolidge and Dawes informed Houghton that Dwight Morrow, a senior partner with J. P. Morgan & Company, had been selected as the agent general to supervise reparations payments and German finances once the Dawes Plan had been ratified. Houghton objected vehemently to Morrow's candidacy on the grounds that Germany's extremist parties would capitalize on the selection of a Wall Street banker and thereby make problematic Berlin's unconditional acceptance of the plan. Owen Young, he argued, had already demonstrated that he was the ideal person for the agent general position. In the end, Houghton persuaded Coolidge, Dawes, and Hughes. The ambassador torpedoed Morrow on foreign policy grounds, but the decision had obvious domestic benefits as well. There was little political gain in linking the administration's foreign policy, even if indirectly, to the likes of the Morgan banking house and Wall Street. The president was quite disingenuous when he proceeded to tell reporters that the appointment of the agent general was strictly a European matter having nothing to do with the U.S. government.

As Europe's acceptance of the Dawes Plan became increasingly important to Coolidge politically, he ensured no shortage of American representatives at the July London Conference, where the final terms for putting the plan into effect would be negotiated. At his regular press conferences, the president suddenly began to speak of America's "direct interests" in a reparations settlement. When asked to which interests he was referring, Coolidge pointed to Germany's obligation to pay an estimated $750 million in American war claims and occupation costs. He announced that Frank B. Kellogg, America's new ambassador to Great Britain, and James Logan had been appointed as official delegates to the London Conference. Treasury Secretary Andrew Mellon and Hughes would visit London unofficially. Young represented the international experts' commissions, and he insisted that Houghton be sent to London as an adviser. Together, these Americans helped to mediate between British and U.S. banking interests and the French government. The Germans were not immediately invited, so news of Houghton's participation came as a relief to Berlin. Stresemann told reporters that he trusted the ambassador's "impartial attitude" and his ability to promote the cooperative "spirit" of the Dawes Plan.[29]

The first weeks of the London Conference were acrimonious. In brief, the moneylenders, represented by British Treasury officials and Thomas Lamont of J. P. Morgan & Company, believed that the Dawes Plan had set reparations unrealistically high, thus making default likely and private lending too risky. To counter these concerns, they sought to grant collateral priority to Germany's foreign bankers over the reparations-hungry Allied governments. They also wanted to give the new agent general and his transfer committee considerable independence from the French-dominated Reparations Committee in the matter of default declarations. France, as the primary recipient of reparations, was understandably reluctant to concede so much authority to a quasi-neutral body. Nor was it eager to withdraw its security forces from German territory. As the conference veered toward collapse, British Prime Minister Ramsay MacDonald, Kellogg, Young, Logan, and unofficial advisers such as Houghton labored to find a compromise. Besides aiding Young and the others, the ambassador played a valuable role by allaying German fears of a regressive and dictated settlement. By July 31, some progress had been achieved, with each side agreeing that German loan payments should have top priority and that a new special arbitration panel might be created to settle disputes over the management of reparations defaults.

With this progress, Houghton returned to Berlin because Hughes was scheduled to arrive for a brief, unofficial visit. On August 2, the day before Hughes appeared, the State Department was informed of renewed efforts in London to appoint Morrow as the permanent agent general for reparations. Young had agreed to take the post only temporarily. There had been some initial agreement that Thomas Nelson Perkins, a Boston lawyer, would succeed him. But the British and Morgan still wanted Morrow. When Acting Secretary of State Joseph C. Grew informed Coolidge of the changing situation, the president grew livid. Grew described "Cool Cal" as "about the maddest white man I had ever seen." Houghton cabled Washington that neither he nor Hughes had any knowledge of Morrow's renewed candidacy, and that he still opposed it. Coolidge and Grew agreed with Houghton, thinking it "a great mistake" to risk controversy in Germany or incite the president's domestic critics. The issue, however, remained unresolved.[30]

In Berlin, Houghton introduced Hughes to Germany's most influential political and industrial leaders. In a private meeting at the Presidential Palace, the duo urged Ebert to impress upon the German delegation, then preparing to join the London Conference, the absolute necessity of reaching a quick resolution. A few days earlier, Hughes had taken the same position with French Prime Minister Herriot and the still-influential Poincaré. Houghton returned to London on August 5, leaving the British ambassador in Berlin to note that his American counterpart had been "active since the visit of the Dawes Commission here, and has undoubtedly contributed largely to the satisfactory progress of events."[31]

In London, Houghton continued to support the American representatives who promoted cooperation. He was especially helpful because he understood German political conditions, including the true extent of Berlin's willingness to compromise—despite tough rhetoric—on the timetable for French evacuation. The ambassador personally thought that the bankers were taking advantage of the French, and he concluded that if left to themselves the two opposing sides would wreck the conference. By August 16, the inexperienced Herriot, forced by France's economic weakness and its dependence on foreign capital, conceded to most of the bankers' conditions regarding loan security and default management. On the controversial issue of troop evacuation, Herriot agreed to remove French troops one year after the Dawes Plan was implemented. And, after considerable jousting between Britain and the bankers, on one hand, and Houghton and the Coolidge administration, on the other, the choice of agent general was resolved by the compromise selection of former Treasury Undersecretary S. Parker Gilbert, a brilliant young protégé of Andrew Mellon.

As the conference ended, Houghton returned to Berlin to gauge German reaction. He reported to Hughes, back in Washington, that a majority of the population appeared to favor the London agreement, although many extremists on the political Right denounced it, especially the delayed evacuation of the occupied territories. Hughes responded with a letter of commendation, congratulating the envoy on his unique contributions to the conference. He also encouraged him to aid the Marx government in passing all the necessary Dawes Plan legislation in the Reichstag. The ambassador needed little prodding.

On the night of August 20, Houghton met secretly with leaders from the conservative Nationalist party. Professor Hoetzsch, Oskar Hergt, and Graf Cuno Westarp informed the envoy that the London terms of the French evacuation were wholly unacceptable to the DNVP and that the party would oppose all related legislation in the Reichstag. Moreover, they warned that new elections or even a referendum on the issue would fail unless France withdrew from the Rhine and Ruhr. Houghton took a hard line. There would be no further negotiations. The United States, he stated, supported the London agreements unconditionally, and he threatened that the party's opposition would "turn American opinion unquestionably, sharply and defiantly against Germany and render either private or public loans impossible or difficult." This only left the conservatives to inquire if Houghton could guarantee the conference's promise of a $200 million international loan for Germany should the appropriate legislation pass in the Reichstag. The ambassador affirmed this, adding that even more loans would follow. Houghton interpreted the encounter favorably. He believed that enough "sober," or moderate, Nationalists would fight through the party's divisive rhetoric and support the Marx government. The conservatives had to cooperate or the United States would completely abandon Germany. The ambassador wired Hughes: "They do not dare to accept the consequences and responsibility of [opposition]."[32]

After he received word that the president wanted him to return to America, Houghton assured Hughes that all looked promising, and that he could leave Berlin in "perfect safety." Besides, he offered somewhat disingenuously, "I can have and should have nothing to do" with issues "of purely domestic politics. . . . It would be dangerous at this time for me to take any further action which might result in making the situation worse rather than better." Houghton left Germany aboard the *George Washington* on August 22. By the time he reached New York, the Reichstag had approved, by a large majority, all legislation necessary to comply with the Dawes Plan and London agreements. Roughly half of the Nationalists supported the measures.[33]

Once in America, Houghton rallied public support for the proposed $200 million German loan, of which U.S. investors were expected to take $110 million (equivalent to $1.18 billion in 2003). He promised that the Germans would fulfill the Dawes agreement and guaranteed the safety of investing in Germany. The ambassador's visit, however, had more to do with domestic politics than with international finance. He met with Coolidge on September 5, and they decided that he should campaign in the Midwest throughout October. Houghton's eagerness to take to the stump placed the two men on intimate terms. From Washington, Houghton went to "The Meadows," his summer home on the Massachusetts coast. The *New Bedford Standard* pronounced the ambassador a viable, if not the probable, successor to Secretary Hughes. A month earlier, there had been reports that Houghton would run for New York's governorship against the formidable Al Smith. Indeed, there was some question as to Houghton's future, as he had informed several confidants that he did not wish to return to Berlin on a permanent basis. All agreed that for now, however, the November elections took priority. Later in the month, the ambassador participated in GOP strategy sessions in New York and Chicago. By September's end, he had resettled in Corning to make final preparations for the campaign.

Republican leaders were optimistic that Coolidge would win the popular vote in November. The Democrats had conducted an acrimonious nominating convention, settling on John W. Davis, a former ambassador and Wall Street attorney. Davis did little to excite the party faithful, and, at most, the Republicans conceded him the South and a few minor states. They could not foresee a Democratic majority in the electoral college. What concerned them most was the threat posed by Republican Senator Robert La Follette's Progressive third-party candidacy. As early as February, Dwight expressed to Houghton the party's worst fears: "The old wild-eyed progressives seem to be flocking to La Follette. Whether he can carry enough of those [Republican] Western states . . . is a problem. . . . It might throw the election into the House of Representatives" and "God only knows" what would happen. The idea that neither Coolidge, Davis, nor La Follette could secure the necessary majority constituted the central concern of the 1924 presidential election.[34]

Republican strategists agreed to concentrate against La Follette, whose strength resided largely in the Far and Middle West. The progressive, or "radical," political doctrine espoused by the senator appealed to a diverse group of farmers, intellectuals, and industrial laborers. His core constituency included German Americans who appreciated, above all, his stand against America's involvement in the Great War and the harshness of the Versailles Treaty. In early September, La Follette received the endorsement of the (Baron von) Steuben Society, the largest German-American association in the United States. Although few people believed that the society could deliver six million votes as pledged, its enthusiasm for La Follette worried Republicans and Democrats alike. According to the *New York Herald Tribune*, the endorsement "undoubtedly" reflected "the feeling of the great majority of Americans of German birth or descent." This seemed confirmed when 30,000 cheering German Americans greeted La Follette at rallies in New York at Madison Square Garden and Yankee Stadium.[35]

The Republicans organized a two-pronged attack on key La Follette territories. While Coolidge remained "presidential" at the White House, Dawes and Hughes waged well-publicized campaigns throughout the Midwest. Houghton, on the other hand, quietly courted groups of business, labor, and religious leaders who represented German-American communities. He wrote to a friend that he had embarked on a new "evil career" as an orator, because the "blessed German-American seems to have made up his mind to vote for La Follette and there are a powerful lot of him, and if [La Follette] is successful in his effort, he will throw the election into the House."[36]

Houghton campaigned tirelessly in Chicago, Milwaukee, St. Paul, St. Louis, Cincinnati, Omaha, Bismarck, and elsewhere. Because of his diplomatic experience, he was perceived as the leading U.S. expert on German affairs, and he communicated a thoughtful and activist foreign policy message. He stressed to his audiences the interdependence of the world economy and the importance of the Dawes Plan and U.S. foreign investment to Europe's revitalization, which, he argued, would directly benefit American farmers and factory workers. Economic recovery was also vital to protecting Europe's democratic institutions, which were threatened because of lowered standards of living. Houghton admitted that prior to the Dawes commission, the United States had failed to deal adequately with "the German problem," but there was now a commitment by the Coolidge administration to rehabilitate Germany. The speeches were well received, and the ambassador was ecstatic to learn on October 14 that American investors had overbought the $110 million loan to Germany. He informed Charles Hilles, the vice chairman of the Republican National Committee: "I am inclined to think on the whole that the efforts we have all been making have broken La Follette's vote by German Americans, and I think further that now the break has come, the movement away from La Follette will be very rapid."[37]

Republican leaders took no chances. Hughes's speeches warned of political chaos if the election was decided in the House. Others complained that La Follette and Davis were conspiring to prevent

Coolidge's election in the electoral college. Such attacks and the party's richly funded campaign in the West and Midwest upset the Progressives and the Democrats. At La Follette's behest, a Senate committee began to investigate Republican campaign financing. La Follette and the Democrats also demanded that Houghton and other diplomats espousing "political propaganda" be subpoenaed to testify about their political activities. When the State Department refuted the charge of politicization and issued a detailed accounting of its diplomatic representatives, it conveniently forgot to mention Houghton's whereabouts. Dwight told the ambassador: all the "pain about your being [here] . . . indicates that you have been doing good work. I do not know of any other ambassadors or ministers who have raised their fingers."[38]

After twenty-six days on the campaign trail, Houghton returned to Corning on November 1. He was confident and predicted that La Follette would be fortunate to win his own state. Three days later, Coolidge won by a landslide. La Follette carried only Wisconsin but placed second in twelve states. Credit for the GOP victory belonged to the robust economy, Coolidge's personal popularity, and well-funded and effective campaigning, which included Houghton's active participation. The president of a Cincinnati bank wrote to him, "No small part of the success of Mr. Coolidge is due to the intelligent manner in which you placed the German situation before the people of this country." Letters also reached Coolidge, including one noting that Houghton had influenced thousands by appealing to their "heads instead of their hearts." Hughes and Dawes heaped praise on him, too, and on November 7, Coolidge told Houghton over lunch that "no one had contributed as much as he had personally to the success of the campaign." Even Hughes's efforts did not rate such a comment from the president.[39]

When Houghton returned to Europe in mid-November, there had been meaningful economic and political progress. French troops had withdrawn from the town of Dortmund, and the Reparations Committee had reported positively on economic recovery. As he traveled through Germany, Houghton observed improved commercial activity and public sentiment. He was "much struck," he noted in his diary, "by signs of activity along the Rhine [and] from Cologne to Berlin, and in particular by the evident change in mental attitude. There are signs of cheerfulness now and the place looks wholly different than it did a few months ago."[40]

In Berlin, Houghton learned of Marx and Stresemann's failure to build a broad coalition government and of the dismissal of the Reichstag in October. Germany's political parties had reverted to full-throttle campaign mode, although the December 7 elections proved largely inconsequential. Houghton accurately predicted that the positive economic developments meant losses for the Communists and far-right *völkisch* parties, but there had not been sufficient progress to rally meaningful support for what he called the "compact middle" parties. As a result, Marx and Stresemann again sought to construct a majority "bourgeois bloc" with the newly enlarged DNVP. Stresemann hoped that economic recovery, underwritten in large part by the influx of American loans, would entice the DNVP and curb its criticism of his conciliatory policies toward the West. This approach appeared sound to the ambassador, but he warned political leaders not to overextend the economy with international loans. He told Stresemann and Hermann Bücher, of the Reich Association of German Industry, that "Germany must be very careful not to abuse the credit she now enjoys in America and that . . . the only loans that should be favored were those tending directly to put men and factories into production. Loans for other purposes, being non-productive, were open to objection."[41]

The ambassador also warned Americans, including Parker Gilbert, the recently arrived agent general for reparations. Gilbert, who spoke no German, became a regular visitor to the embassy and relied heavily upon the ambassador's counsel and his Berlin network. Gilbert impressed Houghton as intelligent and capable, but he demonstrated a lack of diplomatic finesse. His poor management of the international press corps, for example, alarmed the ambassador. Houghton understood the political dangers of an antagonistic press and had always provided journalists with prompt and reliable information. The ambassador explained to Gilbert how trustworthy the correspondents had been during the past two-and-one-half years, and that good press relations were critical if he wanted his view of events to reach the United States without slant. The press corps appreciated Houghton's intervention, as did Gilbert, who asked him to remain in Berlin through the summer to ensure "a good start in his work." But a prolonged stay in Berlin was the last thing Houghton wanted. He believed that Germany's apparent return to stability provided the ideal opportunity for the introduction of a new ambassador who could work with Gilbert on a permanent basis.[42]

Before the new ambassador arrived, Houghton witnessed the formation of yet another German cabinet. With the two largest parties, the Socialists and Nationalists, refusing to cooperate, the Catholic Center Party determined the course of events. But contributing to the political difficulties was a new crisis with the Allies, who postponed their evacuation from Cologne after Germany's failure to comply fully with disarmament provisions in the Versailles Treaty. Nevertheless, Hans Luther, an independent politician, was finally able to form a new right-of-center government that included "expert" representatives from the Center, the Bavarian People's Party, the German People's Party, and the DNVP. Luther had served as finance minister the previous year and was widely respected. Houghton approved, characterizing him as "a very human and well-poised, well-balanced man." The ambassador assured Washington that there should be no worry over the government's shift to the right. There will be no "monarchical intrigues," he promised, as the coalition rested largely on shared economic interests and opposition to the "radical" Left. Moreover, with the moderate wing of the DNVP in the ascendancy, support for the Dawes Plan had grown. A solution to the recent disarmament flare-up, he added, would be found shortly.[43]

As the Germans adjusted to political change early in the New Year, so did the Coolidge administration. On January 10 the president accepted Secretary Hughes's resignation. The move came as a shock to nearly everyone, as did the appointment of Frank Kellogg as his successor. The sixty-eight-year-old Kellogg had served ably as ambassador in London for the past year, but, nervous and irritable, the one-term senator from Minnesota, described by some as a "weak little cup of tea" and a "doddering political hack from the cow country," inspired little confidence and much speculation. Houghton was not surprised by the pronouncements. He had been informed of the coming changes, including the political aspect of Kellogg's nomination, by which the president hoped to improve relations with the Senate. Nor was the ambassador shocked by a third declaration, that he was to replace Kellogg in London. Houghton's influence on the reparations settlement had made an enormous impression on Coolidge. Also endearing, of course, was his contribution to the presidential campaign.[44]

Reaction to Houghton's nomination was overwhelmingly positive in the United States. Congratulatory cables poured into the embassy as did a legion of scoop-seeking reporters. Any thoughts that Houghton's promotion came as simple patronage were quickly dispelled by laudatory reviews in the Democratic press. The newspapers characterized Houghton as a keen intellectual who, by drawing on his diverse background, had championed progressive solutions for world problems. Joseph Pulitzer's *New York World*, hardly a friend of the Coolidge administration, gushed that Houghton's

> grasp of details, facts, personalities, extending over the whole range of post-war economic and political problems . . . [is] astounding . . . his universal and impartial vision, his apprehension of these terribly complicated problems are merely aspects of his vision of unity and multiplicity. . . . [He is] a statesman who not only puts forward as a thesis, but passionately believes in the biggest and broadest and most enheartening gospel of peace and co-operation. . . . Mr. Houghton has emerged . . . as one of the greatest of American diplomats at a time when the world indeed needs diplomats of vision, courage, and character. . . . [He is] the apostle of a "larger synthesis" by which vexatious hates and quarrels are to be merged into at least temporary peace and order throughout the world. His idealism contains nothing of the vague, the woolly, the familiar vote-catching nebulosity. It is made of New England granite, not soft soap.[45]

Such a reaction contrasted sharply with the treatment given Kellogg. Frank Lowden was not alone when he wrote that the former senator's appointment "is somewhat of a mystery to me." State Department officials considered the Minnesotan "a come-down" after Hughes. Many assailed Kellogg as a discredited politician whose diplomatic skill and experience were negligible. By comparison, Houghton, according to the progressive journal, *The Nation*, "stands head and shoulders above Kellogg both as a man and as an official." The contrast led to rampant and persistent speculation that Kellogg's was only a temporary appointment and that Corning's glassmaker would eventually assume the mantle. On January 20, *The Nation*'s publisher, Oswald Garrison Villard, wrote to Houghton in Berlin, "It will interest you to know it's being freely declared in Washington that you will be Secretary of State within six months to a year."[46]

Houghton brushed aside the speculation and began to prepare for his reassignment. News of his impending departure created a swirl of activity at the embassy. Gilbert and his staff visited even more frequently. Others, German and American, came to exert indirect influence on the agent general. Houghton hosted private "cocktail hours" for Stresemann and Gilbert to encourage better personal

and professional relations. There continued to arrive an endless
stream of friends from America, including General Electric's President Gerard Swope, Westinghouse executive Walter Cary, and *Wall
Street Journal* publisher Clarence Barron.

During his final days, Houghton was moved by the praise and
thanks showered on him by the German people. The press extolled
the ambassador's diplomatic accomplishments and personal vir-
tues. From the time of the Reparations Commission's formation
through the London settlement, he had been cast as a progenitor
and the "guiding spirit" of the Dawes Plan. But affection for the
ambassador ran deeper than the plaudits for his official diplomacy.
Since his 1922 address at the Metropolitan Club, he had demonstrated courage by calling for the abandonment of wartime hatreds
and for the restoration of hope, stability, and prosperity. Moreover,
the Germans reflected on the ambassador's many acts of kindness,
including his substantial but little publicized gifts to charity. In three
years, Houghton had become a trusted friend and an inspirational
leader. The most common word uttered regarding his departure
was *"Reue,"* or regret. Chancellor Luther and Foreign Minister
Stresemann implored him to maintain his "friendly attitude" toward Germany while in London. On February 17, two days before
his departure, Ebert brought Houghton to the Presidential Palace
and presented him with a finely crafted cigarette case. On behalf of
his countrymen, he awarded the ambassador the German Red Cross
Medal of the First Class.[47]

Houghton's swan song in Berlin was bittersweet. He felt pride
in his diplomatic performance, in Germany's economic revival, and
in the diminution of anti-American sentiment. It had been more
than two years since someone had brushed against him on a
crowded street and murmured, *"Schweinhundt."* In a farewell speech
to a German and American audience, Houghton recounted how
cold, gray, and cheerless he had found Berlin in 1922 and contrasted
it with the "new Germany"—bright, clear, and "flooded with sun-
shine." Only those who had lived through "the fateful years," he
continued, would ever be able to appreciate the economic "miracle"
that was transforming the country. In a final letter to William Castle,
he remarked that he would soon turn his back on "three of the most
interesting and, I hope, useful years of my life. I get a sort of twinge
when I try to realize that my work in Germany has come to an end,
and that I am about to start off on another Great Adventure." The
ambassador left the capital aboard a night train on February 21,
1925.[48]

Houghton stands as the most important figure in U.S.–German relations from the Republic's ascendancy through 1924. His relentless diplomacy and mounting influence in Germany and the United States were unparalleled. A primary source of his authority in Berlin stemmed, naturally, from the fact that he represented a leading world power. But also key to his effectiveness was his understanding of German society and his apparent and sincere commitment to restoring peaceful international relations. Evidence of his determination took many forms, from his championing of the war claims treaty and the Dawes Plan to his repeated calls for American involvement in European affairs. Houghton's effective diplomacy also increased his influence in Washington, exemplified when he single-handedly vetoed the administration's plans to name Morrow as agent general. Hughes confirmed the ambassador's success in a letter on January 27, 1925: "You have such a complete command of trustworthy sources of information, and such a just appreciation, that I contemplate with dismay your leaving Berlin, yet I believe with you that you have accomplished the main purposes of your mission. . . . I shall never forget your constant helpfulness and cordial support."[49]

But Houghton never considered his Berlin ambassadorship a complete success. German–American relations were much improved, and he had made strides toward involving the United States in Europe's economic and political problems, but he considered the Dawes commission a much belated and severely limited American initiative. The conservative Republican administrations had refused to use postwar U.S. economic strength to press for the political settlement of reparations and European security. Even Houghton's brazen threats to German Nationalists came by his own volition, not from officials in Washington. The Ruhr crisis, the hyperinflation, and the long delay in reaching the Dawes settlement embittered French–German relations and undermined the Weimar Republic. Whether the United States could have altered these negative developments will never be known, but it is certain that Washington did little to prevent them. For the next four years, Houghton's pursuit of progress in international affairs would focus frequently on issues of peace and security, and here, promoting better American–British relations would be paramount. In his report on the heads of foreign missions in Berlin, British envoy D'Abernon reminded his government that the incoming ambassador "is genuinely anxious to see America take a large part in European affairs."[50]

Notes

1. Houghton to Hughes, July 24, 1923, Houghton Papers.

2. Pusey, *Charles Evans Hughes*, 586; Hughes to Coolidge, August 15, 1923, Calvin Coolidge Papers, Library of Congress, microfilm edition, reel 53 (hereafter cited as Coolidge Papers).

3. Hughes to Henry P. Fletcher, August 17, 1923, *FRUS, 1923*, 2:66–68.

4. Houghton to Hughes, August 27, 1923, Houghton Papers.

5. Castle Diary, September 26, 1923.

6. Dwight to Houghton, September 29, 1923, and Houghton to Hughes, October 7, 1923, Houghton Papers.

7. *Press Conferences*, October 9, 1923, and November 6, 1923.

8. Horace Green, "An Unloquacious Ambassador: Alanson B. Houghton, Who Practices Diplomatic Silence in Berlin," *New York Times Magazine*, November 4, 1923.

9. Robert Murphy, *Diplomat among Warriors* (Garden City, NY, 1964), 13–16.

10. Houghton to Arthur Houghton, October 9, 1923, Houghton Papers; Houghton to Castle, November 20, 1923, Castle Papers.

11. Castle to Warren D. Robbins, November 19, 1923, Castle Papers; Hughes to Houghton, November 17, 1923, Houghton Papers.

12. Houghton to Castle, December 3, 1923, Houghton Papers.

13. Houghton to Frank I. Kent, December 21, 1923, and Houghton to Hughes, November 12, 1923, ibid.

14. ABH Diary, January 7, 1924.

15. Ibid., January 10 and 16, 1924; Charles G. Dawes, *A Journal of Reparations* (London, 1939), 88.

16. ABH Diary, January 14 and 17, 1924.

17. Houghton to Hughes, February 19, 1924, Houghton Papers.

18. Charles G. Dawes, *Notes as Vice President, 1928–1929* (Boston, 1935), 133.

19. Houghton to Hughes, March 3 and 25, 1924, Houghton Papers.

20. Ibid.

21. ABH Diary, March 29, 1924.

22. Ibid., March 31–April 2, 1924.

23. Houghton to James A. Logan, April 27, 1924, Houghton Papers.

24. ABH Diary, May 8 and 20, 1924.

25. Ibid., May 20, 1924; Houghton to Hughes, May 8, 1924, Houghton Papers.

26. Dwight to Houghton, February 29, 1924, Houghton Papers.

27. Department of State to Houghton (cable), June 18, 1924, ibid.

28. Chandler P. Anderson Diary, June 26, 1924, Chandler P. Anderson Papers, Library of Congress, Washington, DC; *New York World*, July 1, 1924; Houghton to Arthur Houghton, July 7, 1924, Houghton Papers; Joseph C. Grew Diary, June 18, 1924, Joseph C. Grew Papers, Houghton Library, Harvard University.

29. *Press Conferences*, June 26, 1924; *New York Times*, July 13, 1924.

30. Grew Diary, August 2–4, 1924.

31. Edgar Vincent D'Abernon, *The Diary of an Ambassador: Dawes to Locarno, 1924–1926*, vol. 3 (Garden City, NY, 1931), 83–85.

32. Houghton to State Department (cables), August 17 and 20, 1924, Houghton Papers.

33. Ibid., August 20, 1924.

34. Dwight to Houghton, February 25, 1924, ibid.

35. *New York Herald Tribune*, September 23, 1924.

36. Houghton to R. W. Husted, October 3, 1924, and Houghton to M. E. Hanna, October 7, 1924, Houghton Papers.

37. Houghton to Charles D. Hilles, October 18, 1924, ibid.

38. *New York Times*, October 23, 1924; Dwight to Houghton, October 26, 1924, Houghton Papers.

39. Charles A. Hinch to Houghton, November 7, 1924, Houghton Papers; Fred A. Britten (R-IL) to Coolidge, October 24, 1924, Coolidge Papers, reel 168; Chandler P. Anderson Diary, November 7, 1924.

40. ABH Diary, November 24, 1924.

41. Ibid., November 26 and December 8, 1924; Houghton to State Department (cable), November 27, 1924, Houghton Papers.

42. Houghton to Arthur Houghton, December 29, 1924, Houghton Papers.

43. ABH Diary, January 29, 1925; Houghton to State Department (cable), January 16, 1925, Houghton Papers.

44. Lewis Ethan Ellis, *Frank B. Kellogg and American Foreign Relations, 1925–1929* (New Brunswick, NJ, 1961), 6.

45. *New York World*, January 14, 1925.

46. Frank O. Lowden to Houghton, January 15, 1925, Frank O. Lowden Papers, University of Chicago Library, Chicago; Castle Diary, January 11, 1925; *The Nation* 120 (January 28, 1925): 1; Oswald G. Villard to Houghton, January 20, 1925, Houghton Papers.

47. "German Newspaper Clippings," Houghton Papers; ABH Diary, February 18, 1925.

48. "Toast to Dr. Maltzan at American Luncheon Club in Berlin" (speech), January 29, 1925, Houghton Papers; Houghton to Castle, February 19, 1925, ibid.

49. Hughes to Houghton, January 27, 1925, ibid.

50. Edgar Vincent D'Abernon, "Annual Report on Heads of Foreign Missions in Berlin," March 9, 1924, FO 371/9831/C4335/4335/18, PRO.

5

America's Honest Broker

1925–1926

> If the [Locarno] Security Pact is concluded, as now
> seems likely, it will of course ensure a relatively
> longer period of peace and at the same time tend to
> fix the point where the next great war will begin,
> i.e., the German–Polish frontier.
> —Alanson B. Houghton, 1925

The involvement of the United States in the Dawes Plan
represented a high watermark in Republican world
leadership during the 1920s. Washington's attempt to
solve the reparations problem, however, had come slowly
and reluctantly, and U.S. leadership on the Dawes Commission did not signal the beginning of a new era of political interventionism in the Old World. This became
evident in 1925 when the United States shunned direct
involvement in the negotiation of a European security arrangement known as the Locarno Treaties. On the other
hand, American aloofness never restrained the active diplomacy of Ambassador Alanson Houghton. International
acceptance of the Dawes Plan and the envoy's promotion
and transfer to Great Britain only enhanced his desire to
transform the United States into a more engaged and responsible world leader. His appointment to the top position in the Foreign Service and his unusually close
relationship with the German government made him the
most powerful ambassador in the world, and he meant
to exercise his influence.

Three issues dominated Houghton's attention during
his first year in London: the Locarno security negotiations,
the Anglo-American rubber trade, and international

disarmament. Operating without official instructions, and sometimes without Washington's knowledge, the ambassador immersed
himself in the movement for a Western European security pact. Because of his special standing with the German government,
Houghton's participation in the negotiations was appreciated not
only by Berlin but also by senior British and French officials who
relied on the American as a liaison and sounding board for German policy. Houghton considered a European security pact fundamental to the "high policy" of perpetuating peace and prosperity
among the major powers, and thus he deemed it vital to American
interests. He also deemed a strong and dependable Anglo-American
relationship central to postwar rehabilitation. Houghton found this
latter mission complicated by controversial bilateral conflicts over
"low policy" issues such as the regulation of trade in raw materials, especially crude rubber. Although he was critical of Washington's nationalistic approach to such economic disputes, the extent
of the ambassador's disapproval there paled when compared to
his opposition to the Coolidge administration's impetuous approach
to international arms control. Houghton's self-anointed role as
America's peace broker proved an arduous one.

Prior to his arrival in London, American–British cooperation
had improved significantly. Immediately following the war, the
relationship had suffered from Washington's failure to ratify the
Versailles Treaty (or join the League of Nations) and from its rejection of a U.S.–British military guarantee of French security. The
British felt betrayed, and rightly considered America an unreliable
partner in postwar international affairs. For the next decade, the
Foreign Office, always sensitive to the American strain of Anglophobia, often cast Britain's relationship with the United States as
of secondary importance. Nevertheless, after 1922, an informal entente had developed between the two countries that often promoted
private and public collaboration on economic issues, including
Britain's return to the gold standard in the spring of 1925. Perhaps
more important in improving bilateral relations were the negotiated settlement of Britain's war debt to the United States in 1923
and Anglo-American cooperation on the Dawes Plan a year later.
This is not to say that political distrust and economic rivalry no
longer existed; certainly, they did. In fact, the newly established
rapprochement began to falter just months after Houghton settled
into his new embassy.[1]

After leaving Berlin in February 1925, Houghton enjoyed short
vacations at a resort in Germany and one in Switzerland, where his

daughter attended boarding school. He planned to go to London immediately afterward, but when he heard that King George V had fallen ill, he delayed his arrival until mid-April. The envoy returned to America instead, dividing his time among Corning, Washington, and New York City. When his ship, the *Aquitania*, docked in New York on March 10, reporters asked him for his reaction to the sudden death of President Friedrich Ebert. Houghton expressed shock and sadness at the news and proclaimed Ebert the most significant German leader since Otto von Bismarck. He then seized the opportunity to assess Germany's future, not its past. He commented on the country's remarkable economic progress since the formulation of the Dawes Plan and stressed that this development augured well not only for Europe's stability and prosperity but also for America's.

While in Washington, Houghton stayed at the White House. He found there a letter of commendation from the outgoing secretary of state. "It has been a great privilege to be associated with you in the important work of the last three years," Hughes wrote, "and, as I have frequently said, you have performed a service of incalculable benefit to our country. I am sure that you will enter upon a period of great usefulness in London." Invigorated by the praise, the ambassador whisked through several days of conferences with Coolidge, State Department officials, and Senator William E. Borah (R-ID), a leading progressive and the new chairman of the Senate Foreign Relations Committee. Borah announced to reporters that he was immensely impressed by Houghton, whose unexpected return to the capital fed the rumor that he would soon replace Secretary of State Frank Kellogg. Such talk seemed substantiated when members of the Republican National Committee informed the administration that they preferred Houghton.[2]

From Washington the ambassador journeyed home to Corning. Though he hoped for an extended respite, he found himself shuttling to and from New York City, where he maintained an office in the Corning Glass Works building on Fifth Avenue. By the first week of April, he had returned to the State Department for a final round of briefings and a farewell dinner hosted by John Dwight and attended by a bevy of judges, senators, and congressmen. Later, the Foreign Policy Association organized a banquet in his honor. Houghton's keynote address elucidated the problems and progress of postwar world affairs, which led international financier Paul M. Warburg to claim that he had "never heard a more significant and sound analysis of the European situation." The following day, the ambassador received an honorary Doctor of Laws degree from New York University. The progressive *New Republic* commented on Houghton's constant motion, declaring his private sessions with leaders in the business and journalistic communities "a decided success," due to his obvious "knowledge of the European situation, his broadly tolerant viewpoint, and his vigorous and forthright personality." Just prior to sailing for Europe, Houghton informed reporters that he was returning "with a full sense of responsibility" and "the belief that the greatest independent factor" in international affairs was strong relations between the United States and Great Britain.[3]

By the time the ambassador arrived in London, Britain's relationship with continental Europe, not the United States, had taken center stage. Months earlier, Edgar D'Abernon, the British ambassador in Berlin, had encouraged the German government to propose a new security agreement with the Allies, one based partly on Houghton's jettisoned 1922 nonaggression pact. The Germans were receptive. Fearful of a Anglo-French military alliance and a prolonged occupation of the Rhineland, Foreign Minister Gustav Stresemann proposed to London, and then to Paris, a security treaty to sanction formally Germany's western borders with France and Belgium. Herein lay the origins of the Locarno Treaties. By spring 1925, the Conservative Baldwin government in London had come to accept the premise that Britain should act as the principal guarantor of a Rhineland border pact. France, too, had expressed interest in a security agreement but wanted to negotiate the precise terms of the British guarantee. Moreover, France refused to discuss a military evacuation from Germany until Britain had satisfied all French concerns. Stresemann took comfort from these early developments, although he feared that his policies might be endangered by the presidential candidacy of retired Field Marshal Paul von Hindenburg.

Supplied with confidential information from Stresemann and other officials in the German government, Houghton carefully monitored the preliminary security pact negotiations and Germany's presidential campaign. Like Stresemann, he was apprehensive about Hindenburg's candidacy. In short, the ambassador feared that the elevation of a war hero to political power would throw into question Germany's desire for peace. On April 25, the day before the election, Houghton wrote to retired diplomat Henry White: "I, for one, am hoping that [former Chancellor Wilhelm] Marx will come triumphantly through. . . . Of course, Hindenburg's election would only appear as a mistake." Nevertheless, the mistake transpired and the seventy-eight-year-old Hindenburg became Germany's second democratically elected president.[4]

The German election set the stage for Houghton's keynote address to the British Pilgrims' Society. His speech, broadcast over radio, was a landmark in interwar diplomacy that highlighted the potential influence of America's postwar economic power and the ambassador's personal attempt to establish U.S. leadership in world affairs. On the evening of May 4, hundreds of dignitaries packed the ballroom of the Hotel Victoria to welcome America's glassmaker-turned-diplomat. Houghton sat to the right of Prime Minister Stanley Baldwin, whose preparatory remarks praised recent U.S.–British cooperation and underscored the necessity of peaceful conflict resolution. Houghton followed, opening on a lighter note by poking fun at British trade restrictions against Maine potatoes. The ambassador hoped aloud that "Justice, substantial Justice, British Justice, will ultimately be done to that really excellent American tuber." After the laughter had subsided, he recalled the hardships wrought on Europe by the war, only to emphasize the improving economic conditions propelled by the Dawes Plan and the inflow of U.S. capital. The ambassador informed his audience that Americans were again investing abroad, because the Dawes agreement had finally signaled Europe's postwar commitment to a "peaceful up-building." But, he warned, America's "helpful processes which are now in motion must inevitably cease" if intra-European cooperation was not substantively reaffirmed in the coming months. In other words, if the Allies and Germany did not conclude a new security pact, the United States might cut off the flow of capital necessary for Europe's reconstruction.[5]

Reaction to Houghton's "peace ultimatum" was immediate and widespread. The headline of the *New York Times* was typical: "HOUGHTON DEMANDS PEACE IN EUROPE OR OUR AID CEASES." Attitudes across Europe were mixed. The British were most supportive. Britain's foreign secretary, Austen Chamberlain, had approved the text in advance, and Queen Mary personally congratulated the envoy at Buckingham Palace. Germans also viewed Houghton's remarks favorably, interpreting his admonition as diplomatic cannon fire directed at Paris. Ago von Maltzan, the new German ambassador in Washington, wrote to Houghton that he appreciated the speech and assured him that all Germany shared his perspective. The French, on the other hand, flailed at Houghton for not singling out Germany as the primary cause of Europe's dubious state. Many in Europe construed Houghton's threat as a warning to Hindenburg.[6]

Esme Howard, the British ambassador in Washington, accurately reported that American support for Houghton was "extraordinarily unanimous." Democrats and Republicans, conservatives and progressives, quickly aligned themselves with Houghton on European policy. Morgan banker Thomas Lamont considered the address excellent, as did Owen Young, who contended that no postwar speech had received "such universal approval." Even Senator Henrik Shipstead, the Farmer/Labor party member who had ousted Frank Kellogg from the Senate in 1922, climbed aboard the Houghton bandwagon. "I am glad that Ambassador Houghton has spoken plainly," he said. "The views he expressed I have held over since the signing of the armistice. I know we are being accused of being selfish isolationists, but what other policy can we pursue if Europe insists upon going back to its own vomit." Several newspapers printed features on this unusual breed of diplomat, whose effective method and manner they concluded had developed from his diverse forays into scholarship, industry, and politics. Congratulatory letters and cables flooded the London embassy. "If there is anything in the old fashioned theory that a man's ears burn when people are talking about him," John Dwight wrote to the ambassador, "you ought to have a couple balls of fire hung onto your head . . . [as] you have been the most talked about man in the United States, not even excepting President Coolidge. . . . The net result of all this is that you are being talked about on all sides as the successor to Secretary Kellogg."[7]

As usual, Houghton brushed aside the banter over his "imminent" promotion. Responding to congratulatory letters, he told friends that the purpose of his "frank statement" on American policy had been to warn political extremists on the continent against polluting the "atmosphere" needed "to conduct the further negotiations necessary to a peace." He wrote to former Illinois governor Frank Lowden, "The time had come for a statement of some sort" signaling America's pivotal role in Europe's reconstruction. Houghton grew concerned that the immense publicity generated by his speech might anger Coolidge and Kellogg, and this was especially true after the administration announced that the ambassador had spoken on his own accord. But, writing four days after the speech, Coolidge eased the envoy's mind, noting: "Your address seems to have [been] taken very well, and I think is having a very wholesome effect. I am very much hoping that something can be done in the way of providing a treaty of security." Soon afterward, Coolidge began to support Houghton's position publicly, stating that future American loans should be contingent upon a new European security agreement. The praise heaped upon the ambassador served to validate his aggressive and direct diplomacy and steeled his determination to be a constructive force in international affairs. An Allied–German security pact remained his primary concern.[8]

UNCLE SAM'LL BE MORE INCLINED TO HELP IF YOU'LL CHANGE TOOLS.
—Berryman in the *Washington Star*. *Reprinted by permission of the* Washington Post

During spring and summer 1925, Britain, France, and Germany secretly negotiated the framework for a European security conference, and Houghton labored unofficially as a mediator among the parties. On June 3, Foreign Secretary Chamberlain read to Houghton from an official communiqué that specified Britain's willingness to guarantee the borders separating France and Belgium from

Germany. When Chamberlain made clear that London had no desire to guarantee Germany's eastern border with Poland, Houghton
immediately recognized a potential problem and asked a hypothetical question: Would French soldiers be permitted to cross German
soil to defend Poland from an attack by a third party, say, Soviet
Russia? Chamberlain replied that such questions would be decided
by the League of Nations, but that Britain would not sign such a
pact with France. The ambassador then inquired whether Germany
would be forced to join the League. The foreign secretary answered
yes, but not as a preliminary condition to signing the security treaty.
Houghton believed that the British note represented a reasonable
basis for the security talks, and so instructed the German embassy.

Like the British, the French government sought to keep Houghton updated on the early negotiations. On June 16 the French ambassador in London delivered a copy of his government's note to
Germany. The document expressed sincere interest in pursuing a
mutual security pact based on four conditions: that Belgium participate; that Germany join the League without reservations; that
France play a role in Germany's proposed arbitration agreements
with Poland; and that the security agreement require no modifica-
tion of the Versailles Treaty, especially the timetable for Allied
evacuations from the Rhineland. In a cable to the State Department,
Houghton judged the French note rational, even "friendly in tone."
In a confidential letter to Edward Norris, his former secretary in
Berlin, the envoy observed that, despite some obvious points of
exchange, the French offer indeed provided Germany with a "substantial basis" for an agreement, and as a result, "the end of the
long road is now in sight."[9]

By July, however, it had become clear that the Germans were
less enthusiastic about France's condition-laden response.
Stresemann informed Houghton that he had expected, among other
things, a French pledge to evacuate the Rhineland early, and ab-
sent this good faith showing, the prospects for a security pact appeared bleak. William R. Castle, the State Department's West
European bureau chief, who was then visiting London, noted: "The
French being clever at diplomacy may be maneuvering the Germans
into an untenable position. But wherever the blame may lie, the Pact
is in danger and it gives the only hope for European tranquility."[10]

Disturbed by the thought of Germany's obstruction to a formal
security conference, Houghton promptly intervened. On July 3 he
crafted a compassionate but sternly worded letter to Stresemann.
He expressed dismay over Germany's demand for an early Rhine-

land evacuation, stating that such conditions could be negotiated later. He also gave assurances that Paris and London wanted a satisfactory accord as much as Berlin because the French desired Britain's military guarantee, and the British depended on stable continental trade. Houghton balanced such promises with a threat. Germany's failure to conclude a security agreement would force a military alliance between Britain and France, and for that reason alone, he urged Stresemann to accept the French note.

At this hour, Castle fully realized the magnitude of Houghton's standing and influence. He described the letter to Stresemann as "straight from the shoulder," a remarkably stark document made possible only by Houghton's "peculiar position vis-à-vis the Germans." Castle also witnessed Houghton's stern admonition to German diplomats in London regarding their government's intransigence. When Houghton considered traveling to Berlin to pressure the cabinet and Reichstag leaders, Castle supported the idea: "I cannot help feeling that perhaps the only hope lies in a talk between Houghton and the Germans. He might put the thing across as [Secretary Hughes said] he did the idea of the Dawes Plan." The ambassador was operating without official sanction from the State Department, which dreaded any accusation of meddling in Old World politics, yet Castle believed that Houghton's covert activities pleased Coolidge, and thus Secretary Kellogg.[11]

On July 20 the Berlin government delivered to Houghton a copy of its official reply to the French. The communiqué suggested Germany's willingness to proceed with formal conference negotiations, but it elaborated on various security issues including the desire for early evacuation of the Rhineland. Houghton believed the deadlock was finally broken. The British and French, however, informed the ambassador that they were disturbed by Berlin's note and suspected that the Germans meant to stall. Houghton, without consulting Berlin, insisted that the Germans did not desire further delay and he encouraged the Allies to accept the note and initiate direct and formal security negotiations.

Despite the consternation caused by the German note, Houghton remained optimistic about a European security conference. The Allies' decision to evacuate Germany's Ruhr district on July 31, a full two weeks ahead of schedule, only boosted the ambassador's confidence. He advised the State Department to expect protracted negotiations, yet a pact was certain to come, he argued, because of France's dependence on both British protection and American investment. The ambassador's understanding of

French foreign policy had improved while in London, not only because of his intimate conversations with Chamberlain but also because of frequent contact with French officials, especially the French ambassador. When Foreign Minister Aristide Briand visited London for negotiations with Chamberlain, he arranged a private luncheon with Houghton at the French embassy. There, the foreign minister explained the limits of France's security objectives and emphasized his desire to reach a settlement with Germany. Houghton held a similar meeting with Finance Minister Joseph Caillaux.

In August a jubilant Chamberlain informed Houghton that he and Briand had agreed to organize two multilateral conferences. The first, beginning September 1 in London, would include German, French, and British legal experts who would negotiate the technical details of proposed arbitration agreements between Germany and its neighbors. A second conference of foreign ministers would meet afterward in Locarno, Switzerland, to resolve the political aspects of the security arrangement. Houghton supported these plans, and when German officials approached him to discuss the advisability of the arbitration conference, he strongly encouraged their complete cooperation.

Houghton played a unique supportive role in these preliminary security negotiations. He notified Washington of his intimate and routine contact with French, German, and British officials and concluded that his "steady pressure for a conciliatory attitude on the one hand and a reasonable attitude on the other has had some effect." France's conciliatory leadership had particularly impressed him, and the French had changed their attitude toward Houghton, whom they had dismissed earlier as a rank Germanophile. Reparations agent general Parker Gilbert and banker Paul Warburg informed the ambassador that French officials felt "extremely obliged" for his selflessness in pursuing a fair settlement between France and Germany. Nor did Houghton's influence as a mediator go unnoticed in the press, which described him as "the father" of the security talks. Similarly, Bernadotte E. Schmitt, a University of Chicago professor, recently returned from Europe, announced at a foreign policy conference: "In well informed European quarters, one is told that [Houghton] is the spiritual author of the negotiations."[12]

Success at the September arbitration conference in London paved the way for the meeting of foreign ministers in Locarno, beginning on October 5. The Foreign Office and diplomats at the German and French embassies in London kept the ambassador abreast of developments. The spirit of conciliation and compromise that pervaded the twelve-day Locarno conference validated Houghton's long-standing optimism. He learned that Briand and Chamberlain had dropped the idea of making France the guarantor of the arbitration treaties between Germany and Poland and had accepted Berlin's demand that it be exempted from any League sanctions against Soviet Russia in case the latter attacked Poland. The Allies also promised to negotiate later a timely evacuation from Cologne and to reduce the number of occupation troops remaining in Coblenz and Mainz. For their part, the Allies received Germany's commitment to join the League, to arbitrate disputes in the East, and to maintain the status quo in the West.

In mid-October, while the Locarno talks were coming to a successful close, Houghton found himself engaged in a round of personal, corporate diplomacy. A crisis had developed between Corning Glass Works and its second largest customer, Westinghouse Electric Company. New contract negotiations had faltered. The most serious concern to the glassmakers was Westinghouse's threat that it might begin manufacturing its own lightbulb casings. In March, Houghton had persuaded Westinghouse to abandon the idea and to focus instead on a new twenty-year contract. But by late summer, the talks had broken down and Houghton's brother Arthur concluded that the ambassador's involvement was needed to clear the impasse. By fall, both parties had reconvened in London. After ten days of wrangling, the Houghton brothers emerged with a five-year agreement. The new pact could be expanded to ten years if a satisfactory cost-plus formula could be devised later, or if the Houghtons granted Westinghouse an option to buy the family firm. The ambassador explained to his son that the London negotiations had been an overwhelming success because a "spirit of mutual fairness and good-will" had brought the companies together. He expected the same cooperative spirit to permeate U.S.–European diplomacy.[13]

Houghton's satisfaction with his business diplomacy mirrored his gratification with the Locarno Treaties. In a speech to the Knights of the Round Table, the ambassador explained that there was no "mystery" to achieving success in foreign relations. As in domestic life, international harmony depended on "a spirit of mutual accommodation and good-will." The compromises reached at Locarno, he argued, affirmed this fact, and as a result, all nations could again contemplate the future with a measure of confidence. Houghton gave ample credit to Chamberlain and congratulated him personally at the Foreign Office on October 21. Chamberlain briefed the ambassador and expressed high regard for Briand, Prime Minister Luther, and Stresemann, especially the first two. In addition, the foreign secretary asked Houghton to publicize his personal approval of the accords in the hopes that the envoy's influence might "hold down" extremist opposition in Germany and France. Houghton consented gladly.[14]

Although most plaudits for the security pact justly flowed to Chamberlain and his counterparts in Berlin and Paris, many in Europe and the United States recognized Houghton's contributions. The British magazine *Punch* printed a full-page drawing of the ambassador holding onto the leashes of a smiling German eagle and British lion. The *Berliner Tageblatt* noted that the envoy rarely received proper accolades for his effective diplomacy because it was "mostly carried on unobtrusively and in reticent forms," and the newspaper concluded that his influence on the European security pact was "of far greater importance . . . than is known today." Likewise, the *New York Times* advised its readers not to be surprised if the "dusty archives" of future years reveal that the "first impulse" for a security pact actually came from Houghton while he was stationed in Berlin. Adolph S. Ochs, the newspaper's publisher, knew the extent of Houghton's diplomacy and gave him "much of the credit" for the Locarno movement. James G. McDonald, chairman of the Foreign Policy Association, elaborated in a letter to Houghton: "It now seems a long time since [Chancellor] Cuno made his initial [security] offer to France. Nonetheless, the Locarno achievements are directly related to that initial German move. You personally, must therefore have much satisfaction in your knowledge of the genesis of the Cuno proposal. Those of us who know of the way in which Germany came to make her initial peace offering to France are very conscious of the world's debt to you." Probably no American comprehended the nature of Houghton's diplomatic activities more than his friend Owen Young, who sent "heartiest congratulations" for his most "excellent work" in support of the Locarno accords.[15]

Houghton's personal sense of mission fueled his constant motion on behalf of the security pact. As an industrialist and politician, he considered himself a pragmatist, a problem-solver, and a promoter of a progressive ideology. He interpreted his diplomatic role similarly. Never content to play the part of observer, he acted as a facilitator of progress in international relations. Houghton also acted with regard to America's global position. The United States, the most industrially advanced and prosperous nation, had a re-

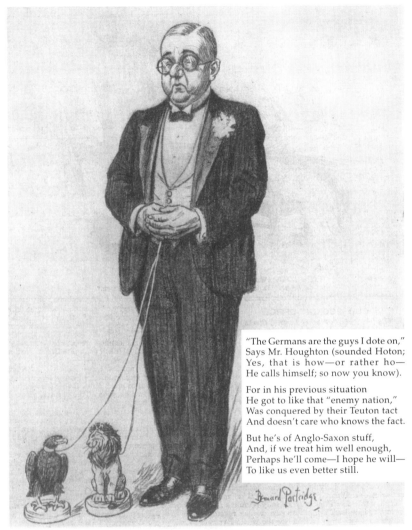

"The Germans are the guys I dote on,"
Says Mr. Houghton (sounded Hoton;
Yes, that is how—or rather ho—
He calls himself; so now you know).

For in his previous situation
He got to like that "enemy nation,"
Was conquered by their Teuton tact
And doesn't care who knows the fact.

But he's of Anglo-Saxon stuff,
And, if we treat him well enough,
Perhaps he'll come—I hope he will—
To like us even better still.

MR. PUNCH'S PERSONALITIES. IV.—H. E. THE AMERICAN AMBASSADOR. *Reprinted by permission of* Punch *Limited*

sponsibility to lead in international affairs. Moreover, he reasoned that active and thoughtful Great Power leadership had taken on increasing importance in the postwar era because of the awesome capabilities of modern weaponry. As America's top diplomat, he felt a personal obligation to exercise his influence constructively, but he never wavered from his belief that ultimate responsibility for world leadership rested with the president of the United States.

Prior to departing for London, Houghton promised President Coolidge a memorandum outlining a major policy initiative. In late June, he apologized for having failed to file the report, and in July, Castle reminded him that the president was still expecting the memo. Finally, in August, with the security pact negotiations moving forward, he completed his design for a new American-led peace offensive. His principal justification for urging the bold proposal rested upon his conviction that a second world war was possible within his lifetime and that it would be "infinitely more deadly and more destructive" than the first. While he remained optimistic regarding the Rhineland security pact and believed that it would promote a "relatively longer" peace in Europe, he also recognized its practical limitations, especially the ongoing uncertainty regarding Germany's eastern border. In a stroke of remarkable prescience, he instructed Coolidge that the Rhineland agreement, when finally concluded, would only "tend to fix the point where the next great war will begin, i.e., the German-Polish frontier."[16]

In his August memorandum, Houghton did not propose that the United States promote world peace by means of a new alliance system. He believed that such military commitments ultimately forced other countries to form counteralliances. What he advocated instead was a partial revival of his 1922 peace plan: a "radical" worldwide "political experiment" whereby the leading industrial nations formally renounced warfare as a means of settling international conflicts. He proposed that the Great Powers—Germany, France, Britain, America, and Japan—sign a hundred-year nonaggression pact. Moreover, they should adhere to national referendums as democratic means for declaring future wars. The war referendum had become increasingly popular among peace activists and American liberals after 1914, and by 1924 it had been incorporated into the convention platforms of the Democratic and Progressive parties.[17]

Houghton freely admitted that concepts such as the renunciation of war and the war referendum might appear "quixotic," but he assured Coolidge that these proposals presented no political or military risks and their public articulation held certain advantages for the Republican administration. For example, the United States could assert its proper leadership role by offering to the world a "democratic method" of bringing the politics of war "under better control." Also, the plan formed the "necessary foundation" for the rational settlement of international disputes by way of compromise, arbitration, conciliation, and, if need be, the World Court. Houghton assured the president that domestic opponents of the League of Nations would not assail these progressive antiwar initiatives. The antiwar treaty, he argued, represented merely an obligation not to wage *offensive* campaigns. Should any country violate it, America remained free to protect its national interests by any means necessary. Coolidge received the ambitious twenty-five-page report during the last week of August. To the ambassador's dismay, the president tabled it for nearly two years.[18]

In 1925, amid the Locarno security negotiations and Houghton's efforts to sustain the postwar peace, there arose a serious Anglo-American conflict over trade policy. The "rubber controversy," the second major issue dominating Houghton's first year in London, demonstrated Houghton's ongoing differences with the Coolidge administration and revealed his sharp disagreement with Commerce Secretary Herbert Hoover, whom scholars frequently credit with being the most enlightened Republican of the New Era.

Through its colonial possessions Malaya and Ceylon (now Sri Lanka), Britain dominated the world's crude rubber supply. It controlled production and exportation through a quasi-governmental advisory committee that reported to the Colonial Office. In the United States, the largest consumer of rubber, businessmen worried about material shortages and their negative effects on manufacturing output and market prices. Indeed, when prices spiked in July 1925 due to increased crude rubber demand and inadequate supply, Frederick C. Hood, an executive of the Rubber Association of America, pleaded with the State Department to intervene. On July 18, Kellogg instructed Houghton to press the Foreign Office for relief on this "very great concern."[19]

The ambassador understood the importance of rubber to the American economy and the risks of being dependent on a foreign supplier. He also recognized, however, that the issue, if not managed prudently, could damage U.S.–British relations, which he considered crucial to international stability. Hood apparently knew Houghton well and frantically cabled London: "PLEASE HELP US MY DEAR ALAN." The ambassador reviewed the matter with his London staff, and later met with W. O. Rutherford, president of the Rubber Association and a key executive with B. F. Goodrich Company. Houghton concluded that American rubber buyers and users, not British producers or the advisory committee, had mismanaged inventories, and thus were more to blame for the crisis.[20]

Therefore, on July 22, when the ambassador approached Foreign Secretary Chamberlain, he took a conciliatory position. He admitted that U.S. companies had been "caught by their own folly" and that he respected British attempts to stabilize rubber prices at "a fair and a remunerative level." Still, it was in neither country's best interests for Britain to exploit its strong position by not releasing more rubber to the market. Houghton explained the gravity of the situation from the U.S. perspective and warned that American rubber consumers might attempt to bypass British suppliers by developing independent plantations or substitute materials. The ambassador also alluded to possible congressional retaliation by means of export restrictions and duties on American cotton and copper. Yet, he confessed to the foreign minister, he was personally opposed to retaliatory maneuvers, as they would prove "quite disastrous" for all concerned.[21]

In the end, Houghton recommended that the two nations seek a reasonable and mutually beneficial compromise. He underscored for Chamberlain the utter necessity for dependable U.S.–British collaboration on the larger work of Europe's postwar reconstruction—what he termed "high policy"—and asked that the critical bilateral relationship not be jeopardized by a narrow trade dispute. Chamberlain agreed that the rubber issue needed attention on "a statesmanlike plane" and promised to consult with his government.[22]

Houghton's presentation favorably impressed the British foreign secretary. "I have no doubt in my own mind," Chamberlain informed the Baldwin cabinet, "of Mr. Houghton's genuinely friendly disposition. I am sure he speaks the truth . . . when he says that he wants our two countries to co-operate increasingly in international affairs. . . . He talked with gravity and persuasively—I might even say pleadingly. . . . I am sure that the fear which he expressed . . . was genuine, and I must admit I was impressed by what he said. . . . [we should] avoid the dangers which must arise to our international relations from the growing agitation in America." Chamberlain exhibited his appreciation for Houghton further when he criticized the Colonial Office for proposing a hardline response to the United States. "And I must add," he wrote to his colleagues, "that we are thinking too much of how we can score and too little of how we can make it easiest for a very friendly Ambassador and obviously a not unfriendly Government to do the right thing." A few weeks later, the British released tons of stored rubber and sanctioned an increase in colonial crop production—though not to the extent desired by the American trade group. Kellogg praised Houghton for "proceeding wisely," and the ambassador informed Hood of the Rubber Association that the British Foreign Office had done all it could.[23]

Houghton realized that the British move was only a stopgap, that further disputes lay ahead. He was not surprised when, in October, the Rubber Association again pressured the State Department to intervene. Houghton undertook informal talks with the British government and recommended that Washington dissuade the Rubber Association from inflaming the press and public opinion. With Chamberlain away at Locarno, the ambassador explained the position of American manufacturers to Prime Minister Stanley Baldwin, who promised to review the situation with the Colonial Office. When Chamberlain returned in late October, Houghton cautiously reintroduced the vexing subject of rubber. By month's end, Britain agreed to increase rubber exportation by 10 percent. Despite the nagging problem, Chamberlain applauded the ambassador's diplomatic poise. He wrote to Ambassador Howard in Washington that he wanted "to record here my sense of the really friendly feelings towards this country that animate the Ambassador, and my appreciation of the way in which he has handled this [rubber] question in his interviews with me."[24]

Despite Britain's willingness to increase rubber exports, the Rubber Association continued to complain to the State Department about price and supply problems. Just before Thanksgiving, Kellogg asked Houghton to press for further relief. The ambassador met with Chamberlain, but believing that Britain was acting responsibly and that market speculators were causing price volatility, he simply informed the foreign minister of the renewed complaints and of his personal sympathy for British policy. Chamberlain promised to investigate further and informed Houghton that members of the Rubber Association had begun secret contract negotiations with the British government without notifying the State Department. That news infuriated Houghton. The Rubber Association had used the ambassador and the State Department to pressure London into concessions, while at the same time keeping them in the dark about its concurrent negotiations. He vented his anger to the State Department and to Frederick A. Sterling, his embassy counselor: "The rubber situation has developed into an awful mess. . . . It looks to me, offhand, as if I had been made the prize fool of the century, and I am frank to say that I don't enjoy the distinction."[25]

Shortly afterward, Rutherford of B. F. Goodrich informed Houghton of a new price-fixing agreement between Britain and an

American banking and rubber syndicate. Rutherford and the British needed Washington to approve the deal. Still piqued, Houghton and Kellogg opposed the scheme. The ambassador delivered the State Department's official rebuff in early December, and the agreement never materialized. The American note specifically protested Britain's willingness to jeopardize "the whole fabric of international commerce and even wholesome international relations" by sanctioning monopolies and price-fixing contracts. The long-term consequences for American consumers, Houghton reported to Kellogg, were "not wholly pleasant."[26]

Upon studying the U.S. communiqué, the Foreign Office accurately detected the influence of Commerce Secretary Herbert Hoover. During November, Hoover had aroused British ire by publicly lashing out against the Colonial Office's regulation of raw materials, especially crude rubber. In January 1926 the politically ambitious Hoover escalated his assault on the British rubber "monopoly," which he claimed "mulcted," or extorted, some $600 million annually from American consumers. The issue resonated with voters, and in speech after speech Hoover attacked the British bogeyman and promoted retaliatory countermeasures of domestic conservation and the development of independent rubber resources. His testimony before a House committee caused extra concern at the Foreign Office.[27]

The anti-American and anti-Hoover reaction in Britain was hardly surprising. The London *Times* feared that "Hoover's laments" might reverse the trend of cordial international settlements and engender autarchy and trade wars. Few in London disputed the *Spectator*'s conclusion that Anglo-American relations had reached a low ebb. Ambassador Howard reported from Washington that Hoover believed sincerely in his campaign against foreign raw-material monopolies, and because of his "strong political ambitions and his passion for the limelight," the attacks were likely to continue. Robert Vansittart, the manager of the American desk at the Foreign Office, railed against Hoover *and* Houghton. The American ambassador "is much to blame for this; for his impertinence has been staged and promoted by Mr. Hoover, and had Mr. Houghton been wise or straight he could at least have helped to restrain, and not incite, the Secretary of Commerce, and the latter would have been less inclined to stampede Congress. . . . Mr. Houghton might be [made] the audience of some well-deserved plain speaking."[28]

Vansittart's outburst against Houghton was unjust, and his attitude found little sympathy from Chamberlain. On the issue of rubber, the ambassador had consistently respected the British position. Moreover, he had worked hard to temper the Republican administration's handling of the issue. Houghton understood that in the postwar economy, Britain and other European powers desperately needed trade and dollars to extinguish their international debts. That the United States maintained high trade barriers, demanded repayment of war loans, dictated terms of new financing, and then protested European raw-material monopolies all appeared "a bit ludicrous" to Houghton. He especially opposed Hoover's campaign for developing American rubber plantations abroad. He believed such a costly program was not only unnecessary but "exceedingly dangerous" for national security. To undertake large-scale raw material programs in Asia or elsewhere, he wrote Young, would only lead to "a colonial policy," the building up of a huge naval force, and an attempt to "conquer" a worldwide position similar to Britain's. "The more I contemplate the activity of Hoover and his no-monopoly slogan," he wrote Dwight, "the more I see a sorry time ahead for us. . . . Hoover's influence seems to me, frankly, thoroughly bad. Worst of all, he seems to have gained influence in the State Department and has messed things up rather considerably in consequence."[29]

Houghton and the British were not alone in their disapproval of the commerce secretary. Parker Gilbert complained to Treasury Secretary Andrew Mellon that Hoover's agitating was complicating his work as the agent general for reparations. Young wrote to Hoover directly and warned that Washington's foreign economic policies risked pushing Europe "to the breaking point." At the State Department, William Castle believed that the commerce secretary was "insanely ambitious for personal power" and warned his colleagues that Hoover's antics were complicating U.S. foreign policy. Knowing Houghton's good standing with Coolidge, Castle even suggested to the ambassador, if he were in "a blood-thirsty mood," that he visit the White House, take a strong stand, and "deliver the coup de grace" against Hoover.[30]

Increasingly concerned over the implications of Hoover's nationalistic crusade, Houghton drafted a frank and confidential report to Kellogg. First, he presented a sympathetic portrait of the rubber controversy from the British perspective to remind the secretary that, in matters of free trade, "we do not come into court with clean hands." He also discussed the extraordinary economic hardships placed upon Europe after the war, the additional burden of America's war-debt policy, and the "desperate eagerness" of Europeans to capitalize on any commercial advantage against the United States. He explained that the British needed to develop their colonial possessions to stimulate economic growth, just as they had exploited their coal and iron reserves after the Napoleonic Wars. "These overseas peoples," he stressed, "are hungry for trade," and if the United States was sincerely interested in opening raw material markets, it should enter into serious trade negotiations instead of taking an ostentatious "pose." Houghton even offered the British view, if not his own, that Hoover's economic strategy for America was analogous to Lenin's self-serving New Economic Policy for Soviet Russia.[31]

Moreover, the ambassador appealed for the State Department, not Commerce, to take the initiative in formulating a broader, more coherent foreign policy agenda, of which economics was only a part. Specifically, he recommended that the rubber issue be placed in the larger context of the international economy. And since Britain already dominated raw material markets in the tropics and subtropics and America held sway over the world capital markets, a natural "trading basis" existed for bilateral cooperation. "The problem is essentially diplomatic," and the diplomatic arena, he concluded, "must always be the field of the State Department."[32]

The Anglo-American dispute over rubber contributed to a general rise in anti-American sentiment in Europe. When the Allies celebrated the official signing of the Locarno Treaties, many rejoiced that the security arrangement had been reached without Washington's formal participation. Houghton wrote to the State Department of the powerful "jubilation" regarding Europe's newfound ability to solve "her own quarrels." Above all, the ambassador feared the development of a European bloc hostile to American commerce. In letters to Castle, he forecast a trade war if Washington continued to pursue shortsighted economic policies such as demanding the repayment of war debts. The United States has forced "a union of interests" on the nations of Europe, he declared; "we have forced on them . . . increased taxation . . . [lower] living standards . . . and how serious this may be in the end I hesitate to think." He insisted that with more assertive leadership from Washington, the American public would recognize the economic and strategic dangers of nationalistic economic policies. "The

American people are [not] fools," he growled; they can be shown "precisely what debt collection means to them in trade and politically," and they can be convinced that the country would be "infinitely better off" by "our growing trade and commerce and industry." In a revealing speech on economics to the British Reform Club, he praised his audience, stating that in foreign commerce "you people stand alone. The rest of us are children in our knowledge of international trade."[33]

If the Republican party had not yet mastered farsighted leadership in world commerce, it did consider itself the postwar champion of multilateral disarmament and arms limitation agreements. The Washington Conference's naval treaty of 1922 had established maximum tonnage limits for capital warships and required the leading naval powers to scuttle dozens of vessels. Coolidge and Kellogg both wanted to enhance this achievement, which had been orchestrated by their predecessors. The Coolidge administration's incessant drive for naval disarmament constituted the third major diplomatic issue of Houghton's early tenure in London. In October 1925 the president floated a trial balloon for a second Washington arms conference. Houghton, asked to gauge European reaction and advise the administration, concluded that Britain alone might favor a naval convention, but there was scant enthusiasm in Europe for an American initiative. He informed the State Department that the Locarno settlement, with its reliance on the League of Nations for arbitration supervision, had dramatically boosted European confidence and hostility toward the United States. "We are not popular in Europe just now," he reminded Kellogg. "Our refusal to join [the] League and our insistence upon debt repayments have left us without friends."[34]

Europeans viewed multilateral disarmament as the logical sequel to Locarno, and in September 1925 the League formed a special committee to discuss plans for a formal preparatory commission. The commission would negotiate the agenda for a future disarmament conference. Given rising anti-U.S. sentiment and America's likely exclusion from the League's preparatory commission, Coolidge's idea for another Washington conference seemed futile. Houghton, who believed any near-term arms talks would fail, advised the president to make a public statement before America was formally excluded from participation. To minimize political fallout, he wanted Coolidge to express support for the idea of a League-only disarmament program and to state that the United

States would intervene only if its assistance were directly requested. Coolidge could argue that a similar policy of watchful waiting had proved successful with the Dawes Plan.

In short, the ambassador feared that America's exclusion from the League's preparatory commission would be used by the administration's critics as proof of Coolidge's weak leadership. Consequently, Coolidge needed to take preemptive action. "In other words," Houghton cabled the State Department, it was better that "the administration, rather than its enemies [at home or abroad] . . . should define its position." Taking "such an attitude on our part would unquestionably have a salutary effect here and serve to bring to the minds of the powers concerned that any real withdrawal on our part [from world affairs] would affect them adversely and possibly disastrously." Kellogg accepted the envoy's recommendations, even presenting them to Coolidge as his own. The president formally adopted Houghton's recommendations in his annual message to Congress on December 8.[35]

Meanwhile, British officials began to pressure League members to invite the United States to join the preparatory commission. The Baldwin government made clear that it had no interest in pursuing further naval limitations without Washington. By mid-December, League members agreed, and word of America's invitation was leaked to the press. Secretary Kellogg immediately asked Houghton to comment on the surprising turn of events and indicated that the ambassador might be recalled to Washington for private consultations.

Houghton had already made clear his belief that the preliminary arms conference would fail. He argued correctly that the European powers disagreed fundamentally on the proper approach to disarmament. France insisted on coordinated reductions in naval, land, and air weaponry based on each nation's industrial capacity. Such a sweeping formula was entirely unacceptable to Germany and Britain. Moreover, Houghton believed there were no significant forces to compel compromise, and the proposed arms talks represented "merely a game which the powers are playing wholly and altogether for individual advantage." Still worse, America's inclusion would only complicate the discussions, and its participation offered a convenient scapegoat for the conference's assured failure. Consequently, the ambassador urged the administration to decline the League's invitation. He proposed that League members first ply the "troubled waters" of disarmament. After being disturbed by never-ending disagreements and the political and financial costs of maintaining large militaries, they would eventually agree to a Washington-led compromise. To participate in the "unwholesome welter" of the preparatory conference, he said, would prove "fatal," and thus end any hope of disarmament in the foreseeable future.[36]

Despite Houghton's warnings, Coolidge accepted the League's invitation. In an apologetic tone, Kellogg conveyed the president's appreciation for the envoy's perspective, but explained that public and congressional opinion had made it impossible to do otherwise. Houghton had, however, successfully pressured the administration to take a cautious approach. When the president requested a congressional appropriation for the preliminary conference, he emphasized that the United States was not obligated to participate in the actual disarmament conference that was to follow. In addition, the United States would be represented by a low-level delegation, headed by Hugh Gibson, the inconspicuous minister to Switzerland, who was instructed to solicit input from Houghton.

Despite its political popularity, Houghton opposed the administration's decision. He clung to his belief, and colleagues in the State Department had come to agree, that the preliminary conference would fail to reach a consensus. His disapproving communiqués to friends and government officials amounted to a biting criticism of Republican foreign policy leadership. Participation in the disarmament conference, while popular in the short term, entailed certain risks such as emboldening League advocates to wage a divisive political campaign in the upcoming midterm elections. Worse, the American delegation might be blamed for the conference's failure, and this would further degrade U.S.–European relations and the chances for a new arms control agreement. The ambassador appreciated the "compelling force" of public opinion and recognized that governments must either "follow . . . or lead it." But Coolidge again failed to make the proper choice.[37]

At bottom, Houghton did not believe that the administration understood the complexities of British or French imperial policies. Arms control could never be approached with the simplicity that America preferred. Nor did the envoy think that the administration realized the implications of affiliating itself so closely with Geneva. The League, as he saw it, was handicapped as a manager of world peace because of Britain's limited commitment to collective security and France's selfish determination to guide League policy toward its own political and military objectives. Houghton instructed Dwight that "keeping clear of the League was the one sound fact on which to base" U.S. foreign policy. "The trouble," he continued, "is that when you sup with the aforementioned divil [*sic*], you need a long, long, spoon. I wonder if we have such a utensil somewhere in the cupboard?"[38]

The administration did not dissuade Houghton from conveying his critical views. Kellogg offered several times to bring the envoy to Washington for personal consultations. In a private letter, Coolidge strongly encouraged the ambassador to share his opinions directly "on the general situation at anytime." Castle pleaded for Houghton's return: "I hope with all my heart that you will take advantage of the Secretary's suggestion that you may want to come to Washington . . . to talk about the Disarmament Conference and various other matters, which I think you can put up to the President perhaps better than anybody else." Knowing that his views ran contrary to official policy, Houghton resisted calls to cross the Atlantic. But after Kellogg, and perhaps Coolidge, read his confidential telegram of February 27, which elaborated on the complexities of British and French foreign policy and the inherent risks of America's participation at Geneva, the secretary ordered the ambassador's return. When he arrived in the United States in March 1926, Houghton allowed his discontent and an emerging crisis at the League of Nations to get the better of him. The public dissemination of his pessimistic views ignited a political firestorm that was fanned by the international press.[39]

The announcement of Houghton's return to the United States generated immediate speculation in European and American newspapers. News stories emphasized the Coolidge administration's concern for disarmament and the possibility that Houghton would replace the aged and often ailing Kellogg. When the envoy reached Washington on March 16, the declining prospects for arms control had taken center stage due to a major conflict at the League of Nations. The League had convened a Special Assembly to welcome Germany back into the world community by granting it membership with a permanent seat on the executive council—a position equal to that of Britain, France, Italy, and Japan. A resurgent Germany, however, worried France and Poland, and caused French Prime Minister Aristide Briand and British Foreign Minister Austen Chamberlain to labor behind the scenes to counterbalance Germany's admission by elevating to the council a second country such as Poland. To much of the international press, these "slimy" backroom deals seemed all too reminiscent of prewar alliance diplomacy, and the intrigues threatened not only the Locarno spirit but also the popularity of the ruling British, French, and German governments. By March 17, the League conference had deadlocked, leaving the London *Times* to conclude that the failed assembly had exhibited the "crudest manifestations" of nationalism, which were capable of driving "desperate nations into blind arbitrament of war."[40]

Echoes of the League debacle reverberated in the United States. Just a few weeks earlier, Americans were still riding a wave of euphoria buoyed by the Dawes Plan and the Locarno achievement. It seemed as if the Europeans had finally attained the elusive U.S. objective of augmenting French security without permanently debilitating Germany or entangling the United States. But the League's rebuff to Germany put Europe's future into question, especially the idea of further arms control. The *New York Times* described the Geneva assembly as a "deplorable exhibition of petty nationalism" and "the most serious [setback] in world politics" since the Paris Peace Conference.[41]

Houghton, although deeply disappointed, was not completely surprised. Like other Americans, he considered Locarno a great stride forward, but he had no illusions about the accomplishment. Peace in Western Europe depended largely on the British guarantee of the Franco–Belgian border with Germany, and thus the Locarno agreements had formally reinstituted power politics. The revival of realpolitik under British auspices did not upset Houghton, as he deemed it necessary to postwar rehabilitation. Given Britain's geographic position and its economic and military strength, he believed that the British had the ultimate responsibility for maintaining peace and stability in the region. But Britain's fair treatment of a disarmed, occupied, and insecure Germany was pivotal. The backdoor machinations at the League's Special Assembly fully exposed Europe's balance-of-power diplomacy and the necessity for a cautious outlook regarding the further enhancement of European security. Houghton concluded that political discord and arms competition would reign in Europe for several years until extended economic hardship impelled the major powers to reduce military expenditures. Such pessimism permeated his reports to the president and secretary of state.

Houghton met with Coolidge and Kellogg on St. Patrick's Day morning, and afterward Hugh R. Wilson, the State Department's publicity officer, asked the ambassador to lead a press conference on European affairs. With the consent of Undersecretary of State Joseph C. Grew, Houghton agreed. Wilson and Castle told the ambassador that the reporters were "reliable" and "trustworthy," and that he could speak "very freely." Although the press interview was not premeditated, the ambassador had long wanted the administration to be more outspoken on European affairs, and this meeting with reporters allowed for a little "frank speaking."[42]

Many in America admired the ambassador's determined approach to U.S. foreign policy and hoped that he would soon succeed Kellogg. The *Boston Herald* editorialized that if he were made secretary of state, "The definite Houghton view will supplant [Kellogg's] more or less foggy and nebulous" European policy. Houghton could find no greater proponent than the State Department's Division Chief for Western European Affairs. Castle confided to his diary that the ambassador's return "makes me wish he was here for good as Secretary of State. He is thoroughly courageous and we need courage." Above all, Castle admired the ambassador's "clean-cut break" with the administration regarding the necessity of publicly articulating a foreign policy vision and acting on it. Few diplomats, he concluded, thought "as clearly and as vigorously."[43]

Late in the afternoon of March 17, 1926, the ambassador, accompanied by Wilson and Castle, met with some forty members of the Washington press corps. He spoke "wittily and picturesquely" about the deteriorating state of European affairs and explained his pessimistic outlook on disarmament. According to the envoy, the continent was reverting to balance-of-power politics, and he openly doubted the League's ability to control the forces of nationalism and international rivalry. He answered all questions candidly and, after more than an hour, concluded with an earnest request that he not be quoted directly. Astonished by Houghton's bald honesty, Castle feared that any extensive news coverage might upset Kellogg. Still, he approved of the ambassador's message, concluding that "it is just as well that people should be told how things actually are, not fed up on 'the beauties of Locarno' and all that sort of bunk." Hugh Wilson considered the interview "a breath of east wind blowing across the warm over-optimism of the country with regard to disarmament and European peace." Stunned reporters discussed the difficulties of presenting the story while maintaining Houghton's anonymity. Some contended that the ambassador's remarks had been the most "clear-cut and comprehensive" ever uttered by "a public man" to the Washington press. In the end, most journalists assumed that the administration shared his perspective and that the State Department wanted it disseminated. Coolidge, on receiving word of his father's rapidly deteriorating health, departed for Vermont before the papers went to press.[44]

The Houghton controversy began to unfold on March 18 when more than a dozen American newspapers reported on the administration's disillusionment with European relations, especially the bleak prospect for disarmament. The banner in the *New York Herald Tribune* read, "U.S. to Keep Hands Off, Houghton Advises Coolidge to Ignore Geneva Arms Parley, Europe Rapidly Reverts." Although not quoted directly, many stories implicated Houghton as the person most responsible for the stark pessimism. Readers were treated to the gloomy details of Houghton's views on European conditions. The object of his official reports, according to the press, was to convince Coolidge of the futility of pursuing near-term disarmament as Germany's resurgence pressured France and its Central European allies to remain fully armed. Moreover, the major powers disagreed on the proper formula for disarmament. Only the exorbitant economic costs of maintaining large militaries would compel the Great Powers to disarm, and not until then should the United States intervene.[45]

The extensive press coverage alarmed administration officials. Kellogg roared over the impropriety of the interview and, according to Castle, called the ambassador into his office and gave him "the dickens." Houghton defended himself, stating that his views were known to the administration and that the press conference had been arranged and sanctioned by the State Department. That evening, before leaving town for a short vacation, Houghton described the day to Castle as having an "Alice in Wonderland" quality, and he took some pleasure in recounting how the excitable Kellogg had "climbed into the chandelier." Meanwhile, with Coolidge out of town, the secretary took precautionary measures. As news of Houghton's interview reached London, Kellogg issued a department circular to the press and to key European embassies stating that Houghton had not divulged to reporters the content of his official reports to the administration.[46]

The Houghton interview and the State Department's tepid denial, which had not refuted the envoy's alleged views, caused a sensation in Europe. The British, French, and German governments rejected outright the thesis that Europe was reverting to power politics. Some in the press accused Coolidge of orchestrating a publicity scheme against the League's disarmament agenda. Coming in the aftermath of the recent League crisis, however, many in

Germany and Britain sympathized with Houghton's concerns. The U.S. embassy in London reported: "The majority of people realized down in their hearts that what he said is in the main true, even if unpalatable." But the French were outraged and attacked Houghton as a reckless, ignorant Germanophile plotting against good U.S.–French relations. The *Journal des Débats* denounced the ambassador as possibly the world's "worst enemy of peace." European diplomats, many familiar with Houghton's personal views, were less shocked by his negative portrayal than by its public circulation. Editors at the London *Times* feared his influence on American policy, concluding that the ambassador's report on the deteriorating state of European power politics would push U.S. foreign policy "in the direction of isolation."[47]

Spurred by the uproar in Europe, Kellogg arranged an official press conference on March 20 to proclaim that U.S. foreign policy had not changed as evidenced by Washington's upcoming service on the League's preparatory disarmament commission. Meanwhile, the controversy was politicized at home. Opponents of America's involvement with the League and the World Court rallied behind Houghton's report that Europe had returned to power politics. In a widely printed editorial, William Randolph Hearst supported his old Harvard classmate's warning about "foreign entanglements either by means of the League or the League's World Court." Proponents of the League and the Court divided over the issue. The *New York Evening World* claimed that Washington had been "besieged" with protests over Houghton's "anti-league propaganda" and by demands for his censure. *The Independent* assailed the ambassador for "amateurish" and "deliberate meddling" in European affairs and declared that he had committed a diplomatic blunder "worse than a crime." A political cartoon in the *St. Louis Post-Dispatch* depicted Houghton's interview as an American brick flung at Europe. In contrast, the pro-Court *New York Herald Tribune* appreciated Houghton's position. The diplomat's warnings, the newspaper contended, would have the positive effect of shielding the United States from blame when the League's disarmament program failed. Moreover, Europe's renewed instability further necessitated America's leadership in the World Court.[48]

The debate over the Houghton incident spread to the Senate chamber on Monday afternoon, March 22. Several Republican senators, who had recently voted for U.S. membership in the Court, feared that the League crisis over Germany and Houghton's criticism of Europe might jeopardize their reelection. Pat Harrison, a

DOING OUR BIT FOR EUROPEAN PEACE. *Reprinted with permission of the* St. Louis Post-Dispatch, *2004*

Mississippi Democrat and firm League supporter, launched a broadside against the administration's "embarrassing" conduct of foreign affairs. He lampooned the president, the secretary of state, and the ambassador as "Careful Cal," "Nervous Nellie," and "Gloomy Gus," respectively. He assailed Coolidge for failing to lead and accused the administration of reverting to "dark-lantern diplomatic procedures." Such practice was evident, he claimed, in the State Department's refusal to repudiate the substance of Houghton's remarks, which the boisterous Mississippian characterized as "repugnant." He suggested that the ambassador had acted as an "assassin" in the White House's elaborate scheme of "subtle propaganda." Accordingly, Houghton's unofficial and pessimistic representations of Europe enabled Coolidge to retreat from the World Court and

capture "a little glory" by calling for an American-sponsored disarmament conference before the midterm elections.[49]

"Careful Cal," "Nervous Nellie," and "Gloomy Gus" were not
without defenders, however, and rancorous debate broke out after
Harrison's volley. Senator Simeon D. Fess chastised Harrison for
his undignified and "far-fetched" criticism. The Ohio Republican,
a former history professor and college president, lectured his colleagues on the state of international affairs. "Composure" had been
brought to "confusion," he stated, through the Washington naval
conference and the Dawes Plan. European security had arrived in
the form of the Locarno Treaties. The recent League crisis, he insisted, had, as Houghton said, demonstrated a disturbing regres-
sion to power politics that jeopardized peace. The American public
had the right to an explanation of this turn of events, and Houghton,
who had done so much to bring about the Locarno accords, was
"best qualified" to explain it. League proponents challenged Fess
and argued that the ambassador had severely damaged the League's
credibility. Since the United States had "eschewed all association"
with the League, Carter Glass (D–VA) demanded to know "what
right" an American ambassador had in "interfering" in Geneva affairs. Claude A. Swanson, Virginia's other Democratic senator, asked
perceptively, if the Locarno spirit was so crucial to world peace,
why did Houghton "come here and do all [he could] . . . to de-
stroy" it? To the surprise of many, Republican progressive William E. Borah (ID), the chairman of the Senate Foreign Relations
Committee, defended the administration's senior diplomat. In the
process, he clarified some confusion over the true nature of Houghton's views. He announced that press accounts of Houghton's interview were entirely consistent with the ambassador's opinions
as personally expressed to him in a recent private consultation.
Borah argued that Houghton, an "honest" public servant intimately
"familiar with the facts" of Europe, felt obliged to inform the country of the current threat to peace and disarmament.[50]

The administration took a keen interest in the wrangling on
Capitol Hill, and the press reveled in the story. The irascible Kellogg
urged Coolidge to censure the ambassador publicly for having
"made trouble" for the department. According to the *Washington
Post*, the president had returned from his father's funeral to find
U.S.–European relations in possibly "the most confused state since
the war." On March 23 an unusually large crowd gathered at the
Executive Office for a prearranged presidential news conference.
Coolidge, though shifting his cigar about, appeared calm. He ig-

FIFTEEN CENTS

TIME
The Weekly News-Magazine

VOL. VII, No. 14

ALANSON B. HOUGHTON
. . . does not throw stones
(See Page 6)

APRIL 5, 1926

ALANSON B. HOUGHTON DOES NOT THROW STONES. *Reprinted by permission of* Time *Magazine*

nored all questions directly related to Houghton, but did reconfirm America's commitment to the League's preliminary disarmament conference. Reporters interpreted his refusal to criticize Houghton or refute his view of European affairs as support for the ambassador and a willingness to let matters take their course. Coolidge also left the impression that Houghton spoke for the administration and remained the president's chief European policy adviser.[51]

Throughout the controversy, Houghton received considerable and typically glowing publicity. He was depicted as a highly accomplished industrialist and diplomat with unique influence on administration policy. The London *Times* noted that the president depended on Houghton "to a peculiar degree" and that he acted as the "guiding rod" for U.S. policy in Europe. The *Brooklyn Daily Eagle* declared Houghton "the outstanding figure of American diplomacy," with Kellogg "simply swept aside under the impact of Mr. Houghton's logic." The *Boston Herald* reported that the ambassador "has always been regarded in Washington as the diplomatic apple of Mr. Coolidge's eye," and the Pulitzer chain even insinuated that Houghton was presidential material. The whole affair landed the diplomat on the cover of Henry Luce's *Time* magazine.[52]

Despite the favorable press coverage, Houghton feared that he had embarrassed and upset the president, who once told members of his cabinet: "If you blunder, you can leave or I can invite you to leave." The ambassador returned to Washington from Corning in late March. In a private meeting with Coolidge at the White House, he offered his resignation. The president refused it and instead expressed his confidence in the envoy. Houghton later confided to his diary that he left Pennsylvania Avenue with a "much lighter heart than I had had for several days. My only feeling then regarding the episode was a regret that the [press] conference had ever taken place."[53]

The "Houghton controversy," the first blunder of the ambassador's public career, had been derived in large part from his deep-seated frustration with the Republican leadership. For four years, he had worked tirelessly to improve U.S.–European cooperation. It was unfortunate, and supremely ironic, that the incident centered on his opposition to the League's preparatory disarmament conference, giving the erroneous impression that he, not the administration, sanctioned an isolationist attitude toward Europe. Houghton failed to appreciate that spurning the League conference would jeopardize his personal campaign to promote constructive American engagement on the world stage. The ambassador favored arms limitation, but his diplomatic experience informed him that conditions abroad were not ripe for a successful conference, and as a result he believed that the administration was better off educating the public about this fact and preserving the nation's clout until more promising circumstances arose. To Houghton, the administration's attempted leadership on disarmament smacked more of political expediency than responsible action. In other words, his dispute with Republican arms policy was more a matter of timing than of objectives. In short, Houghton's predictions about the conference's failure ultimately proved accurate, but Coolidge demonstrated a superior understanding of the disarmament issue, especially its significance in domestic politics.

In the broad context of U.S.–European relations, the Houghton controversy, though highly embarrassing for Washington, proved a fleeting diplomatic bungle. The ambassador's expressed concern over renewed power politics in Europe never endangered world peace, as ardent League supporters claimed. The effects of the controversy abroad were nominal, especially compared to the League's failure to welcome Germany to its governing council. In fact, the excitement over Houghton's comments had subsided by early April, after the foreign ministries in Britain, France, and Germany publicly reconstituted their commitment to the Locarno spirit and their respective governments survived new votes of confidence. Fears emerging from the Geneva crisis and the Houghton controversy were further allayed six months later when the League finally accepted Germany as a full-fledged member.

Aside from the press conference blunder, Houghton's early work as ambassador to Great Britain had again demonstrated his importance as a diplomat in the postwar era. He effectively advanced European stabilization by helping to broker the Locarno security accords, never hesitating to take advantage of his position as America's leading representative or as a trusted adviser to the German government. His "ultimatum" speech at the British Pilgrims' Society dinner, his frequent collaboration with British and French officials, and his occasionally stern counsel to Berlin all provide evidence that he was less a Germanophile and more an Atlanticist seeking Europe's rehabilitation. The ambassador's untiring activities on behalf of European reconstruction earned him the respect of Foreign Minister Austen Chamberlain and won him broad praise in the American press. Several leading journalists hailed him as a superior diplomat. Mark Sullivan touted him as "one of the best America has ever had in any country." Frederick L. Collins described him as "by long odds the ablest man in Europe," and Frank H. Simonds characterized him as one of the "architects" (the only American) of the "New Europe," and stated further that his contributions to the Dawes Plan and Locarno Treaties could "neither be indicated nor exaggerated. No man who has represented

us in Europe during or since the war has more completely earned
the rank of diplomat than Houghton; and his share in . . . [Europe's
reconstruction] remains unmistakable."[54]

For Houghton, it was not enough for him to personally assume
an active role in international politics. Foreign policy leadership,
he believed, must emanate from the White House and State Department. Houghton had pleaded, apparently to no avail, with the
president to seize the initiative with an antiwar treaty and the war
referendum, issues that the ambassador believed were popular
among the masses and thus could encourage sustained American
engagement. Coolidge's reticence on these matters, however, was
less problematic to Houghton than the president's determination
to force U.S. leadership on the disarmament question, which the
ambassador considered unanswerable in the near term. Any
progress on arms control required Great Britain's cooperation, and,
as Houghton discovered upon his return to London, U.S.–British
relations were deteriorating rapidly.

Notes

1. B. J. C. McKercher is the preeminent historian of Britain's interwar
relations with the United States. For a recent overview of the 1920s, see
the prologue to *Transition of Power: Britain's Loss of Global Pre-eminence to
the United States, 1930–1945* (Cambridge, 1999), 1–31. For U.S. perspectives, see John E. Moser, *Twisting the Lion's Tail: American Anglophobia between the World Wars* (New York, 1999); Michael J. Hogan, *Informal Entente:
The Private Structure of Cooperation in Anglo-American Economic Diplomacy,
1918–1928* (Columbia, MO, 1977, 1991).
2. Charles E. Hughes to Houghton, March 3, 1925, Houghton Papers.
3. James G. McDonald to Houghton, April 16, 1925, Houghton Papers; T.R.B., "Washington Notes," *New Republic* 42 (May 13, 1925): 317;
New York Times, April 16, 1925.
4. Houghton to Henry White, April 25, 1925, Houghton Papers.
5. Houghton, "Speech of the Ambassador to the Pilgrims," Houghton
Papers.
6. *New York Times*, May 5, 1925.
7. Howard to Chamberlain, May 15 and 18, 1925, FO 371/10645/A2492,
A2500, PRO; Young to Houghton, May 17, 1925, Houghton Papers; *New
York Times*, May 5, 1925; Dwight to Houghton, May 12, 1925, Houghton
Papers.
8. Houghton to Schuyler Merritt, May 15, 1925, Houghton to Isaac
Siegel, May 18, 1925, Houghton to Lowden, June 9, 1925, and Coolidge to
Houghton, May 8, 1925, Houghton Papers.
9. ABH Diary, June 16, 1925; Houghton to Norris, June 17, 1925,
Houghton Papers.
10. Castle Diary, July 5, 1925.
11. Ibid., July 6, 1925.

12. Houghton to Castle, August 18, 1925, Castle Papers; Gilbert to Houghton, June 6, 1925, and Warburg to Houghton, August 3, 1925, Houghton Papers; *New York Times*, August 6, 1925.

13. Houghton to Amory Houghton, November 2, 1925, Houghton Papers.

14. Houghton, "Knights of the Round Table Speech," October 28, 1925, Houghton Papers; Houghton to Kellogg, October 22, 1925, Telegram #326, National Archives Record Group 59 (hereafter cited as NARG59), File 740.0011/181.

15. *Punch* 169 (November 25, 1925): 585; *Berliner Tageblatt*, November 27, 1925; *New York Times*, October 30, 1925; Adolph S. Ochs to Houghton, November 2, 1925, James G. McDonald to Houghton, October 19, 1925, and Young to Houghton, November 2, 1925, Houghton Papers.

16. Houghton to Coolidge, August 19, 1925, Coolidge Papers, reel 53, series 66.

17. Ibid.

18. Ibid.

19. Kellogg to Houghton, July 18, 1925, Telegram #232, NARG49, Files 841.6176/5, 5.

20. Frederick C. Hood to Houghton, July 19 and 22, 1925, Houghton Papers.

21. Chamberlain Memorandum, July 22, 1925, FO 371/11060/w7067/5208/50, PRO.

22. Houghton to Kellogg, July 23, 1925, Telegram #240, NARG59, File 841.6176/6.

23. Chamberlain Memorandum, July 22, 1925, FO 371/11060/w7067/5208/50, PRO; Colonial Office to Chamberlain (includes his comments), August 13, 1925, FO 371/11060/w7756/5208/50, PRO; Kellogg to Houghton, July 27, 1925, Telegrams #233, NARG59, Files 841.6176/6.

24. Chamberlain to Howard, October 22, 1925, FO 371/11060/w9977, PRO.

25. Houghton to Frederick A. Sterling, November 30, 1925, Houghton Papers.

26. Kellogg to Houghton, December 1, 1925, Telegram #352, and Houghton to Kellogg, December 4, 1925, Telegrams #352, #372, NARG59, Files 841.6176/42-5.

27. *New York Times*, December 15, 1925; *London Times*, January 5, 1926; "On Hating America," *Spectator* (January 30, 1926): 157.

28. London *Times*, January 5, 1926; "On Hating America," 157; Howard to Chamberlain, January (?), 1926, FO 371/11061/w11864, PRO; Vansittart to Chilton, December (?) 1925, FO 371/11061/w11722/5208/50, PRO.

29. Houghton to Castle, December 7, 1925, Houghton to Young, February 13, 1926, and Houghton to Dwight, December 18, 1925, Houghton Papers.

30. Young, quoted in Hogan, *Informal Entente*, 201–2; Castle to Houghton, January 7, 1926, Castle Papers.

31. Houghton to Kellogg, February 1, 1926, Houghton Papers.

32. Ibid.

33. Houghton to Kellogg, October 24, 1925, Telegram #332, NARG59, File 500.A12/71; Houghton to Castle, November 3 and 23, 1925, Houghton Papers; Houghton, "Reform Club Speech," December 15, 1925, Houghton Papers.

34. Houghton to Kellogg, October 24, 1925, Telegrams #322, #332, NARG59, Files 500.A12/71a, 71.

35. Houghton to Kellogg, October 29, 1925, Telegram #337, NARG59, Files 500.A12/77, 86.

36. Houghton to Kellogg, December 22, 1925, Telegram #384, NARG59, File 500.A12/17.

37. Houghton to Castle, February 3, 1926, Houghton Papers.

38. Houghton to Dwight, February 20, 1926, ibid.

39. Coolidge to Houghton, February 11, 1926, and Castle to Houghton, February 15, 1926, ibid.

40. London *Times*, March 12 and 18, 1926.

41. *New York Times*, March 17, 1926.

42. Castle to Frederick A. Sterling, March 23, 1926, Castle Papers; ABH Diary, March 17, 1926.

43. *Boston Herald*, March 22, 1926; Castle Diary, March 17, 1926; Castle to Houghton, December 7, 1925, and Castle to Sterling, March 18, 1926, Castle Papers.

44. "Worse Than a Crime—A Blunder," *The Independent* 116 (April 3, 1926): 400; Castle Diary, March 17–22, 1926; *St. Louis Post-Dispatch*, March 28, 1926.

45. *New York Herald Tribune*, March 18, 1926.

46. Castle Diary, March 22, 1926; Castle to Sterling, March 23, 1926, Castle Papers.

47. Sterling to Castle, April 6, 1926, Castle Papers; *Living Age* 329 (May 8, 1926): 306–10; London *Times*, March 19, 1926.

48. *New York American* reprinted in *San Francisco Examiner*, March 24, 1926; *New York Evening World*, March 22, 1926; "Worse Than a Crime—A Blunder," 400; *St. Louis Post-Dispatch*, March 23, 1923; *New York Herald Tribune*, March 21–22, 1926.

49. *Congressional Record*, 69th Cong., 1st sess., 1926, vol. 67, 5977–86.

50. Ibid.

51. Castle Diary, March 22–23, 1926; Castle to Sterling, March 23, 1926, Castle Papers; *Washington Post*, March 22, 1926.

52. London *Times*, March 22 and 24, 1926; *Brooklyn Daily Eagle*, March 20, 1926; *Boston Herald*, March 21, 1926; "Houghton Stumbles," *Time* 7 (April 5, 1926): cover, 6.

53. Donald R. McCoy, *Calvin Coolidge: The Quiet President* (New York, 1967), 283; ABH Diary, March 29, 1926.

54. Mark Sullivan, "A Quiet Reform in Our Foreign Service," *World's Work* 51 (November 1925): 45–52; Frederick L. Collins, "Abroad with Our Ambassadors II—The Ablest American in Europe," *Woman's Home Companion* 53 (January 1926): 15, 60; Collins, "Under the High Hats," *Collier's, The National Weekly* 77 (March 13, 1926): 8–9, 41; Frank H. Simonds, "After Locarno—A New Era," *American Review of Reviews* 72 (December 1925): 593–605.

6

America's Ambiguous Internationalism

1926–1927

> There is enough of responsibility attached to the [London embassy] job . . . to absorb a man's energies without bedevilling the situation unnecessarily. Frankly, I am about fed up.
> —Alanson B. Houghton, 1926

After a year in London, Houghton disapproved of Washington's management of the Anglo-American relationship. He thought that lasting international stability and prosperity depended on close political and diplomatic cooperation with Great Britain, the world's other dominant industrial and military power. Houghton, not the administration, believed that the perimeter of America's vital economic interests had expanded outside the Western Hemisphere to Western Europe. He no longer believed in American self-sufficiency and understood that the United States, as a leading power, possessed significant responsibility for underwriting Europe's postwar recovery. This meant making economic sacrifices such as forgiving billions in Allied war debt. The ambassador's opposition to ultranationalistic economic policies had also been manifested during the Anglo–American conflict over crude rubber. He refused to take a hard line against Britain's monopoly and chose instead to rail against Herbert Hoover's anti-British campaign. When another dispute surfaced in the spring of 1926 over war claims, Houghton again intervened and attempted to promote conciliation and a better bilateral understanding.

Houghton was far more supportive of the Republican administration's handling of international relations in Latin America and Asia. When Coolidge ordered Marines into Nicaragua in 1926 to bolster its conservative government, the ambassador immediately backed the policy and encouraged the administration to explain the deployment to the public. Later, when a violent revolution erupted in China, Houghton supported the president's opposition to U.S. military intervention. In essence, the ambassador and the administration agreed that Latin America, not Asia, fell within the purview of vital national security interests.

The indisputable high point of 1927 was Charles Lindbergh's solo transatlantic flight. Shortly after his Paris landing, Lindbergh flew over the English Channel and spent a week with Houghton at the American embassy. The ambassador persuaded the young aviator to cancel his plans for an Asian tour and to return home for a well-deserved hero's welcome. In contrast, the nadir of international affairs was the development of a sharp breach in Anglo-American relations, one brought on by the Coolidge administration's unceasing push for naval arms limitation. Although Houghton believed that his superiors had mismanaged the arms issue, he worked diligently to broker a compromise between London and Washington. The ultimate failure of the 1927 "Coolidge disarmament conference" caused both the president and his chief ambassador to reconsider their futures as public servants.

Houghton returned to London on April 9, 1926, and moved quickly to smooth the diplomatic ruffle caused by his March press conference. Austen Chamberlain and officials at the French and German embassies generously expressed their ongoing confidence in the ambassador. Then an economic crisis struck. On May 3, British workers launched the first general strike in the nation's history, which led Houghton to note: "Life . . . is certainly one damn thing after another."[1]

While in London, the ambassador had actively publicized his faith in Britain's industrial competitiveness. He hoped to combat local grousing about economic conditions and to bolster confidence in the nation's sluggish postwar recovery. Coal remained a pivotal factor, and after the war, the industry had enjoyed a temporary resurgence thanks to government subsidies and strong continental demand. But that demand foundered in 1925 when faced with intensified German and Dutch competition and with Britain's return to the gold standard, which made British coal more expensive. In May 1926, when mine owners demanded wage cuts and extended work hours and the Baldwin government refused to defend labor, the coal miners struck, and other unions walked out in sympathy. Given the serious dilemmas facing the coal industry, Houghton predicted that the general strike could last weeks, if not months. The specter of fuel rationing, newspaper shortages, and soldiers in the streets reminded the ambassador of his previous assignment: "It is almost like Germany all over again."[2]

But 1926 Britain was not 1923 Germany. The Baldwin government was prepared for the general strike, and it even enjoyed some support from the opposition Labour Party. Under government supervision, middle-class volunteers operated key transportation networks and distributed food and supplies. The American ambassador was thoroughly impressed by the government's ability to provide essential services. Only a week into the crisis, he wrote to Coolidge, "To my mind, the Strike is now broken," and "a compromise certainly is not far off." Two days later, on May 12, the Trade Union Council cancelled the sympathy strikes on a faint government promise that the coal miners would be dealt with fairly. But the coal workers' impasse with mine owners could not be bridged so easily, and the miners remained on strike through the summer. The debilitating economic conditions troubled Houghton, who described the perpetual fuel rationing as forcing a "sort of paralysis" on British industry "with a good deal of bitterness thrown in."[3]

Bitterness also plagued the faltering Anglo-American relationship. The British viewed America's nationalist economic policies, such as high trade barriers and mandatory war debt repayment, as additional brakes on postwar recovery. They further resented renewed calls to reimburse U.S. shippers and businessmen for cargo and transit losses resulting from the Royal Navy's blockade during the three years preceding America's entry into the war. Robert Vansittart, the head of the American desk at the Foreign Office, informed Chamberlain that the U.S. war debt policy had "already made the average Englishman think the Americans are dirty swines" and that even the renewal of the war claims issue could not "make him think them very much dirtier." Houghton, who opposed America's war debt policy, had assured the foreign secretary that the severity of British attitudes regarding the debt had caused him much personal anxiety. The ambassador was, therefore, extremely sensitive to any new threats to either cordial bilateral relations or Britain's economic recovery.[4]

The "blockade claims conflict" first surfaced in October 1925 when the State Department threatened to press for the payment of outstanding war claims. Chamberlain immediately explained to Houghton that the renewal of the claims issue had landed in Britain like a "thunder-clap," because President Woodrow Wilson had forgiven them at the Paris Peace Conference. For London to concede their validity years later, he argued, would not only cause other neutral nations to assert similar claims but would also call into question the legitimacy of British naval rights. More important, Chamberlain stressed that the claims issue would further enrage the British public, which already held a jaded opinion of America due to its "morally unjust" demand for war debt repayment. The foreign secretary then read a cable he had sent to Washington, asking Esme Howard, the British ambassador, to intervene directly with Coolidge. Houghton, who according to Chamberlain spoke "with his usual frankness," expressed his ignorance of any new initiative regarding the shipping claims. Caught off guard, he first reacted by stating that American public opinion also needed consideration, and that if just claims existed, then "they must be paid by somebody." Upon gathering his thoughts, the ambassador readily conceded that a conflict over war claims, no matter how just, was not worth disturbing the bilateral relationship. "There could be no greater disaster than a quarrel between the United States and Great Britain," Houghton attested, and he promised to help settle the issue. In a telegram to Kellogg, he explained Chamberlain's "highly emotional and excited" state and concluded by confessing his sympathy for the British position.[5]

Houghton explained his views more fully to William Castle. "I do believe that we should approach this matter with a great deal of caution. Otherwise," he warned, "I am afraid . . . a tremendous agitation may follow," and "in the interest of all concerned, the present seems to me an ill-advised time for such a discussion." Castle supported the ambassador in his discussions with Kellogg and Assistant Secretary of State Robert E. Olds. Acting on Chamberlain's order, Ambassador Howard conferred with Coolidge and Kellogg at the White House on November 7. The secretary of state suggested, perhaps disingenuously, that he was unfamiliar with the specifics of the claims issue. Irregardless, the president gave his personal assurance that the matter would be investigated. Coolidge, moreover, stressed that there was no cause for alarm because America did not wish to jeopardize its good relations with Britain. The Foreign Office was relieved that Washington had no immediate plan to assert the financial claims. To do so, Houghton declared, would "invite a tempest of indignation" against the

United States and represent yet "another tactical error" in the conduct of America's postwar foreign policy.[6]

In March 1926, Senator William Borah resurrected the blockade-
claims controversy. A well-known Anglophobe, he introduced a
resolution demanding that Kellogg provide the Senate with a status report on all outstanding war claims. Borah's broadside
prompted anti-American protests in the British press and led
Ambassador Howard to issue a written complaint to the State
Department. He objected to the claims, arguing that America had
eventually aligned with Britain in the war and thus had actually
benefited from the blockade. Howard and his American counterpart in London played central roles in resolving the claims conflict
as both were determined to build more dependable Anglo-
American ties.

During his recent trip to Washington, Houghton had worked
to control the uproar. He conferred with Borah and State Department officials, urging them to settle the war claims quickly and
amicably so as not to disturb larger policies of peace and recovery
in Europe. He endorsed a suggestion that British and American
officials meet informally to review all private and governmental
claims. Moreover, he agreed that they should dismiss the vast majority of claims and quietly adjudicate the balance. Throughout
March, however, the British rejected the legitimacy of America's
private-party claims and discussed the settlement only of official
intergovernmental claims. This approach was completely unacceptable to Borah and the Coolidge administration.

In early April, the State Department proposed that the two governments conduct an informal preliminary survey of *all* claims to
help prepare for the disposal of illegitimate petitions. Houghton
met with Chamberlain and received his approval for the investigation, but only on the condition that it be carried out informally in
Washington. Soon afterward, the British representative, John J.
Broderick, and his American counterpart, Spencer Phenix, began
to review some three thousand claims. They were able to dispense
with roughly two-thirds of them in short order. But the issue became more ominous when Kellogg insisted that Phenix be allowed
to review all private-party claim files in London, an idea that the
British had heretofore delicately skirted.

In mid-May, Houghton was asked to inform the Foreign Office
of Phenix's planned visit to London and to ascertain the government's receptivity. Houghton met with Chamberlain and Permanent Undersecretary William Tyrrell, and when he failed to report

home immediately, Kellogg suspected the worst. The secretary fired off a telegram to London instructing the ambassador that if Chamberlain did not acquiesce to Phenix's mission, the State Department would terminate the claims review under way in Washington and begin a more public and formal investigation without regard for British sensitivities. Houghton met again with the foreign secretary and read Kellogg's telegram. When Chamberlain continued to resist Phenix's "roving mission of enquiry," Houghton pleaded with him, in the interest of the all-important bilateral relationship, "not to slam the door" on further discussions. The ambassador's obvious distress affected Chamberlain, who told Houghton that he would reconsider Phenix's trip if he could read the ambassador's next report to Kellogg and after he heard from Howard in Washington.[7]

(From left to right): Queen Mary, King George V, and Alanson B. Houghton. *Courtesy of the Houghton Family and Corning Incorporated*

Houghton cabled the State Department that Chamberlain was "disturbed" by the U.S. insistence on a London "fishing excursion," especially since the work in Washington had not yet been completed. In addition, Chamberlain had grown apprehensive because the U.S. Navy had postponed its planned London trip to examine the separate intergovernmental war claims, which were most important to the British. Chamberlain's position infuriated Kellogg. The secretary ignored Houghton's comments about the delayed naval investigation even though they served to remind Kellogg that Chamberlain was willing to support a simultaneous review of private and government claims in London. Kellogg transcribed a blistering memorandum for Houghton to read at the Foreign Office. The secretary declared a premature end to the confidential investigation into the blockade claims because of "the absence of cordial cooperation" in London. But before Houghton could deliver the message, Howard managed to assuage Kellogg's anger by promising his personal support for the Phenix mission. Houghton was instructed to hold the note temporarily.[8]

Believing that Kellogg had overreacted and that he might injure the Anglo-American relationship, Houghton continued to defend Chamberlain, who had left for League meetings at Geneva. He explained to the State Department that, for political reasons, the foreign secretary needed to minimize the publicity surrounding the investigation of America's private-party war claims against Britain. And that without the simultaneous arrival of the U.S. Navy delegation, Chamberlain feared that Phenix's appearance in London would become suspect, and thus embarrass the Baldwin government. Moreover, Houghton argued that the foreign secretary wanted to prevent any possible debate over the legitimacy of British maritime rights. The ambassador repeatedly assured Kellogg that his interviews with Chamberlain had always been conducted in a friendly manner and promised that Phenix's mission would eventually be approved by the Foreign Office. Despite Houghton's attempt to calm Kellogg, the secretary remained disturbed, and he informed the ambassador that a continuation of the claims investigation rested on the Foreign Office's willingness to capitulate to his position.

When Chamberlain returned to London in mid-June, he was greeted with the news that Borah's resolution demanding a public account of all outstanding American war claims had just passed the Senate. Wondering "what in the love of Mike" was going on, he called for Houghton. The ambassador explained that he had done everything possible to prevent the crisis. He read aloud his cable to Washington defending Britain's position and urged Chamberlain to approve the Phenix mission. Chamberlain immediately withdrew his objection. Unlike some members of his staff, the foreign secretary recognized Houghton's sincere efforts to safeguard the Anglo-American relationship. He wrote to Howard that the

American envoy "showed a clear appreciation of the goodwill of His Majesty's Government and of the perplexities caused us by the sudden change in the [joint naval delegation] plan on which we had agreed. It was evidence in support of the view which I had formed of Mr. Houghton's attitude, and proved that he was exerting himself to prevent friction and promote a friendly settlement."[9]

Phenix and his British counterpart, John Broderick, arrived in London on September 1. The American began his work unimpeded, and he consulted frequently with Houghton. After eight weeks, all relevant British records had been examined. Remarkably, the number of meritorious claims had been successfully whittled to eleven, totaling less than $3 million. Houghton recognized that the most difficult work had been completed, and he reveled in the fact that a serious breach in British–American relations had been avoided. "It is really a tremendous achievement to have cleared the slate," he wrote to Castle, "and to have ended once and for all such possibilities of real trouble as these claims presented. . . . It is a bully piece of work." The Phenix–Broderick report was issued in November. After a round of secret negotiations in Washington, a formula was agreed upon whereby the value of the legitimate private American claims was essentially to be offset by the official intergovernmental claims favoring the British. Although a formal and final exchange of notes did not occur until May the next year, the Anglo-American crisis over blockade claims was over.[10]

Unfortunately, the revival of the war claims controversy paralleled the ongoing U.S.–British conflict over the rubber trade. Just one day after Borah had reopened the claims controversy, Commerce Secretary Herbert Hoover gave a widely publicized address on the need for America to develop "the potent weapon" of independent rubber supplies. Hoover had privately boasted to Houghton about the success of his rubber conservation campaign, and he informed the ambassador that the British government's control over rubber production was "a most wildly foolish thing" that circumvented the natural laws of supply and demand and forced the United States to take retaliatory measures. The public revival of the rubber conflict angered Houghton. He believed that its overall significance to U.S. foreign policy had been blown out of proportion and hence threatened progress on more substantive issues pertaining to postwar stability and rehabilitation.[11]

The ambassador vented his frustrations to a sympathetic Castle, who agreed that "we are making ourselves absurd and . . . the British are quite right in considering us insincere." In March 1926,

Houghton had expressed his dismay in a lecture at the U.S. Foreign Service School. Half of the address was dedicated to the rubber controversy. He reminded the students of Britain's ongoing struggle to recover from the war and of London's understandable satisfaction with being able to "plaster us" with rubber after "we had first plastered them with debt." For America to complain about the "horror" of foreign monopolies would not, Houghton claimed, "take us very far" in rebuilding a war-torn world. Moreover, he insisted that the rubber issue had only brought to the fore "a greater question of policy": whether the United States should embark on a colonial program that would "put us head on with England." To take an imperial path, he argued, was economically superfluous and strategically dangerous. In sum, the ambassador challenged the students to put diplomatic crises in proper perspective and to view controversies as opportunities to promote cooperation and goodwill.[12]

By the time Houghton had returned to London in April, he found waiting a copy of a new British memorandum on rubber restrictions that had been forwarded to the State Department. The note was a belated response to the December 1925 Hoover–Kellogg telegram attacking British export controls. Phrased with diplomatic care, the memo defended Britain's rubber policy, but also pledged support for the promotion of freer world trade. The latter issue, Secretary Chamberlain noted, must be examined broadly because high tariff rates, as found in America, were integral to the problem of government-sponsored trade restrictions. Officials at the Foreign Office, who still believed that Houghton was conspiring with Hoover on the rubber issue, considered the British note a much needed "love-tap" to the "solar plexes" of their American cousins.[13]

Kellogg shared the memorandum with the commerce secretary. Hoover interpreted the communiqué as mere confirmation of British intransigence and wrongheadedness. He informed Kellogg that any official response would prove futile and that America's best "weapon of defense" on rubber remained retaliation through conservation, substitution, and self-sufficiency. Whereas Kellogg concurred, Houghton objected. And because of his opposition to America's hard-line policy, he tried, when possible, to avoid the thorny subject with the Foreign Office. The ambassador was only too happy, however, to send the State Department press clippings that smartly defended the British position and protested the hypocrisy of America's economic foreign policy. Among the articles he forwarded was a thoughtful essay in *The Nation* written by John

Maynard Keynes, the economist whom Houghton had befriended years earlier in Berlin.[14]

Despite the State Department's official silence on the rubber issue, the British continued to complain about the inflammatory rhetoric of Secretary Hoover. The controversy came to a head in late July when Ambassador Howard informed Kellogg of his government's desire to publish several of the diplomatic notes on rubber that had been exchanged between the two countries. Howard, like Houghton, had worked hard to defuse the rubber crisis, and he complained about the constant "misassertions" and "misconceptions" in the United States over Britain's "safeguarding" of rubber supplies. He also reminded Kellogg of America's self-interested regulation of Filipino exports. The publication of official notes, Howard argued, could prevent "the recrudescence of the recent agitation," which could only "be harmful to the harmonious relations between the two countries."[15]

Surprised by the proposal, Kellogg reached out to Houghton for advice. In a slight rebuff, the ambassador simply and curtly informed the secretary that the department was in possession of all official documents relating to the rubber issue. Kellogg next turned to the commerce secretary. Hoover's response was immediate and unambiguous—the British request should be refused. Hoover argued that the diplomatic exchanges did not fully articulate the American position and thus represented a "totally distorted statement of the facts." Kellogg stalled the British.[16]

Meanwhile, Houghton contemplated the matter in London. He considered the problem of foreign raw material monopolies a threat to Anglo-American relations and shared his views with Philip Kerr, a British foreign policy adviser in the Liberal Party. Word of Houghton's concern (and Ambassador Howard's) circulated in the Foreign Office, but Robert Vansittart of the American Department again dismissed Houghton as Hoover's tool. "We have had this Hoover–Houghton tosh bowled at us before," he snapped, "one of them at either end. It is the old story. . . . The less said of the Hoover–Houghton bowling in that [rubber] match the better."[17]

Vansittart proved a poor judge of the American ambassador. In late August, a month after Howard's call to publish the diplomatic exchanges, Houghton finally proffered his views to Kellogg. He instructed the secretary that the British must think their position completely "sound," and therefore wanted it made available to the American public. Houghton reiterated that the original spike in world rubber prices had not been caused by British production controls, but rather by unforeseeable increases in demand. He also stated that, if left unadjusted, the one-sided regulation of rubber by Britain would in the long run have a "more disastrous effect" on British rubber producers than on American consumers. He admitted that Chamberlain's April note represented "a direct attack on our tariff policy," yet he was not opposed to publishing the exchanges. His only recommendation was that a single paragraph of an earlier telegram be omitted because it revealed the ambassador's personal belief that American commodity speculators had contributed to inflated rubber prices. After receiving Houghton's analysis, Kellogg asked the department's Economic Adviser's Office to investigate the matter further. In November, when a Commerce Department analyst published yet another attack on the evils of "Foreign Government Price Fixing," a furious British delegation descended upon the State Department demanding that the notes on rubber be publicized. Kellogg staunchly refused, and the controversy eventually petered out when Dutch colonies in the Pacific began to supply U.S. manufacturers with new and cheaper sources of rubber.[18]

While attempting to minimize the fallout from disagreements over crude rubber and blockade claims, Houghton also waged exhausting battles against State Department bureaucracy. The conflicts over embassy property and personnel only added to Houghton's general frustrations with Washington. While the ambassador was in Berlin, his childhood classmate, J. P. Morgan Jr., donated to the U.S. government two townhouses to serve as the new American embassy in London. By late summer 1926, with a major renovation of the Princess Gate properties nearing completion, Houghton let his lease expire on the old Crewe House residence and its furnishings. The only obstacle preventing a smooth transition was the procurement of new furnishings and equipment for Princess Gate. The ambassador reminded his colleagues that during his Berlin tenure he had personally spent $150,000 to overhaul, equip, and maintain the embassy. This time, he had Coolidge's promise that Congress would foot the bill.

A congressional appropriation was made in July, but it stipulated that all furniture and equipment must be acquired in the United States and then shipped to England. The embassy staff thought the proviso ridiculously inefficient and expensive. Houghton's request to make minimum purchases in London was rejected, and he received little support from Kellogg. When the ambassador moved into Princess Gate in October, no furniture had arrived, forcing him to draw upon his own resources. He retrieved from storage some belongings from Berlin and invested $20,000 in new acquisitions ranging from rugs to dinnerware. One embassy staffer described the affair as "red tape gone mad." The British press ridiculed the "strange niggardliness" of the U.S. government. When Morgan offered Houghton $50,000 for the immediate procurement of furniture, Washington made the gift subject to the same spending restriction. The episode took on farcical proportions when the department informed Houghton that it would not reimburse him for ordinary operating expenses such as cleaning services and heating fuel. The first shipment of government furniture arrived seven months late. "All this tom-foolery," the ambassador ranted, "has cost me $20,000 at least, but it is no doubt what I ought to have expected" when dealing with the American government. "Efficiency when discovered in Washington should be spelled with a small 'e.' "[19]

The State Department's mishandling of embassy personnel also provoked Houghton. Under usual conditions, the London embassy operated with one counselor and five ranked secretaries. In spring 1925, one of the ambassador's junior secretaries was transferred but not replaced. Believing that the position was somewhat superfluous, Houghton thought it wrong to demand a substitute. But when a second secretary was transferred in February 1926, the ambassador expected a replacement. None came. To make matters worse, one of Houghton's best informed men, Percy A. Blair, was due to be rotated out. Already piqued over the furniture tangle, Houghton put his foot down, reminding the administration that he was managing the embassy with two men less than Kellogg had when he was ambassador. The secretary reluctantly sent Houghton a new secretary and postponed Blair's transfer. But the next year, when the embassy's counselor was made the first American minister to Ireland, the State Department never transferred in a replacement, and as a consequence, the embassy carried on indefinitely with two secretaries short of the standard operating staff. The ambassador noted the toll of the constant bureaucratic infighting: "There is enough of responsibility attached to the [London] job . . . to absorb a man's energies without bedevilling the situation unnecessarily. Frankly, I am about fed up."[20]

Needing a rest, Houghton went to the States for a Christmas vacation. His trip during the winter of 1926–27 was hardly peaceful. He enjoyed the holidays in Corning, but was forced to challenge several frivolous lawsuits filed by amateur blackmailers.

Worse, his brother Arthur became seriously ill. The envoy remained stateside for a month, shuttling between Corning, New York City, and Washington.

Houghton conferred with Coolidge, Secretaries Mellon and Kellogg, and Senator Borah on a variety of issues. Debate continued to rage over the president's decision to reoccupy Nicaragua. His objective was to bolster the newly "elected" president, Adolfo Díaz, against leftist rebels. The ambassador supported the deployment on the grounds that the United States bore responsibility for regional stability. He strongly advised the administration to provide a detailed and rational explanation to the American public. By "covering the whole ground," he argued, any criticism of the policy would be minimized and, more important, popular support galvanized.[21]

At the State Department, Houghton found the staff fatigued and demoralized. Castle, Assistant Secretary Robert Olds, and others complained that the department's bureaucratic structure encouraged constant opposition and delay. There was a palpable feeling that the nation's foreign policy was adrift. Hoover's foreign policy influence and public posturing were disliked. One afternoon, when Hoover intruded upon a luncheon shared by Castle, Olds, and Houghton, the secretary "got rather a cold shoulder."[22]

Many inside and outside the administration deemed Kellogg the source of the State Department's problems. His abilities had been questioned from the onset, and the secretary had weakened physically and mentally under the strain of the office. Castle chronicled his decline:

> I am thoroughly worried over the general disintegration of the Department by reason of the Secretary's state of mind. I fear a complete nervous breakdown. Olds looks at things quite as seriously as I do. The Secretary is wildly inaccurate, intolerably rude, unwilling to read memoranda or listen to an oral statement. Olds thinks he is incapable of making a decision in a crisis. . . . He is desperately afraid of criticism. To him the accusing voices of Borah and of the *New York World* are more terrifying than a chorus of approval would be assuring . . . the Department suffers and the country may suffer.

Houghton agreed. The seventy-one-year-old secretary, often ill, appeared haggard and done in. The ambassador's low opinion of Kellogg's leadership was reconfirmed, and rumors of the secretary's imminent retirement and the envoy's succession persisted. Just before Houghton returned to London, Charles D. Hilles, the vice chairman of the Republican National Committee, informed him that he would replace Kellogg as secretary of state as early as February. The ambassador took note of the prediction and, just before his departure, wrote to his son from on board the *Albert Ballin*: "Hilles and the other wise men here tell me that I shall be returning within a month. I do not believe . . . but if it comes you will receive the [cabled] word 'excellent' or something of the sort and if it doesn't come you won't hear anything at all."[23]

After Houghton's return to London in late January 1927, war clouds over East Asia cast a shadow on the diplomatic scene in Europe. The United States had ordered its Asiatic fleet to China's central coast. The British went one better, dispatching some 13,000 soldiers equipped with tanks and airplanes. The object of these maneuvers was the defense of American and British interests in Shanghai. The coastal city appeared threatened by the northerly advance of Chinese revolutionaries, the Kuomintang. Aided and advised by Soviet Russia, these Nationalists, including Communists and non-Communists, sought to consolidate political rule in China by wresting away the authority and privileges of regional warlords and of the imperial powers. Kuomintang and British forces narrowly averted battle at Hankow when the British abandoned their defenses and evacuated to nearby warships. Tensions mounted in London and Washington, because the large international settlement at Shanghai lay in the path of the rebels' "Northern Expedition."

None of the leading powers wanted war with China. Though they continued to enjoy special commercial, political, and judicial privileges at China's expense, they had recently become more conciliatory regarding Chinese demands for tariff autonomy. But the imperial powers insisted upon the protection of their property and citizenry. Britain moved to pacify the Nationalists by offering to concede municipal control of Hankow and two small cities in return for protective guarantees. This proposal left the rebels in a predicament: to accept would gain them political legitimacy, but it would also give the appearance of striking a deal with an imperialist devil. The issue remained in suspension.

Houghton monitored developments from the London sideline. "No one is thinking of Europe at the moment," he reported to Olds on February 7. "There is a terrible dread here" that the crisis may lead to war, and all were anxious for the Chinese reply on Hankow. A week later, the Nationalists accepted the British offer, but Houghton thought that the bargain would only produce "a temporary period of quiet." His pessimism stemmed from fears in Britain of Soviet Russian influence. There was considerable evidence that Moscow had assisted British workmen during the general strike in 1926, and there was little doubt of Soviet support for the Kuomintang. Sir William Tyrrell, the permanent undersecretary at the Foreign Office, had noted that intensive Soviet propaganda campaigns left Britain "virtually at war with Russia." The pervasive fear of Soviet machinations within the British Empire led military leaders in London to contemplate battle plans. Pressured by Chancellor of the Exchequer Winston Churchill and others to break off diplomatic relations with Moscow, the cautious Chamberlain issued a formal note of protest instead. It appears that the Soviets "have declared a silent war" on Britain, Houghton wrote, and any Communist success in China could have disastrous consequences for India and the Malay States, where "half a million Chinese coolies are at work on the rubber plantations." The ambassador dismissed Chamberlain's protest note as a "dud." Still, he admitted that little could be gained from breaking diplomatic ties, and besides, maintaining formal relations allowed the British the best means for gathering intelligence on Soviet intrigues. By May, this would no longer seem sufficient, and Britain broke off diplomatic relations with Russia.[24]

As Houghton had predicted, the reprieve from turmoil in China was short-lived. On March 24 a new crisis emerged, not at Shanghai where foreign troops had been deployed, but farther west at Nanking. Chinese rioters looted the city, and several foreigners were killed, including an American university administrator. Attempting to defend refugees lodged at the Standard Oil compound on Socony Hill, U.S. and British gunboats fired upon Nationalist troops. News of the engagement shocked Americans and Britons alike. "We have not had as much excitement in the popular mind" since the war, a former New York congressman informed Houghton. On April 11 the Great Powers—Japan, Britain, America, France, and Italy—agreed to issue a joint protest over the Nanking incident. They made four demands: financial restitution, the punishment of offenders, the protection of lives and property, and the issuance of a formal apology. The British wanted to stipulate a timetable for compliance and possible punitive sanctions, but Kellogg blocked this to avoid any commitment that might compel further American intervention.[25]

Houghton supported the administration's cautious policy. He did not believe that vital U.S. interests were at stake in China. The Pacific fleet should protect American lives and property there, but if that became too dangerous, the expatriates should be evacuated. In other words, the United States should ask for compensation, but revolution in China did not threaten American security, and a war over damaged property or treaty rights seemed irrational. He agreed with Assistant Secretary Olds that it would be preferable to "prevent the bolshevization of China," but there was little that the United States or the other powers could do until the violent and volatile situation stabilized. This outlook on China was analogous to Houghton's position on Soviet Russia. As he had frequently said in Berlin, sometimes political situations "must get worse before they can get better." The ambassador reported his personal views directly to Coolidge, and the president concurred: "From such observations as I have been able to make I judge you are correct in your deductions about the situation in the East. It seems about all we can do is try to protect our citizens and work the situation along from day to day." A note of confirmation also arrived from Kellogg: "Great Britain is perhaps in a different position; that the rise of Bolshevism in China is a great menace to her but I do not believe she can gain anything by extreme measures in China." The U.S. policy of patience proved wise, and when the Nationalists came to power the following year, Washington quickly recognized the new government.[26]

The spring of 1927 also witnessed the excitement of Charles Lindbergh's spectacular solo transatlantic flight. As the American ambassador in London, Houghton was fortunate enough to become associated with several revolutionary advances in long-distance communication. For example, news of his return to Washington in March 1926 constituted the first story transmitted across the Atlantic by wireless telephone. A month later, Houghton sent the first "photo-radiogram" (a precursor to the modern fax) to his New Hampshire alma mater, St. Paul's School. This feat was surpassed when a picture and a drawing of the ambassador became the first human images "radioed" across the ocean. By 1927, Houghton was listening to live radio addresses from America and placing telephone calls to Corning. "In the words of Uncle Ephraim," he wrote to a friend, "the world do move."[27]

Of the many technological achievements of the 1920s, few captured the public imagination as the advancements in human flight did, and here too, the ambassador became at least indirectly involved. In May 1926 he hosted an embassy luncheon in honor of Commander Richard E. Byrd, who had just completed a dangerous flight over the North Pole for which he and his copilot were both awarded the Medal of Honor. Less daring shuttles over the English Channel had become commonplace after the war, and the ambassador's family adopted this means of travel for excursions to Paris. But even these shorter flights were not without peril, a fact demonstrated in September 1926, when the embassy's assistant naval attaché died in a crash. Two years later, the same fate befell Baron Ago von Maltzan, the German ambassador to the United States.

The daring and danger surrounding long-distance air travel produced "Atlantic fever" in early 1927, with pilots scrambling to make the first solo transatlantic flight. The victor would ultimately meet with Houghton at the London embassy. Almost everyone expected Robert Byrd to carry the day, but a pair of French aviators lifted off the ground first in May. When they crashed somewhere over the Atlantic, a window of opportunity opened for Lindbergh, a twenty-five-year-old air mail carrier who had been turned away from Byrd's North Pole expedition. On May 21, after flying for 33 hours and 30 minutes, "Lindy" landed his monoplane, the *Spirit of St. Louis*, at Le Bourget Air Field in Paris. An exuberant crowd of 150,000 greeted him. Reporters rushed to U.S. embassies throughout Europe asking for comment. Houghton announced, "We are all proud of Lindbergh, he is no 'flying fool' after all. It is a wonderful achievement."[28]

At first, Lindbergh planned to traipse about Europe for several weeks before flying home by way of Greece, Asia, and the Pacific islands. Once in Paris, however, he changed his mind, plotting short visits only to Brussels and London on his way to the Pacific. Houghton insisted that the "plucky airman" be his houseguest and that the embassy coordinate his stay in London. After a week of congratulatory celebrations in Paris and a brief layover in Belgium, "Lindy" landed at Croydon Field, just south of London.[29]

The English reception was overwhelming. Using a megaphone, Lindbergh shouted to the adoring masses, "This is a little worse than Le Bourget, or, I should say, better." The crowd responded by singing "For He's a Jolly Good Fellow." The ambassador captured the event in his diary:

> I motored to Croydon to join representatives of the Air Ministry in greeting Captain Lindbergh. . . . Some 150,000 lined the field and as Lindbergh descended [the crowd] broke through the barriers and the police lines to such an extent that he failed in his first effort to find a landing place. When he finally did alight, his plane was instantly surrounded and the reception committees

were separated from him by a huge, enthusiastic crowd, and it
was many minutes before we could finally greet him. He was acclaimed by the crowd with great enthusiasm, and it was only after great effort by the police that we were able to leave the field
in the car and start back to town.

Houghton hosted luncheons, dinners, and press events for Lindbergh. On Memorial Day, in the presence of several American Civil
War veterans, he and Lindbergh placed a large wreath at the Tomb
of the Unknown Soldier. One evening after dinner, Lindbergh informed the ambassador of his plans to fly on to Asia. Houghton
objected, wanting the hero to go home directly, and by ship no less!
The two debated into the night. The envoy "pressed his case against
the fair haired youth" who did not want to surrender his plane to a
shipboard "coffin." At one point, the flyer asked if he was being
"ordered" home. Houghton replied no, that he was only concerned
for the captain's safety and the national interest. Lindbergh countered, "I have been in the army and know what you mean. I will go
back as you advise." They agreed that he should travel aboard a
U.S. warship. Houghton cabled Secretary Kellogg that his guest
would "prefer to fly home via Japan. I am frankly afraid some un-
toward occurrence may negative [*sic*] the splendid reception he has
so far received. Lindbergh has agreed to go home direct but is most
eager to make the journey on a destroyer. . . . I cannot too strongly
advise that our best national interests will be served in this way. If
presidential action is necessary, take it to him immediately." On
June 4, Lindbergh departed Britain aboard the USS *Memphis*.[30]

Against the backdrop of Lindbergh's historic flight and the
Nationalist revolution in China, the Coolidge administration
steadily pushed its disarmament agenda forward. Disarmament,
or at least arms limitation, amounted to the Holy Grail of Republican foreign policy in the 1920s. The fiscal benefits of decreasing
government spending and taxes were especially attractive to the
conservative Republican administrations. There were also gains to
be had in international relations, because of the widespread belief
that the curtailment of arms spending weakened rivalries and the
likelihood of war. Having already demobilized most of its wartime
army, the United States wanted to limit international naval power,
and, because Great Britain maintained the largest navy, Houghton
found himself at the center of dissension over this critical defense
policy. The disarmament issue presented the ambassador with a
peculiar problem. Although he lauded the administration's will-

ingness to take the lead on the matter, he worried about the impracticality of new arms talks and their possible pitfalls. Above all, Houghton feared that contentious negotiations might threaten relations between Britain and the United States.

The League-based preparatory commission on international arms control first convened in May 1926 in Geneva, with the objective of establishing a viable framework for a major disarmament conference. Given Houghton's forewarnings, the Coolidge administration participated reluctantly and cautiously. Because of the widely divergent opinions among commission members, most of the administration agreed with Houghton that the commission was likely to be unproductive. Three primary goals of the American delegation, led by Ambassador Hugh Gibson, were to skirt entanglement with League politics, to oppose the complicated French disarmament formula that correlated military and industrial strength, and to avoid becoming the scapegoat for the commission's expected failure. Before the May meeting, Houghton had secured for Coolidge a British declaration that the work of the preparatory commission would be independent from and superior to any League committees on disarmament. And, on Kellogg's recommendation, Gibson sent two subordinates, Allen Dulles (the future CIA director under Eisenhower and Kennedy) and Dorsey Richardson, to London to solicit advice from the ambassador.

The meetings of the preparatory commission dragged on for twelve months with little success. Britain and France championed competing proposals designed to guide a future, wide-ranging disarmament conference. The British plan called for the separate treatment of sea, land, and air armaments, while the French underscored the interrelationship of the three forces and other national factors such as population size and industrial capacity. The divide was broad and steep. By late April 1927, with little hope for reconciliation, the preparatory commission adjourned. Ray Atherton of the London embassy left the ambassador a note: "The only thing [the French] really accomplished was fulfilling your prophecy of some eighteen months ago. . . . I think it was the Bible, and not Shakespeare, that said: 'No man is a prophet in his own country.' But, on the other hand, you were in England when you prophesied." Gibson had supplied Houghton with copies of his confidential reports to Washington, always assuring the ambassador that he had prudently avoided the three potential pitfalls of the conference. Houghton applauded his younger colleague's "bully" efforts and expressed his happy surprise that the U.S. delegation had "steered between Seylla [*sic*] and Charybdis . . . safely and with distinction."[31]

The mere avoidance of mistakes, however, was never sufficient for either Coolidge or Kellogg. The administration had been anxious for substantive progress on naval arms control and launched secret negotiations with Britain. As early as July 1926, Kellogg ordered Admiral Hillary Jones and Allen Dulles to consult with Houghton and British officials in London on a plan to extend the 1922 Washington Naval Treaty to all classes of warships. After a series of inquiries, Houghton, Jones, and Dulles concluded that the administration was moving too quickly. The British were sympathetic to the idea of separate naval talks, but London wanted to delay until the futility of the preparatory commission became more fully apparent. Admiral Jones returned to London in November for further consultations with Houghton and Admiral Sir David Beatty, Britain's First Sea Lord. According to Jones and Houghton, Beatty reaffirmed British support for a future naval conference and he supposedly agreed to the principle of Anglo-American parity in all warships.

Three months later, on February 10, 1927, Coolidge formally invited France, Britain, Italy, and Japan to attend a new naval conference. The reception was decidedly mixed. France rejected the invitation, arguing that naval power should not be considered apart from land and air forces. Italy expressed interest, but demanded a guarantee of parity with France. When Coolidge refused that condition, Italy opted out. Japan, ever concerned about the British and U.S. naval presence in the Pacific, accepted. Britain's delayed response sent the administration into panic, and Kellogg directed Houghton to intervene.

The ambassador seized the opportunity to articulate to Washington not only Britain's hesitation but also his personal opposition to the naval conference. The British could not act hastily, he noted, given the ongoing work of the preparatory commission and the negative reactions of France and Italy. Yet he thought the Baldwin government would ultimately accept the invitation, albeit with reservations. The ambassador opined that Britain might grant naval parity to the United States, in principle at least, but the Royal Navy would not countenance a reduction in its substantial cruiser program, which was considered integral to securing the British Empire. He warned Kellogg that, because Britain already possessed a significant advantage in this class, the "net result of [an] attempt to limit cruiser construction may lead directly to an enlarged program of construction" in the United States and Japan. Chamberlain later informed Houghton of Britain's willingness to participate in the conference. As anticipated, Britain's acceptance emphasized the "special geographical position of the British Empire, the length of inter-imperial communications and the necessity for the protection of its food supplies." Implicit was Britain's demand for a large cruiser program.[32]

Coolidge welcomed the British acceptance without question, and the "Three Power" naval conference was set for June. Meanwhile, Houghton worried that the Republicans had made another strategic error in rushing a policy because of its domestic popularity. He again attempted to squelch high expectations. The fundamental problem, he argued, was that, in 1927, the United States had few cards to play at the disarmament table, with the ironic exception of threatening to expand its own navy. "We have taken the initiative," he wrote Owen Young, "and I suppose our friends in Washington realize fully that the temper of mind in which this new conference will be approached differs radically from that existing at the time of the Washington Conference some years ago. Then we had a great deal to offer. Now about all we have is the ability to build a fleet of any dimensions." Moreover, by organizing the conference, the ambassador knew that the administration had assumed the responsibility for ensuring its success. He also feared that Washington failed to comprehend the British position on cruisers, which was "very far-reaching and very deeply thought out." To a former House colleague, he observed, "I wonder sometimes if the good people at home know just what the probable outcome of this 'limitation' conference is going to be, for if any limitation is reached, it will be a limitation up rather than down, and involve an immediate building programme unless we are prepared to surrender our position [demanding parity with Britain]."[33]

Coolidge and his secretary of state were naively optimistic, fully expecting that the conference, to be held in Switzerland, would result in the successful extension of the Washington treaties. They gave considerable thought to the composition of the U.S. delegation. Unlike the preparatory commission, they wanted men of prominence, and offered the lead position to former secretary of state Charles Evans Hughes. After he declined, Kellogg solicited Houghton's confidential advice. In the meantime, Coolidge all but decided to have Kellogg lead the delegation together with Treasury

Secretary Andrew Mellon and Senator Claude A. Swanson, the rank-ing Democrat on the Foreign Relations Committee. A strongly worded letter from Houghton scotched the president's plans.

In a blatant attempt to curb the administration's optimism re-garding the naval conference, the ambassador reiterated that no "large or important outcome" would be reached at Geneva. He fore-cast that "our British friends" would lay out in detail their prede-termined naval program, promising "effective command of the trade routes during the next five or ten years." It would be left to the United States and Japan either to accept that condition or to adjust upward their relative naval standings. "In other words," he predicted, "the net result will be to place before the American people the option either to embark on a new building program probably at least twenty new cruisers or to accept . . . a position of definite inferiority." Regarding the U.S. delegation, he strongly advised Kellogg not to attend the conference, thus avoiding personal re-sponsibility for its negative outcome. He warned the administra-tion not to make mistakes similar to President Wilson's at Versailles. Instead, he proposed sending the Secretary of the Navy, the Chief of Naval Operations, and Ambassador Gibson. In the end, he per-suaded Coolidge and Kellogg not to "overload" the delegation, and they appointed Gibson as the chief American representative. [34]

The so-called Coolidge naval conference opened on June 20, 1927. Five years earlier, the Washington Conference had capped the tonnage of battleships and carriers and established the govern-ing ratio of 5:5:3 for the United States, Great Britain, and Japan. The Americans hoped to maintain this ratio and set new tonnage limits for smaller vessels, especially cruisers, in which the Royal Navy had built a sizable advantage. The U.S. delegation proposed, for example, a 250,000- to 300,000-ton limit for all cruisers, a level already exceeded by Britain, but one that Washington considered sufficient for mutual security. Britain rejected the American plan. London called instead for new restrictions on large capital war-ships, supported the Washington ratio as a guide only for the most powerful cruisers (the heavy 10,000-ton, 8-inch gun class), and pro-moted the Empire's "special" need for a total of some 500,000 tons in cruisers. The conference's collapse appeared imminent from the outset. Gibson wired home that Britain was laboring to justify its need for "preponderant" naval strength via the cruiser class. Backed by the president, Kellogg instructed Gibson to hold his ground, explaining that the administration would not renegotiate the existing Washington agreement on capital warships, and that he saw no "logical excuse" for London's "excessive tonnage demands."[35]

Worried, Kellogg wired the London embassy. The secretary preferred to terminate the conference rather than go "before the world with a proposition which almost doubles [the] present British cruiser tonnage." His telegram set in motion a round of secret negotiations in London. Kellogg asked if it was wise to confer with Baldwin or Chamberlain on the "apparent contradictions" in the British approach to limiting naval power. Houghton doubted that the British could be diverted from their "well-matured" cruiser policy, but he offered to open an unofficial channel with Chamberlain. Houghton promised to explain the U.S. position on the cruiser issue. But he also wanted to emphasize that a failed conference would harden anti-British sentiment in the United States and eliminate any possibility of reducing Britain's war debt. Kellogg approved of the covert talks, but "deplored" any discussion of debt cancellation.[36]

Houghton and Chamberlain met privately on July 8, one day after a rancorous British cabinet meeting wherein the foreign secretary repulsed an excited Winston Churchill, who favored canceling the naval conference. Houghton explained his fear that failure at Geneva would have disastrous consequences for U.S.–British relations. "The big navy people" in America, he predicted, would demand a large building program to reach parity with Britain and reduce Coolidge to a mere "cockle-shell on the waters quite unable to control or direct the storm." Houghton suggested to Chamberlain that they work together to prevent the "impending calamity."[37]

To the charge that the British were attempting to secure a superior naval position through small warships, Chamberlain responded that Britain's proposals were based on the minimum needs for imperial security as opposed to the "unreasonableness" of the American position. Houghton claimed that he understood British naval policy, but argued that "extensive building programs" were currently unjustified. Germany's navy, after all, had "disappeared," and the other leading powers, except the United States, were too weak financially to build imposing fleets. Furthermore, the thought of war between America and Britain was unimaginable, and if new security threats arose later, the development of new arms programs would be justified.[38]

Chamberlain was impressed by the ambassador's "evident feeling" and "complete sincerity." He agreed that an Anglo-American war was inconceivable, and pronounced his support for naval parity. Houghton thought that these admissions undermined British arguments for constructing new warships. But Chamberlain expressed frustration with Washington's insistence on treating large and small cruisers as a single class with one tonnage cap, and with America's intention of maintaining mostly the larger variety. Britain could not, Chamberlain said, accept anything less than parity in these big cruisers, and the Empire also required a sizable small cruiser fleet. The ambassador argued that parity could be achieved through two distinct cruiser categories, but that it was "mere common sense" for the two tonnage limits for cruisers to be set at "low" reasonable levels. Acting on his own accord, Houghton proposed a 400,000-ton total limit for cruisers, a compromise between the American and British positions. If Britain accepted this figure, Houghton promised to use his personal clout with Coolidge to get a separate sublimit on heavy cruisers. Chamberlain appreciated the ambassador's intervention and promised to discuss his proposal immediately with Prime Minister Baldwin and fellow cabinet member Arthur Balfour.[39]

Houghton glimpsed a breakthrough and cabled a hopeful report to the State Department. Although further impressed by Britain's commitment to a complex and well-conceived naval program, he described Chamberlain as very sympathetic and told of his intention to meet with the prime minister. He added that the Coolidge administration should consider it a major concession if the British looked favorably upon a 400,000-ton cap on cruisers. He also instructed Kellogg to prevent the American delegation in Geneva from taking any action that might jeopardize his secret negotiations in London. On the evening of July 8, Chamberlain sent a communiqué to the American embassy. After considering Houghton's proposal, the Baldwin government decided to withhold its response until receiving an update from its Geneva delegation, which might be recalled to London for consultation.

Three days later, Chamberlain asked the ambassador to meet him at the House of Commons, where he proposed additional parameters for a naval agreement. The United States, Britain, and Japan would agree to establish total tonnage limits "in each class" of warship. These caps would be maintained until 1936, when the Washington Treaty expired. If the United States limited itself to twelve 10,000-ton cruisers, Britain would do the same, thereby agreeing to scrap two new large cruisers currently under construction. Houghton greeted the proposition warmly and passed it on to Washington. Kellogg, too, was appreciative and proposed a brief adjournment of the Geneva conference to consider the recent Chamberlain–Houghton negotiations. The ambassador objected to the idea of a recess. He argued that if brought home, the British delegation would be susceptible to the influence of naval hard-liners, and as a result, "any gain we have made by intervention in London will be lost." Moreover, he felt that the administration should not hesitate to accept Chamberlain's proposal. Kellogg backed away from a recess, but when he discovered that, by "in each class," Chamberlain meant to establish tonnage maximums for each type of cruiser, he rejected the British entreaty as "value-less and of no significance to us," and turned back to Geneva, where some progress had been made.[40]

Gibson had suggested that the Anglo-American deadlock might be broken if the British and Japanese delegations reached a pre-liminary agreement. This was accomplished on July 17. Along with other considerations, the two delegations agreed to combine into one category all cruisers and destroyers with a 500,000-ton-maxi-mum limit. They also sanctioned the continued deployment of out-dated cruisers, which were not to be included in the new tonnage totals. But Gibson and the American team opposed the new plan, as did British cabinet officials in London, who arranged for a re-cess and recalled their delegates for consultation.

The Americans grew pessimistic. Houghton informed Castle that an agreement, if possible at all, could only come from private diplomacy set apart from the Geneva conference. "Confidentially," he added, "I am sorry I could not carry through the effort I began with Sir Austen. I think the opportunity was there to really accom-plish something." Kellogg had again dropped the ball, he believed, and allowed tensions to worsen unnecessarily between Britain and the United States. The ambassador remarked further, and with con-siderable disenchantment, that continental Europeans could now revel in the "discord developed between those outstanding advo-cates of peace—the English-speaking peoples." Houghton's disap-pointment was echoed by the progressive publisher Oswald Garrison Villard, one of America's most vocal proponents of disar-mament. He wrote to Houghton that "if a few men like you do not get into the breach now," the arms convention will fail. "Heavens, how we need leadership here! It is simply incredible the way we are drifting." Meanwhile, on July 22, Kellogg informed the presi-dent that the conference would probably dissolve due to the "exor-bitant" British demands for small cruisers. He promised that he was "doing, of course, everything" to reach a settlement, but that British irrationality had created insuperable differences.[41]

The delegates reassembled in Geneva after a weeklong recess. The British presented a modified proposal based on their earlier compromise with Japan. The Americans rejected it. Gibson claimed that it limited the number of large, heavily armed cruisers desired by the United States, while at the same time it provided for extensive light cruiser fleets favored by the Royal Navy. Kellogg asked the president to move for another adjournment, now claiming that a complete breakdown at the conference would be "disastrous" to Anglo-American relations and "to all the world." Coolidge refused to intervene. Despite last-minute attempts at compromise, including one led by Dulles, the conference failed in early August.[42]

As disarmament historian Christopher Hall notes, although the aim of the conference had been to "limit or reduce armaments, not to increase them," the last British proposal would have allowed for the substantial enlargement of the British, American, and Japanese navies. The irony had not been lost on Houghton, who had predicted the conference's fateful outcome. He received a letter from Fred Sterling, his former counselor at the London embassy, who exclaimed: "The Geneva Conference I see turned out word for word as you foresaw!!" Nor was the irony lost on members of the British delegation in Geneva. After his return to London, Sir Robert Cecil resigned his cabinet position in protest. After giving assurances to Coolidge that he had attempted everything possible to reach an agreement, Kellogg concluded that perhaps "the British Navy has gone mad."[43]

The failure of the naval conference came as a great disappointment in the United States, and journalists employed considerable ink in postmortems. The Conservative Baldwin government came under heavy attack for its imperial "die-hard Toryism." The virulent criticism in the United States proved too much for Chamberlain, who lashed out in a letter to his ambassador in Washington: "We are advanced and almost revolutionary reformers compared with the Republican Party . . . the United States seems to resemble England under George III far more than does the democratic England of today. . . . I wonder, by the way, whether it ever occurs to Americans that while many nations fear the United States, they haven't a single friend in the world. We, on the contrary, with all our 'Imperialism' and 'Toryism' have a good many." The American press castigated the Republican administration. Villard's *The Nation*, for example, launched a scathing attack: "The one independent and bold excursion into international affairs by Coolidge ought finally to open the eyes of some of his adorers to the grave danger of having a pitifully weak and inept man in the Presidency."[44]

Although this was an extreme statement, Houghton did not completely disagree. His long-held belief that the Coolidge conference would prove a reckless misstep was reconfirmed when Dulles visited London and provided the ambassador with a first-hand account. "The stupidity," Houghton contended, "was shown in the calling of the Conference. Either we ought to have been prepared to accept what Britain believes to be the minimum number of ships of various kinds that she regards as essential to her existence, or else let the existing situation alone." He thought that Washington's proposal had been a "tactical mistake," which not only failed to produce an arms agreement but also badly jaded the American public's view of the British. Disarmament, like other major issues, he told newly promoted Undersecretary Olds, must be approached from "a larger angle" and coordinated with other significant policies such as arbitration and nonaggression treaties. "But the milk has been spilled," he concluded. "It is best now to turn our attention to the future."[45]

In the aftermath of the Geneva failure, the *New York Times* published for its Sunday readers a detailed feature on Houghton. "He Snips The Red Tape from Diplomacy" amounted to a tribute to the ambassador's five-year diplomatic career, arguing that the badly fractured U.S.–British relationship was perfectly safe in his hands. His calm demeanor and unconventional style explained his success in the crucial posts at Berlin and London. He was described as patient, polite, quiet, smooth, and calculating. Houghton embodied "America's elegance"; "he is suavity personified." Equally important were those qualities more characteristic of an American industrialist. He was pragmatic, forceful, direct, and exacting. Brought together, these ingredients—the "velvet hand" and the "practical brain"—had created a new brand of diplomat, one uniquely capable of solving complicated international problems. The *Times* pointed to the envoy's determination in Berlin to settle the question of Germany's reparations on a fair and logical basis. He was never afraid to "brush aside diplomatic convention" and to argue for compromise over the selfish demands of the Allies and of German politicians and industrialists. "History may yet," the article contended, "allot him the lion's share of the credit for putting the Dawes Plan into operation; certainly one could not find in America or Europe more than a few other men who deserve equal credit." His Berlin years represented "one of the most difficult chapters in the whole history of American diplomacy." Houghton's rare blend of skills had also been effective in London. They had enabled him to calm the frequent "squalls" that surfaced between the United States and Britain. In short, he could be trusted to bridge the breach recently created by the failed disarmament conference. Harmonious bilateral relations would no doubt resume after a dose of his "most efficacious" business methods, administered "with plenty of soothing syrup to disguise the bitter taste."[46]

Despite the public praise, Houghton, who was almost sixty-four, had grown increasingly tired of diplomacy and begun to contemplate his future as a public servant. Any aspirations to become secretary of state had faded. He had resigned himself to the idea that Kellogg would never willingly relinquish his post, and he was convinced that Coolidge wanted a lawyer in control of the State Department. Houghton considered the latter idea a fundamental flaw in postwar Republican leadership. With ultraconservative men in the White House and attorneys at the diplomatic helm, the nation's foreign policies, he believed, were destined to be unimaginative and halting. It would suffice, he once told Dwight, for a progressive-minded secretary of state to have at his fingertips "competent legal advice and assistance."[47]

Since he had transferred to London, Republican leaders had consistently urged Houghton to leave diplomacy for the governorship of New York. The state party, badly divided over Prohibition, suffered at the hands of a united Democratic party led by Governor Al Smith. In the summer of 1926, Senator James Wadsworth (R-NY) had obtained Coolidge's support for the ambassador's gubernatorial candidacy, and when word of the Houghton boom reached the press, some momentum developed. The ambassador was again trumpeted as "the greatest American in Europe," and his return would lift the gubernatorial campaign out of the gutter of Prohibition politics. But when Congressman Ogden L. Mills (R-NY) traveled to London to coax the envoy to run, Houghton steadfastly refused. "Really, it is to laugh," he wrote to his brother. "Two years ago I think I could have been elected Governor and boxed up Al Smith, because I would have the full German-American support and that would have compensated two or three times over for the eighty thousand by which [Theodore Roosevelt Jr.] was licked. I didn't want it then, however, and I want it less now." In November 1926, Smith won reelection easily, and the ambassador's friend

Wadsworth was turned out of the Senate by State Supreme Court Justice Robert F. Wagner.[48]

Throughout the first half of 1927, many embassy visitors discussed presidential politics with Houghton, especially the issue of Coolidge's renomination. The president was unpopular in much of the Midwest because of his veto of farm-relief legislation. In addition, the question arose of whether his candidacy threatened the two-term tradition established by George Washington. Traveling supporters of Senator Borah informed Houghton that he would become secretary of state if their man prevailed. Charles Nagel, a prominent Republican attorney and former secretary of commerce and labor under William Howard Taft, even floated trial balloons for a presidential run by Houghton. The ambassador depreciated such lofty speculation, especially since he believed that Coolidge would run for reelection. Houghton's political mentor, John Dwight, encouraged the ambassador to consider the vice presidency in 1928.

On August 2, 1927, Coolidge gathered the presidential press corps to announce that "he did not choose to run" for reelection the next year. When the "thunderbolt" reached London, Houghton at Princess Gate was hosting two Republican insiders, Chandler P. Anderson Sr. and James Reynolds. All three were shocked by the news. The announcement ignited wild speculation over the word "choose." Did this mean that Coolidge could be drafted at the national party convention? If not, who would be his successor? Houghton informed his friend Thomas Lamont, the Morgan banker, that he thought Coolidge's decision was final.

A multitude of potential candidates came to the fore, including Hughes, Hoover, Borah, Lowden, and Dawes. There now emerged new rumors of a Borah–Houghton ticket and old speculation over the envoy's running for governor. Martin B. Madden, a Republican stalwart and chair of the House Appropriations Committee, described for the ambassador the unsettled state of American politics, and expressed his support for Houghton's presidential nomination: "You know I would like to see you president. You have done well [in] every job that you have had, both private and public and you have not made a noise about it; but my conception of a big man is the fellow who can do things without prattling about them every minute. You have great standing before the American people. Your record in the ambassadorial field is recognized favorably everywhere throughout the country, and personally it would make me very happy to see you in the place." At least a few others agreed with Madden. One lobbied for the ambassador's nomination in a letter to Lamont. The banker relayed the letter to Houghton, who wrote back mimicking Coolidge: "Dear Tom: I have your kind note . . . enclosing my nomination papers. I do not choose to run." [49]

Houghton realized that a presidential bid was impractical. But he did have political influence to wield. He arranged for vacation time, and on October 11, one day after his sixty-fourth birthday, he sailed for New York. He instructed Dwight, "I mean to be home for a month or six weeks, and during that time to make some definite decisions . . . my time here is definitely limited." As usual, his holiday combined business, diplomacy, politics, and leisure.[50]

With the exception of Lindbergh's magnificent transatlantic flight, the year and a half that followed the Houghton controversy had been a dismal period in international relations. The United States deployed troops to Nicaragua to quell civil unrest. The spread of violent revolution in China led to military confrontations between Nationalist soldiers and the U.S. and British navies, and to a joint letter of protest by the five major powers. Great Britain broke diplomatic relations with Soviet Russia, and the League's preparatory commission failed to establish an agenda for a major disarmament conference. Worse, from Houghton's perspective, the aborted Coolidge naval conference heightened hostility and suspicion in Anglo-American relations. The ambassador's personal campaign to enhance cooperation between the two countries had suffered a serious blow.

The Coolidge administration's approach to the disarmament issue and the crises in China and Nicaragua reflected the ambiguous nature of conservative internationalism. The Republican administration intervened militarily in Latin America because it believed that stability in the Western Hemisphere was crucial to American security. In contrast, turmoil on the Asian continent was not considered a vital threat; thus, Washington responded to China's revolution with reticence. For Republicans, Western Europe's importance ranked between Latin America and China's, and the only major political issue worthy of official U.S. engagement was arms control. The Coolidge–Kellogg drive for disarmament sprang in part from the desire to curb the stinging criticism emanating from within and outside the Republican party. The criticism often centered on the administration's failure to assert clear leadership in foreign affairs. Dwight and other Republicans had long complained to Houghton that even with a sixteen-seat majority in the Senate, Coolidge could muster only forty senators to toe the party line;

and worse, there was no "wise political head" in the president's cabinet "who can take the leadership."[51]

Although Houghton supported the administration on China and Latin America, he placed much greater value on cooperative relations with Western Europe, especially with Britain and Germany. This distinction accounts for much of his frustration with Republican foreign policy. The ambassador wanted the United States to pursue a more active, cooperative, and comprehensive agenda that promoted Europe's reconstruction and world peace. He possessed considerable foresight on the issue of arms-control negotiations, and he had worked diligently to educate Washington officials on the British perspective and on the likely outcome of the naval conference. But his influence on defense policy was limited. At best, he had won the debate over U.S. conference representation, persuading Coolidge and Kellogg to scuttle plans for a prominent delegation. Despite his pessimism regarding the prospects for arms control, Houghton had attempted in his typically active fashion to broker a compromise agreement of his own making. To his regret, the administration proved less than conciliatory on the issue. Overall, he was distraught over Republican management of Anglo-American relations. It had been an extremely difficult period in the ambassador's career. The events of 1928 would present him with even greater challenges.

Notes

1. Houghton to S. Parker Gilbert, May 4, 1926, Houghton Papers.
2. Houghton to Castle, May 8, 1926, Castle Papers.
3. Houghton to Coolidge, May 10, 1926, Houghton Papers; Houghton to Castle, July 3, 1926, Castle Papers.
4. Vansittart to Chamberlain, October 27(?), 1925, FO 371/10646/5376/1490/45, PRO.
5. Chamberlain to Howard, November 3, 1925, *Documents on British Foreign Policy*, Series 1A, 6 vols. (London, 1966–1977) (hereafter cited as *DBFP*), 2:867–68; Houghton to Kellogg, November 3, 1925, *FRUS, 1926* 2:214–15; ABH Diary, November 3, 1925.
6. Houghton to Castle, November 7 and 23, 1925, Houghton Papers.
7. Chamberlain to Howard, June 4, 1926, FO 371/11162/a3014/6/45, PRO.
8. Houghton to Kellogg, June 4, 1926, and Kellogg to Houghton, June 5, 1926, *FRUS 1926*, 2:227–32.
9. Houghton to Castle, July 3, 1926, Castle Papers; Chamberlain to Howard, June 16, 1926, FO 371/11162/a3239/6/45, PRO.
10. Houghton to Castle, October 21, 1926, Castle Papers.
11. *New York Times*, March 17, 1926; Hoover to Houghton, May 1, 1926, Houghton Papers.

12. Castle to F. A. Sterling, March 18, 1926, Castle Papers; "Talk by Mr. Alanson B. Houghton, Ambassador to Great Britain," March 18, 1926, NARG59, (Stack Area)250/46/08/05-06, Box 5.

13. Commercial Relations Department to Tyrrell, January 16, 1926, FO 371/11167/a315/10/45, PRO.

14. Hoover to Kellogg, May 18, 1926, and Sterling to Kellogg, June 25, 1926 (enclosing Keynes article), NARG59, Files 841.6176/84, 93, 96.

15. Howard to Kellogg, July 30, 1926, ibid., File 841.6176.

16. Hoover to Kellogg, August 12, 1926, ibid., Files 841.6176/99, 103, 104, 109.

17. Howard to Tyrrell, August 27, 1926, and Vansittart's commentary of September 20, 1926, FO 371/11168/14769/10/45, PRO.

18. Houghton to Kellogg, August 28, 1926, NARG59, File 841.6176/109; Joseph Brandes, *Herbert Hoover and Economic Diplomacy: Department of Commerce Policy, 1921–1928* (Pittsburgh, 1962), 94.

19. Percy Blair to Castle, October 5, 1926, Castle Papers; a British newspaper is quoted in Adelaide Wellington Houghton, *The London Years: The Diary of Adelaide Wellington Houghton, 1925–1929* (New York, 1963) (hereafter cited as Adelaide Houghton Diary), February 2, 1927, 131; Houghton to Castle, October 21, 1926, Castle Papers; Houghton to Castle, October 7, 1926, Houghton Papers.

20. Houghton to Castle, October 21, 1926, Castle Papers.

21. Castle Diary, January 4, 1927.

22. Ibid., January 6, 1927.

23. Ibid., December 31, 1926; Houghton to Amory Houghton, January 20, 1927, Houghton Papers.

24. Houghton to Olds, February 7, 1927, and Houghton to former New York congressman Isaac Siegel, February 21, 1927, Houghton Papers; William Tyrrell Memorandum, December 4, 1926, FO 371/11787/5425/387/38; Houghton to Castle, February 28, 1927, Castle Papers.

25. Isaac Siegel to Houghton, March 25, 1927, Houghton Papers.

26. Olds to Houghton, April 11, 1927, Coolidge to Houghton, April 28, 1927, and Kellogg to Houghton, May 2, 1927, ibid.

27. *St. Louis Post-Dispatch*, March 8, 1926; ABH Diary, April 20 and 30, 1926; *New York Times*, April 21 and May 1, 1926; Houghton to Alexander Falck, February 28, 1927, Houghton Papers.

28. A. Scott Berg, *Lindbergh* (New York, 1998), 100; *New York Times*, May 22, 1927.

29. Adelaide Houghton Diary, May 21, 1927, 152–53.

30. Berg, *Lindbergh*, 147; ABH Diary, May 29–30, 1927; *New York Times*, May 31, June 7 and 13, 1927; Houghton to Kellogg, May 30, 1927, Houghton Papers.

31. Ray Atherton to Houghton, April 13, 1927, and Houghton to Gibson, June 21, 1926, Houghton Papers. The Houghton quotation refers to an account in Greek mythology of the difficulty in navigating the narrow Strait of Messina between a rock personified as a monster, part woman and part fish (Scylla), and a whirlpool (Charybdis).

32. Houghton to Kellogg, February 23 and 25, 1927, NARG59, File 500.A15a1/46, 52; Chamberlain to Howard, February 25, 1927, FO 371/12661/w1581/61/98, PRO.

33. Houghton to Owen Young, March 2, 1927, Houghton to Castle, February 28, 1927, and Houghton to Isaac Siegel, March 7, 1927, Houghton Papers.

34. Houghton to Kellogg, May 13, 1927, NARG59, File 500.A15a1/231; Kellogg to Coolidge, May 27, 1927, *FRUS, 1927*, 1:40–41.

35. Gibson to Kellogg, June 23–24, 1927, and Kellogg to Gibson, June 24, 1927, *FRUS, 1927* 1:52–56.

36. Kellogg to Houghton, July 5 and 7, 1927, and Houghton to Kellogg, July 7, 1927, *FRUS, 1927*, 1:70, 78–79.

37. Chamberlain to Stanley Baldwin, July 8, 1927, FO 371/12671/w6462/61/98, PRO.

38. Chamberlain to Baldwin, July 8, 1927, and Chamberlain to Howard, July 11, 1927, ibid.; Houghton to Kellogg, July 8, 1927, *FRUS, 1927*, 1:84–85.

39. Chamberlain to Baldwin, July 8, 1927, and Chamberlain to Howard, July 11, 1927, FO 371/12671/w6462/61/98, PRO.

40. Houghton to Kellogg, July 12, 1927, and Kellogg to Houghton, July 16, 1927, *FRUS, 1927*, 1:97–98, 108; Houghton to Kellogg, July 13, 1927, Telegram #165, NARG59, File 500.A15.a1/421.

41. Houghton to Castle, July 21, 1927, Castle Papers; Villard to Houghton, August 2, 1927, Houghton Papers; Kellogg to Coolidge, July 22, 1927, *FRUS, 1927*, 1:124–27.

42. Kellogg to Coolidge, July 29, 1927, *FRUS, 1927*, 1:138–39.

43. Christopher Hall, *Britain, America, and Arms Control, 1921–37* (New York, 1987), 48–51; Sterling to Houghton, August 10, 1927, Houghton Papers; Kellogg to Coolidge, August 10, 1927, *FRUS, 1927*, 1:157–59.

44. Chamberlain to Howard, August 24, 1927, FO 371/12040/a4794/133/45, PRO; "The Disgrace at Geneva," *The Nation* 125 (August 10, 1927): 127.

45. Houghton to Dr. John H. Finley, August 15, 1927, and Houghton to Olds, August 25, 1927, Houghton Papers.

46. *New York Times*, August 14, 1927.

47. Houghton to Dwight, April 29, 1927, Houghton Papers.

48. *New York Evening Post* and *New York Times*, July 14, 1926; Houghton to Arthur Houghton, June 21, 1926, Houghton Papers.

49. Robert H. Ferrell, *The Presidency of Calvin Coolidge* (Lawrence, KS, 1998), 192–96; Madden to Houghton, October 4, 1927, and Houghton to Lamont, August 30, 1927, Houghton Papers.

50. Houghton to Dwight, September 15, 1927, Houghton Papers.

51. Dwight to Houghton, January 20, 1926, ibid.

7

Final Opportunities

1928–1929

It is vastly important for the United States to have
men in the Senate who know something about the
practical business of carrying on foreign relations.
. . . The people of New York could render no greater
service to the country than by putting into the Senate such a man as Alanson B. Houghton.
—Elihu Root, 1928

With the final year of the Coolidge administration
approaching, Houghton realized that his chances
to promote assertive and responsible American leadership were rapidly diminishing. The widening rift in
Anglo-American relations caused by the failed naval conference complicated his mission. Moreover, he believed
that important problems, including arms control, belligerent maritime rights, and U.S. trade policy, could not be
resolved effectively until the next administration assumed
power. Nonetheless, there arose several opportunities to
influence the course of America's conservative internationalism, and the ambassador seized them.

The two issues that dominated Houghton's last year
of diplomatic activity were familiar: reparations and security. The Dawes Plan, which Houghton had helped to
arrange, established an elaborate financial system for
managing Germany's reparations payments. The plan stabilized European economic affairs after 1924, but all parties recognized that the complex issue required a more
permanent settlement. In 1928–1929, Parker Gilbert, the
reparations agent general, was working on a new and final program, and he relied upon Houghton for guidance

and assistance. The ambassador played an even larger role in the negotiation of a landmark antiwar treaty among the major powers. He helped to champion this nonaggression accord and reveled in the Coolidge administration's ultimate leadership on the issue, wishing only that it had come years earlier when he had recommended it. Houghton, unlike Coolidge and Kellogg, especially hoped that this peace treaty would encourage public support for sustained U.S. involvement in international politics.

To further this cause, Houghton immersed himself in American politics. He wanted the next administration to appreciate more the vital significance of Western Europe to the United States and to accept responsibility for promoting peace and prosperity among the principal powers. As a result, he tried to prevent the presidential nomination of Herbert Hoover, whose economic foreign policy he considered short-sighted and perilous. He favored, instead, former Illinois governor Frank Lowden, whose outlook on international affairs was more in line with his own. When this strategy went awry and Hoover won the nomination, Houghton was coaxed into running for the U.S. Senate, where he could influence policy from the Foreign Relations Committee.

Throughout much of 1928, Great Britain, France, and the United States engaged in wide-ranging and often intense security negotiations that culminated not in a new arms control agreement but in a multilateral nonaggression treaty known as the Kellogg–Briand Pact. An insecure France, a galvanized American peace movement, and an assertive Houghton spurred the Coolidge administration's participation in these talks.

In April 1927, French Foreign Minister Aristide Briand had bypassed normal diplomatic channels and floated in the press the idea of a bilateral treaty with the United States, one that renounced war as a means of settling disputes. Columbia University Professor James T. Shotwell had inspired Briand's proposal. Shotwell, a leader in the American peace movement, had also developed a friendship with Houghton after witnessing his selfless efforts in Berlin. Shotwell considered Briand's initiative the start of the "last chapter" in the post-Versailles peace movement that began with Houghton's promotion of a nonaggression treaty in 1922.[1]

Ten weeks after Briand's public overture, Houghton delivered an acclaimed foreign policy speech. For two years, he had urged the Coolidge administration to take the lead in advocating war referendums and a nonaggression pact among the major powers. The president remained uncommitted until early 1927, when he finally gave the ambassador approval to promote the ideas. Houghton waited for an ideal time to launch his peace campaign, which came when he accepted an honorary doctorate from Harvard in June. The Harvard Regents had offered Houghton the award twice before, but his diplomatic duties had interfered. He was determined to accept the honor at the 1927 Commencement.

Thomas Nelson Perkins, a prominent Boston attorney and president of the Harvard Alumni Association, urged his friend to make a bold and daring speech. He knew that Houghton often disagreed with administration policy and reminded him that the address offered "a great chance" to educate Americans on their responsibilities toward European stabilization. Perkins, like the ambassador, viewed the war debts–reparations tangle, including the lack of authoritative U.S. leadership, as the "most immediate problem." Houghton was tempted. "I wish I might help," he responded. "I really think I could put the Debt question in a way that would be serviceable" to the country, but "I am pretty sure that such a talk could hardly be regarded favorably by the Administration and naturally, being their servant, I cannot do anything to build up opposition for them."[2]

Instead, the ambassador's speech adhered to the ideas of a multilateral nonaggression treaty and the war referendum as steps toward preventing a second world war. Nations, he believed, had become too integrated and weaponry too destructive to risk another catastrophe. Modern warfare's "proportions have become so formidable," he continued, "and its demands and consequences so ruinous that it threatens to wreck civilization itself. . . . Whatever may be said regarding war in the past . . . to-day the situation is changed. This new democratic [and integrated] world into which we are entering, wherein production is becoming more and more a world process and in which the relations of each of us is becoming more and more vitally dependent upon others, cannot withstand the shock and dislocation and waste of war. . . . Some check . . . must be found." Houghton encouraged new international "experiments" aimed at curbing the historic war-making powers of "little groups of men." He specifically called upon the major powers to sign a hundred-year pact of nonaggression and to adopt the war referendum as a means of declaring war. Because warfare among the industrialized powers had become "all-embracing and all-consuming," he argued, the "democratic impulse" so successful in domestic relations should be tested in foreign relations. Although admitting that these diplomatic and political mechanisms were "inadequate" to abolish war, the ambassador maintained that they offered supplemental "form[s] of security" in the dangerous, modern age.[3]

The idealism undergirding Houghton's peace plan cannot be denied. He did not argue, however, that the war referendum and antiwar pact were panaceas. "War may be in fact . . . the inevitable result of a serious clash of national interests," he told the Harvard graduates. But as he had learned in business, changed conditions demanded adjustment and innovation by leaders. The speech must be understood in the context of the ambassador's long campaign to push the United States away from its traditional mooring of avoiding political engagement with the Old World. He continued to demand progress, a new outlook on international relations. The address, in other words, served as a clarion call to the American people to exert leadership in the postwar era. His 1922 Metropolitan Club speech had contained a similar appeal but lacked a program of action. And although he had been successful in getting the Cuno government to support the war referendum and nonaggression pact concepts, with the latter culminating in the Locarno security treaty, his attempts to have Republican administrations promote these ideas at home had been stymied.[4]

The press and leaders in the international peace movement praised the speech. In New York alone, the *Times*, the *World*, the *Tribune*, the *Telegram*, and the *Eagle* all endorsed the ambassador's message. In an article disparaging Kellogg and Republican policy, progressive historian Charles A. Beard applauded Houghton's address as "one of the most remarkable state papers ever presented to this nation." *The World Tomorrow*, a liberal magazine, noted the ambassador's knack for delivering "significant speeches." *The Nation* proclaimed the "truth-telling" Houghton "an anachronism in our diplomatic service . . . not afraid to speak out . . . and when he speaks he has something to say—which is certainly unusual among those who belong to the statesman class." There were numerous requests to reprint the address, which was entered into the *Congressional Record*, circulated by the Federal Council of Churches and the British World Alliance for Promoting International Friendship, and included in a college textbook, *Readings in Public Opinion: Its Formation and Control*.[5]

Just prior to Houghton's speech, the State Department had received Foreign Minister Briand's official proposal for a bilateral "Pact of Perpetual Friendship" between the United States and France. It was not warmly embraced. Houghton supported the treaty in principle, but he advised the administration to abstain from any bilateral arrangements, arguing that an antiwar accord should commit all the major powers. Kellogg suspected Briand's motives. He believed that the French, having refused to participate in the Coolidge naval conference, hoped to divert attention from arms control negotiations. Kellogg persuaded the president not "to play into [Briand's] hands" by offering a quick response to the proposal. Thus began what historian Robert Ferrell describes as six months of "ingenious inaction."[6]

By December 1927, circumstances abroad and public pressure at home compelled the administration to respond to the French initiative. The Coolidge naval conference in Geneva had failed miserably, making France's antiwar proposal even more appealing to the American peace movement. The proposed agreement gained overwhelming support in the press and in Congress, where the nation's political representatives were bombarded with cables and letters demanding Washington's official reply. The French, increasingly fearful of diplomatic isolation, made it known that they were eager for any treaty with the United States, even if only a renewal of an expiring bilateral arbitration agreement. On December 14 the State Department announced that it had crafted a new "model" arbitration treaty, one that made reference to Briand's peace proposal in the unbinding preamble. When delivered to France two weeks later, the department included with the treaty a separate note that expressed a willingness to negotiate a binding antiwar pact if the accord would be open to other nations.

Paris welcomed the new arbitration agreement, but balked at the suggestion of a multilateral antiwar treaty. The French insisted on concluding an antiwar pact with the United States before inviting others to join, and they also wanted to revise the text of Briand's original proposal by rewording the renunciation of war to the renunciation of "all war[s] of aggression." This change was meant to reserve the right of self-defense. Kellogg refused the French conditions, and a deadlock ensued. The State Department kept Houghton fully apprised of these negotiations, and the ambassador continued to advise the administration on the absolute importance of including Britain and the other major powers in any antiwar treaty. In discussions with Chamberlain, the foreign minister predicted that Briand's initiative, although well intended, would prove immensely difficult to conclude.[7]

After proposing the new arbitration treaty to France, Kellogg informed the British ambassador in Washington that the United

States would make a similar proposal to London. This caused a stir at the Foreign Office, because America's new model agreement no longer excluded from arbitration matters related to national honor and "vital interests." Kellogg had deleted these traditional phrases because he considered them too nebulous to be of value in arbitration settlements. The British, however, interpreted the omission of the vital interests clause as a threat to their wartime right to organize naval blockades. An anxious Chamberlain quickly set up an internal subcommittee on "Belligerent Rights" to examine the issue.[8]

When Houghton renewed his discussions with the foreign secretary on January 23, 1928, the British had just received a copy of the proposed arbitration treaty. The ambassador downplayed the significance of Kellogg's changes, but Chamberlain was not easily won over, claiming that all treaty revisions required deliberate examination. Although the foreign secretary wanted to reach an accommodation on arbitration and belligerent rights, he never overtly explained to Houghton the nature of British apprehension. Still, the ambassador appreciated London's caution, reporting: "Chamberlain approaches the Treaty sympathetically, but evidently and naturally proposes to weigh with great care precisely the meaning of the various changes suggested." The ambassador informed Professor Shotwell that "Chamberlain is still examining with meticulous care provisions of the treaty offered him," and "it will be interesting to discover just how far Britain is prepared to go—or for that matter, the good old U.S.A." The British were in a quandary when the French suddenly announced their acceptance of Kellogg's new arbitration pact. The Franco-American accord was signed ceremoniously on February 6, leaving the Baldwin government to adopt its own version of ingenious inaction.[9]

Meanwhile, buoyed by the success of the arbitration agreement with France, Kellogg decided to push for a multilateral antiwar pact. He called upon Paris to renew negotiations, and delivered a speech to the Council on Foreign Relations arguing that Briand's original, simple proposal should be left intact, with only the exception of expanding the list of signatories to include the other major powers—Britain, Japan, Italy, and Germany. A protracted and complicated diplomatic battle ensued. Paris responded in late March by insisting that the pact include several reservations explicitly acknowledging the right to war in self-defense, the automatic termination of the treaty should it be broken by a single signatory, and the right of *all* nations to participate in the treaty. At first, Kellogg dismissed the French note and on April 13 asked the other four powers to join his antiwar treaty. He included with the treaty a copy of America's diplomatic exchanges with Paris for the previous ten months.

Determined not to be outmaneuvered, Briand delivered to the major powers a proposal of his own. And to forestall sympathy for the French plan, Kellogg, on April 23, dispatched a long memorandum to his ambassadors in London, Rome, Tokyo, and Paris. The memo unofficially recognized the validity of France's reservations such as the right of self-defense and the need for release in case of a breach. Kellogg wanted his ambassadors to argue orally, if necessary, that these interpretations were implicit in the American treaty and therefore should not be made part of the compact. To incorporate the French reservations into the treaty, the secretary argued, would cause the agreement to read more like a justification for war rather than a renunciation of it.

Houghton applauded the secretary's newfound enthusiasm for a nonaggression pact. He also supported his hard line on the French reservations, describing administration policy as "sound as a nut." With no enforcement mechanism in the treaty, the ambassador reasoned that "a few reservations" would have little effect on future belligerency, so why complicate the statement of a worthy principle? But unlike Kellogg, who aspired to the Nobel Peace Prize, the ambassador viewed the proposed treaty not as an end in itself, but rather as a "new starting point" that could facilitate international cooperation and goodwill. He believed that the conclusion of a peace treaty, so popular with the general public, could open the door for progress on other pressing issues such as arms control, belligerent rights, and the final settlement of Germany's reparations. He also hoped that the administration's initiative on the peace treaty would build domestic support for more concerted American leadership on the world stage. He informed Undersecretary Olds: "[The] proposal may be mere sentimentalism," but popular opinion can have "profound significance" on the course of international relations.[10]

As throughout the prior six years, the ambassador continued to furnish the Republican administration with policy advice. His efforts were evident in his response to Kellogg's note of April 23 and in his revealing discussion with Chamberlain on April 26. The foreign secretary urged Washington to be patient with Britain's slow responses to the model arbitration agreement and the antiwar treaty. He also suggested that changes in the treaties were likely because

Britain sympathized with France's desire to clarify rights of self-defense. As an example of the complexities involved, Chamberlain asked if acceptance of the American antiwar treaty meant that the United States would abandon the Monroe Doctrine and allow "European infringement" on Latin America. Houghton replied, no, "that it would be much better to assume that when [the] Powers signed a treaty of the kind proposed, they meant what they said, and in renouncing war they would renounce acts that must produce war." It was a "dangerous" mistake, he continued, to approach the treaty in Chamberlain's hypothetical manner, because the exact circumstances of defensive or aggressive wars could never be satisfactorily defined within the body of the treaty. Instead, the ambassador argued that the antiwar pact should be considered a symbol of a new era of trust and goodwill among the leading powers. Houghton postulated that the peace treaty represented icing on the cake of postwar European security, which had been bolstered by the League of Nations and the Locarno Treaties. On the other hand, world statesmen should not "underrate the effects of a simple broad declaration" against war, especially one in which the United States was willing to take the lead. Speaking on his own accord, he suggested further that the conclusion of the antiwar treaty would not only solidify American support for League sanctions against a future "peace-breaker" but would also have an immediate and "powerful effect" in favor of naval arms control. In the end, the foreign secretary expressed his appreciation for Houghton's perspective and asked that Kellogg be informed of their discussion and of Britain's cautious but general support. A final remark disturbed the ambassador. Chamberlain noted his desire for a new foreign ministers' conference to resolve the outstanding "difficulties" in the antiwar treaty.[11]

In his April 27 report, Houghton described Britain's reservations concerning the peace pact. Equally important, he opined that Chamberlain was angling to serve as the pact's savior by mediating a compromise between France and the United States. The ambassador wanted Washington, not London, to champion this immensely popular issue and recommended that Kellogg act quickly and decisively to conclude the treaty on American terms. Specifically, he suggested the expediency of issuing to the press the essence of Kellogg's confidential memorandum of April 23, which had thoroughly addressed all of France's known concerns. The widespread publication of Washington's position, the ambassador asserted, would break the diplomatic deadlock and "act directly to strengthen popular sentiment everywhere" in favor of the comparatively simple American proposal.[12]

Houghton's communiqué was timely and influential. Kellogg was impressed by the ambassador's "thoughtful personal message" and immediately implemented his "excellent" advice. The secretary was already scheduled to give an address to the American Society of International Law on April 28. He had planned to speak "wholly extemporaneously," but instead stitched together a speech based on the April 23 memorandum. At the last minute, the State Department distributed the speech to the Washington press corps. On the following day, Houghton noted contentedly in his diary, "I see by today's paper that Kellogg followed my suggestion." All the major powers later pointed to Kellogg's address as a turning point in reaching a final agreement.[13]

Kellogg's public statement that France's reservations were implicitly guaranteed in the American treaty sparked considerable diplomatic activity. On May 2, Houghton learned that the Baldwin government was inclined to accept the American pact. The following day he arranged to meet with Chamberlain, who described the encounter as having "the highest consequence." Much to the foreign secretary's disappointment, Houghton expressed his and Kellogg's staunch opposition to a foreign ministers' conference to negotiate the antiwar treaty. When Chamberlain suggested the value of holding a legal experts' conference to ferret out the complexities involved, the ambassador snapped, "What on earth . . . was [there] for the jurists to decide. The question was political and not juridical." To aid his argument, Houghton reminded the foreign secretary that Germany had accepted the American treaty five days earlier (against Chamberlain's expressed wishes) and that this dispensed with the necessity of any conference. Moreover, Kellogg's speech, he claimed, had satisfactorily addressed the concerns over self-defense. The ambassador then urged that Britain follow Germany's lead, because acceptance of this "plain and sweeping declaration [for peace]" would positively affect the "larger aspects" of international relations by bolstering the Anglo-American relationship and Washington's commitment to solving world problems. Houghton even appealed to the foreign secretary's vanity, claiming that acceptance of the treaty would further Chamberlain's place in history as one of the world's "great benefactors" of peace. But Chamberlain continued to emphasize "the necessity of caution" and expressed a fear that without explicit recognition of a "British Monroe Doctrine," Britain's interests in Egypt and elsewhere might be jeopardized by the American treaty. After a ninety-minute debate, Chamberlain thanked the ambassador for the meeting and promised to confer with his colleagues.[14]

This meeting increased Houghton's suspicions of the foreign secretary's motives. While he believed that Kellogg's speech had countered all French objections, performing "the execution of a machine gun," he still saw opponents of the treaty working to bury it. He concluded that Chamberlain, while not opposed to an antiwar pact, "is hoping that he can somehow produce a situation . . . which will enable him to come in as mediator and score another Locarno. I have a [feeling] that he will fail so long as no Conventions [are called]. . . . If we ever get drawn into the discussion of all the possible ways in which one nation may directly or indirectly involve itself in war with another, the treaty will fail. There is no possible way of getting an agreement over so many hypothetical . . . possibilities. The strength of the proposal lies in its simplicity."[15]

Houghton was doing everything possible to further the peace pact negotiations, and the administration greatly appreciated his efforts. After reading the ambassador's account of his meeting with Chamberlain, Undersecretary Olds wrote a glowing commendation reflective of both the ambassador's standing within the government and the importance attached to the treaty:

> I have just been reading your long message. . . and I cannot forbear expressing to you at once my admiration for the way in which you have put the case at this juncture. It is a delight to read such a message. On all points it is most convincing. The same may be said of your earlier communications since we entered the really interesting phase of this discussion. If I may indulge in an indiscretion, I should like to say that you are the only Ambassador of the United States who has thus far betrayed a thorough understanding of the deeper significance of this peace movement and made any notable contribution to its success. It goes without saying that you occupy the key position, and nothing is more gratifying and reassuring than the fact that you are at London at this time. I don't know how you feel about it but my own view is that this is the biggest show any of us ever is likely to take part in.

While this compliment was making its way across the Atlantic, the envoy consulted privately with Aimé-Joseph de Fleuriau, the French ambassador in London. The Frenchman was a confidant of Briand, and during the previous three years, the ambassador and Houghton had struck up an amicable friendship. In their most recent meetings, Houghton had presented the arguments for a quick acceptance of the treaty. De Fleuriau expressed his personal support for the treaty, especially since Kellogg's April 28 address, and he hoped that the speech could be written into the pact's preamble. But de Fleuriau informed his counterpart that his government's acceptance would be delayed because public opinion had not yet "crystallized" in support of it and because "French *amour propre*" had been disturbed by Kellogg's attempts to control the negotiations. Another key to France's approval, he claimed, was the support of its Central European allies, especially Czechoslovakia, which had expressed opposition to the American treaty. In a surprising move, the French ambassador asked Houghton to present his case for the treaty directly to Edvard Benes, the influential Czech foreign minister who would soon visit London.[16]

After Houghton explained the benefits of a meeting with Benes, Kellogg supported the initiative as long as it was held unofficially. The Benes–Houghton conference took place at the American embassy in London on May 9. The tone was cordial. Houghton described Benes as a "distinctly interesting figure [who] has about as acute an intelligence as any one that I have met." Benes reminisced about the pair's sessions several years earlier when working behind the scenes in support of the Locarno Treaties. The foreign minister also expressed appreciation for America's support of an antiwar pact, but explained that he had reservations similar to France's. By reading from a copy of Kellogg's April 28 speech, Houghton addressed Benes's concerns regarding the pact's effect on Czechoslovakia's commitments to the League, the Locarno settlement, and existing military alliances. Houghton assured his guest that if these prior commitments were only "defensive" in nature, then, under the antiwar treaty, the Czechs would be free to act against any "attacking power." Benes left the embassy apparently satisfied with the ambassador's interpretation. "[The] net result of this interview," Houghton reported, was that "Benes is really in favor of the treaty. I think too he will use his influence, which is, of course, great, to bring Paris to a more favorable mood."[17]

Kellogg lauded Houghton's intervention and informed the ambassador that matters were progressing favorably, especially since Austria and Ireland had joined Germany in support of the treaty and because Japan's approval was thought to be forthcoming. The secretary still worried, however, about Britain's delay. Specifically, he feared that the Foreign Office would insist on reserving the right of intervention in the Middle East. As a result, Kellogg asked the ambassador to dissuade Chamberlain from making any assertion of "special interests" in Egypt or elsewhere, because such rights were implicit and not dissimilar to America's rights in Latin America. Before Houghton could act, he received word that the Baldwin government had already formulated its reply. The British note of May 19, while accepting Kellogg's April 28 interpretations and asking that the Dominions and India be invited to sign the treaty, also demanded precisely what Kellogg feared— explicit recognition of Britain's interests in "certain regions" of the world. The Coolidge administration accepted the inclusion of the Dominions and India but not the British reservation.[18]

In late May, when Chamberlain learned of Houghton's imminent departure for Washington, he requested a private meeting. In the course of a long dinner, the foreign secretary labored to explain not only the British note, but also Britain's special relationship with France and the reasons for Paris's reluctance. Houghton countered that Kellogg had adequately addressed France's concerns and objected to British reservations pertaining to spheres of influence. The declaration of a British Monroe Doctrine, the ambassador claimed, had "opened a veritable Pandora's box of difficulties," because the other major powers were tempted to "surround" the treaty with their own security doctrines. Chamberlain expressed some doubt, and when he left the embassy, both men agreed that the treaty was far from settled. When Houghton reached Washington in early June, he reminded the administration that Britain's acceptance of the antiwar treaty ultimately depended on France. Not "everybody is straining at the leash to sign up."[19]

The ambassador's motives for returning to America were personal and political. His brother Arthur, who had helped him transform Corning Glass Works into a modern industrial enterprise, had died in April. As the executor of his brother's estate, he needed to settle family affairs. Also important and in need of settlement was the uncertain state of Republican presidential politics. Houghton had become convinced that the GOP was splintering over Hoover's well-publicized candidacy and that a deadlocked convention was likely. He predicted further that the delegates would eventually turn to Coolidge for a third term, but after receiving the incumbent's rebuff, the party would be forced to find a compromise candidate. Houghton wanted that candidate to be Lowden. The former Illinois governor, who had declined the 1924 vice presidential nomination, remained immensely popular in the Midwest. "Lowden would be my first choice," the ambassador confided to a friend. "I believe profoundly that he would make a great President" because of his balanced temperament and constructive political record. More than anything, the ambassador hoped to head off Hoover's nomination because he felt it would cause an irreparable rift within the party. Houghton respected the commerce secretary's leadership in domestic affairs, especially his nationwide campaigns for improved economic efficiency and voluntary market cooperatives. But the ambassador objected strongly to Hoover's strident nationalism in foreign affairs, including his pandering to the public on complex issues such as war claims, international loans, and raw material monopolies. Houghton had once remarked that the secretary "had stirred up a maximum of bad will [in foreign relations] for no gain whatever, and with that much accomplished, perhaps he will give his attention now to matters other than international, where I think he is more at home." Moreover, the ambassador found Hoover's fondness for self-promotion distasteful and unbecoming to a public servant. All of this made the selection of delegates to the 1928 Republican convention unusually important.[20]

During his Christmas vacation a year earlier, Houghton had received assurances from party officials that he would be a delegate from New York's 37th District. He had even received Coolidge's blessing to take part in the tussle of convention politics. But during late winter, Houghton's promised appointment had grown less certain. Several local Republican leaders had come out strongly for Hoover and demanded that the district's two delegates commit themselves to the commerce secretary in advance of their official appointment and thus before the convention. It was a poorly kept secret that the ambassador favored Lowden, as he had in 1920 and 1924. Much to Houghton's disappointment, a nasty behind-the-scenes fight ensued. To help ease the situation, he agreed to withdraw if the district's delegates went to the convention uninstructed. When this failed to break the stalemate, he took the politically safe path of declaring himself for Coolidge's renomination. The question was finally settled in Houghton's favor after several influential Republicans, including Treasury Secretary Andrew Mellon, intervened on his behalf. Mellon's undersecretary at the Treasury Department, Ogden Mills, who had lobbied Houghton to run for the New York governorship in 1926, wrote to the ambassador: "I have consistently told the local leaders that if you desire to go as a delegate, you are entitled to represent your district, irrespective of whom you favor for the nomination. I am sorry to learn that you do not look with favor upon the Hoover candidacy, as I do not like to find myself in disagreement with you."[21]

By the time the ambassador arrived in the United States on June 2, just ten days before the opening of the Kansas City convention, Hoover's prospects appeared increasingly favorable, but the national scene still remained unsettled. Unfortunately, the envoy had to navigate these political waters without the guidance of his mentor, John Dwight; the retired House whip had died four months earlier. Since Dwight's death, Houghton had grown close to his fellow New Yorker, Charles Hilles. The Republican National Committee vice chairman and many other Republican leaders, including the president and his treasury secretary, disliked Hoover personally. Coolidge once complained, "That man has offered me unsolicited advice for six years, all of it bad!" More important, Hilles doubted the commerce secretary's election chances against Governor Alfred Smith, the likely Democratic nominee. Hilles backed Coolidge first, and former secretary of state Charles Evans Hughes second. Those Republicans who opposed Hoover's nomination were glad that Houghton had returned for the convention. This was especially true for the Lowden supporters, who had asked the ambassador to take over Dwight's Washington "under-cover work" for their campaign. Hoover, of course, was not happy about Houghton's return. As early as February, the commerce secretary had expressed surprise and unease at the envoy's intense interest in presidential politics, and he had stated that the ambassador's involvement at the convention would be improper because it ran contrary to State Department policy.[22]

Houghton's political stature began to crest at the time of the GOP convention. A few weeks earlier, an unauthorized boom had started in New York for his entry into the 1928 U.S. Senate race. The development was not entirely surprising. Party leaders had courted Houghton to run for office before, and they were still smarting from Senator Robert Wagner's surprising victory over the Republican incumbent in 1926. In the upcoming battle with Democratic Senator Royal S. Copeland, the New York Republicans were desperate to field a viable candidate, who, although "dry," would not draw attention to the Prohibition issue and who could help carry the state for the presidential ticket. Also reflective of Houghton's popularity was a pronouncement by New York's Republican machine that it was working for his nomination for vice president of the United States. Unlike the Senate bid, Houghton had a certain affection for this latter movement. These political endorsements even led to the extreme suggestion that Corning's favorite son might emerge from the convention as a compromise candidate for the presidency. Regardless of his true feelings, Houghton played down the speculation. "All the information I have," he informed his friend William C. Boyden, "is that there is some possibility that I may be New York's candidate for the Vice Presidency, but I do not take this possibility very seriously. . . . What you say about [my] dark horse [presidential candidacy] comes to me from time to time, in one form or another, from a good many angles. It is, of course, unthinkable."[23]

A convention deadlock and the emergence of a dark-horse candidate hinged on Coolidge's attitude toward his potential renomination. Hoover had performed well in the spring primary campaign, even without the president's support, and he entered the June convention with the largest number of committed delegates. He was not, however, assured of a victory on the first ballot because of the strength of two discernible anti-Hoover factions. The first, loosely led by Hilles and Mellon, was pro-Coolidge, with its base concentrated in the northeastern states. The other, headed by Lowden, consisted largely of Midwesterners who opposed not only Hoover, but also Coolidge because of his veto of major farm-relief legislation. To complicate matters further, Charles Dawes, the gregarious and ambitious vice president, had supported the farmers against the administration and was a close friend of Lowden. Dawes, Lowden, and Houghton hoped that the anti-Hoover groups would somehow coalesce behind a single candidate.

Coolidge's final signal regarding his renomination shifted the balance of power. On June 12, after word reached Mellon at the convention that the president opposed any effort to place his name on the ballot, the treasury secretary assumed the role of kingmaker. Although Hoover's nomination was not pleasing to Mellon, the prospect of either Lowden or Dawes was even more abhorrent. Coolidge's definite withdrawal made the commerce secretary's nomination certain. There was little Houghton or Lowden could do. Always looking ahead, the ambassador hoped at least to use his position on the Resolutions Committee to champion an agricultural plank satisfactory to the Lowden forces. He did not want the party to replay the divisiveness of the 1912 GOP convention, so he conferred with Lowden. The former governor later wrote to Houghton, "I was surprised and delighted with your familiarity with the farm problem . . . you were not afraid to espouse whatever measure might be needed to remove the farmers' economic handicap." But Hooverites dominated the Resolutions Committee, and they ensured that the party platform supported Coolidge's record on farm policy. Lowden bolted the convention in disgust. On June 15 a substantial majority of delegates, including America's ambassador to Britain, nominated Hoover on the first ballot.[24]

The last major convention issue was the choice of Hoover's running mate, and here the New York delegation pushed hard for Houghton. The ambassador was an attractive candidate. Among other things, he could balance the ticket geographically (Hoover hailed from California), draw the support of German-Americans, and help to carry the critical state of New York over the Democrats' front-runner, Al Smith. However, Senator Reed Smoot (R-UT) lobbied for former Massachusetts governor Channing H. Cox. When this idea was blocked, Smoot opted not for Houghton, but for a Senate colleague, majority leader Charles Curtis of Kansas. Curtis appeared a smart choice. He enjoyed considerable support in the Midwest and could serve as a sop to farmers. The Kansan ultimately prevailed, and evidence suggests that Hoover representatives had broached the issue with Curtis long before the convention. There were, of course, legitimate reasons for Hoover not to want Houghton, an avid Lowden supporter and a known critic of the commerce secretary's foreign policy. But there was another problem. Earlier in his life, Hoover had lived in England, and his Anglophobic critics had begun to snipe at him as "Sir Herbert." As a result, the nominee needed political distance from Britain, which did not help the ambassador's chances. Castle, who attended the convention, touched on this aspect of the ambassador's possible nomination: "At one stage of the game it looked very much as though Houghton would be the nominee for Vice President. He seemed pretty nearly ideal as he came from New York, had the up-state vote, and would get all the German vote. But someone suggested that with Hoover having a 'British taint' it would be hopeless to appoint as his running mate the Ambassador to Great Britain. That was hard luck."[25]

Having failed to win Houghton's nomination as vice president, New York Republican leaders immediately discussed his running for the Senate. According to the *New York Times*, the ambassador was receptive to the idea, although, if elected, he wanted "some assurance" that he would be seated on the Foreign Relations Committee. The newspaper also speculated that Hoover's supporters in the state, including Treasury Undersecretary Mills, might oppose Houghton's candidacy. Such opposition appeared unlikely, however, after the envoy met with Mills and Hoover in Washington on June 21. Houghton remained in the United States for the next eight weeks, dividing his time between the capital, Corning, New York City, and New Bedford, Massachusetts. During that time, the pressure increased for him to make the Senate bid. He reviewed the circumstances in a letter to an old friend: "I was slated, I believe, for V.P. at Kansas City, but owing to the disturbances in the West, it seemed wise to put the nomination out there," and "now I find myself the apparent choice for Senator from New York. I am told it will be easy and that I can go back to England and return for three weeks campaigning . . . but I hesitate very much to take on a new job." Houghton also thought that party leaders were overly optimistic, and that a "horrid political fight" lay ahead in New York. By late July, reports continued that the ambassador held the lead in the Senate nomination race. Castle encouraged him to take the political plunge, reminding him of the material influence he would wield on the Foreign Relations Committee. Before Houghton sailed for London on August 18, he notified Hilles and others that he would not be a candidate for the Senate, but he never ruled out the possibility of being drafted.[26]

While Houghton was in America, significant progress had been made on the multilateral antiwar pact. In mid-June, France, with Britain's support, suggested that the United States add to the preamble statements that the new accord did not run counter to any existing treaties and that its signatories would be automatically released from their treaty obligation in case of its breach. Kellogg immediately revised the American treaty. The new preamble addressed the second issue by denying the benefits of the treaty to any violator, and it also listed among the treaty's participants fifteen nations, including all of the Locarno powers, India, and the British Dominions. Kellogg distributed the new draft to the various countries on June 23 and, to protect the sanctity of all existing treaties, he included a separate note that summarized his April 28 speech. He refused to make any further revisions.

The French and British reacted cautiously. They organized a secret meeting with German officials in Berlin to discuss the legal implications of the treaty. Several weeks later, Germany broke the diplomatic ice by accepting the revised American accord. Not wanting to be overshadowed by its former enemy, France followed suit. The French specified their interpretation that the treaty did not forbid self-defense or jeopardize existing obligations. Paris did not, however, demand that the pact be formally amended. Italy and other nations quickly fell into line. Britain's approval arrived in

Washington on July 18. Its declarations mirrored France's, but also added that the treaty did not infringe upon Britain's right to defend regions vital to the Empire's security. Japan accepted two days later. American leaders dismissed the side-interpretations by the other powers because they were omitted from the official treaty text. Kellogg was elated. Houghton was encouraged, too. He reassured skeptical friends, reminding them to interpret the treaty not as a panacea, but rather as "only a first step" toward better international relations.[27]

Although the antiwar pact had been consummated by the time Houghton returned to England in late August, yet another crisis threatened Anglo-American relations. Five months earlier, the British had initiated secret arms-control negotiations with France. The Baldwin government hoped to break the disarmament deadlock, to limit America's construction of large cruisers fitted with 8-inch caliber guns, and to prevent a separate Franco-American entente. Chamberlain even expressed fear that, if progress were not achieved on arms control, Germany might repudiate the disarmament provisions of Versailles and jeopardize world peace. By July 28, London and Paris had reached a compromise whereby the French accepted the British principle of limiting warships with 8-inch guns, but not the cruisers with 6-inch guns preferred by the Royal Navy. The British, in turn, agreed not to include France's large contingent of reserve soldiers under any cap placed on land forces. They also decided that small submarines (under 600 tons) should not be regulated. The agreement essentially condoned Britain's mastery of the seas and France's dominance of the European continent. Two days later, the British issued a partial copy of the Anglo-French compromise to Italy, Japan, and the United States, asking them to accept the accord as a basis for restarting arms-control negotiations. Hoping to reach consensus on the naval formula first, the British communiqué deceptively excluded all references to the agreement favoring France's reserve army.

News of the secret Anglo-French compromise landed like a bombshell on the State Department, and there was little chance that the United States would accept it. Hostility toward the compromise spread rapidly in the States, especially among Anglophobes and large-navy advocates. No one appeared more upset by the secret dealings than Coolidge, who already blamed London for the failure of his 1927 conference. In Houghton's absence, Ray Atherton, the embassy counselor in London, met several times with British officials to clarify the principles embedded in the Anglo-French negotiations. From these meetings, Washington learned of the hidden counteragreement regarding land-based army reserves, which only fueled administration resentment. The Foreign Office was informed on August 9 that the United States wanted time to study the proposal in full, but that under no conditions would it accede to restrictions on warships with 8-inch guns without limitations on small cruisers bearing 6-inch guns.

When Houghton reached his post in late August, he and Atherton exchanged notes on the situations in Washington and London. The ambassador learned that knowledge of the Anglo-French compromise had also sparked sharp opposition within Britain, and he noted how criticism grew when the Baldwin government failed to justify its secret negotiations with France. The ambassador considered the Anglo-French agreement misguided, believing that substantive progress on arms control could not be attained until after the upcoming elections in the United States and Britain. This proved to be the case, for an Anglo-American compromise on the divisive cruiser issue was not reached until the 1930 London Conference. In the interim, Houghton felt compelled to support a U.S. naval construction program to increase the country's leverage in future negotiations and to dispel speculation that such talk had been a diplomatic bluff. The Foreign Office sensed that an anti-British wave had washed over the U.S. embassy, and some officials complained that American staffers shared their discontent too freely with the London press corps.

The ambassador made his position clear on September 5 in a meeting with Acting Foreign Secretary Sir Ronald Lindsay, who was substituting for an extremely ill Chamberlain. Houghton applauded the Anglo-French compromise as a "bona fide effort" to bring about arms control, but he argued that it had no chance of wider acceptance and, therefore, must "die a natural death." Though Lindsay would not admit the failure of the Anglo-French initiative, Houghton knew that Coolidge would quash it. The day after his meeting with Lindsay, the envoy told Parker Gilbert that the Anglo-French compromise and the fervor over it amounted to a "molehill . . . made into a mountain. Nothing has really happened, nothing has taken place, nothing is going to take place." He repeated this to Kellogg on September 12, and soon after delivered to the Foreign Office Coolidge's rejection of the proposal. Anglo-American relations had plunged to new depths.[28]

Behind these diplomatic machinations loomed the tumult of American politics, and Houghton seemed content to be thousands of miles away. He confided to Ambassador Henry Fletcher that his Senate nomination had been "assured" to him by Republican party officials, and that he probably could defeat the incumbent Copeland in the November election. "But the job," Houghton continued, "has no attraction for me, and my remaining ambition is to complete my work here as well as I can and then retire decently and quietly into the obscurity from which I came." Despite such reticence, Republican leaders did not want the ambassador to slip away so easily. Hoover made a special appeal, through Castle, for Houghton to enter the New York race on the grounds that it would "greatly strengthen the national ticket." The ambassador continued to deny his candidacy, telling Gilbert that a senatorship at this time in his life appeared less as "an ambition to be gratified," and more like "a six year sentence." But Houghton adjusted his outlook in late September when he learned that his draft by the party was probable. In a message to Theodore Roosevelt Jr., who would soon attend the New York convention, the ambassador expressed his hope that an alternative candidate could be found. He admitted that he would acquiesce if nominated, but also that he would enter the campaign with the "same feelings that a horse approaches a bass-drum."[29]

Hilles, the Republican National Committee vice chairman, and George K. Morris, the New York State party chair, had begun the drive for Houghton's nomination after the Kansas City convention. But Morris's sudden death threatened to derail the movement. Moreover, word leaked to the press that opposition to Houghton was building, and the newly elected state chairman, H. Edmund Machold, declared the Senate nomination wide open. Nevertheless, on the eve of the state convention at Syracuse, the ambassador remained the front-runner, and by then he had Machold's endorsement. On September 28, George R. Fearon, a state senator with larger ambitions, led a floor fight against his nomination. Fearon, with a small upstate bloc supporting him, argued that Houghton, "good man though he is," would not be able to win the election because he lacked the "hard hitting" attack style necessary to dislodge the Democratic incumbent. In other words, he was too aloof, too well-heeled, too "ambassadorial" to be an effective campaigner. The argument failed to move many delegates, and Houghton won a landslide victory, defeating Fearon 911 to 119. The press concluded accurately that the nomination represented more of a triumph for Hilles and Machold than for the nominee himself.[30]

Hoover was "much pleased" by the development, believing that Houghton could help the national ticket carry New York and possibly contribute in other states as he had done for Coolidge in 1924. Hoover's positive outlook was dampened, however, when word reached Washington that Houghton had no intention of waging a drawn-out campaign. Hoover telephoned Castle and authorized him to cable the ambassador the message: "Your assistance to the National Ticket in New York is essential and greatly important among German voters everywhere . . . [hope] you will return as soon as possible and take a vigorous part in the campaign." Houghton informed Castle that he would sail for America on October 5 and asked him to assure Hoover of his "earnest desire" to help the party. Houghton considered the Senate bid the "last hurrah" in his career as a public servant. The day before he departed London, he wrote that he had been "caught up in the political whirlwind" and that he approached the "turmoil" at home with considerable apprehension. "The only comfort," he continued, was that the campaign "will be short and that even if I am licked, which is well within the bounds of possibility, I shall be able to return to my former plan to go home as a private citizen."[31]

If Houghton harbored any hope of enjoying a calm voyage before the political storm, it was dashed quickly. The *Mauritania* encountered nasty winter weather during its six-day crossing. The roller-coaster effect resulted in an unpleasant journey for all aboard and served as a harbinger of the ambassador's senatorial candidacy. On October 12, two days after his sixty-fifth birthday, the ship finally docked in New York Harbor. At the moment Houghton came ashore, a brass band struck up "Hail to the Chief," and dignitaries, friends, and reporters mobbed him. After a round of hand-shaking and picture-taking, he was whisked by automobile to the Weylin Hotel, where he disappeared into conferences with political advisers.

For better or worse, Houghton allowed the professional politicians Hilles and Machold to plot his campaign strategy. All agreed that he should avoid a mudslinging contest and take the high road. The ambassador would essentially ignore his opponent, just as he had done a decade earlier in his first congressional race. In 1928 the barnstorming would be carefully calibrated. Plans were laid for a moderately paced speaking tour of large urban areas. The support of New York's rural districts would be taken for granted, although most of the speeches were to be "radioed" across the land. His addresses would embrace the Coolidge-Hoover record and the party's Kansas City platform, especially the foreign policy plank of pursuing world peace. The specific issues of Prohibition enforcement and immigration restriction were to be treated gingerly so as not to arouse ethnic-group opposition.

Houghton left Manhattan for a series of meetings, interviews, and speeches upstate. His arrival at the train depot in Corning created a hubbub unmatched since the Armistice. More than 6,000 people cheered for their "most distinguished as well as beloved citizen," while five bands sounded off in the background. The local fervor was maintained during the next few days when other celebrities visited Steuben County, including campaign-stumper Franklin D. Roosevelt, the Democrats' candidate for governor, and baseball sluggers Lou Gehrig and Babe Ruth, who squared off in an exhibition game. Ruth and Gehrig supported the Democratic party.[32]

Houghton's first major address, titled "Protection, Power, and Prosperity," was broadcast live by WABC and WGY. He praised Hoover and, as planned, dedicated himself to Coolidge's policies and the GOP platform. He singled out Republican tariff policy as a primary reason for the country's general prosperity and also its value as a guard against unfair labor competition. He did, however, make clear his position that current tariff schedules needed to be revised to meet changed world conditions and that Americans should not fear either downward or upward tariff adjustments on particular products. Houghton informed his audience that seven years of diplomatic experience had taught him much regarding the world political economy. It had given him an improved understanding of America's new position and responsibilities as a dominant power. The United States must avoid "direct participation" in foreign "political systems," but the country could not remain isolated; it "must inevitably" assume a leading role in world affairs. The *New York Times* followed the speech with a perceptive editorial focusing on the tariff. In short, the newspaper read into the ambassador's address a recognition that certain tariffs should be reduced to stimulate world trade, but even enlightened Republican candidates such as Houghton could not risk any specific declaration against the party line of high tariffs, "no matter what they think in their hearts."[33]

After spending a week upstate, the ambassador went to New York City to participate in a massive rally for Hoover at Madison Square Garden. While there, his Senate candidacy took a sudden and risky turn. Hoover arranged a conference at the Waldorf Hotel and asked Houghton to leave his own campaign to make speeches

Republican Candidate

FOR

United States Senator

ALANSON B. HOUGHTON

Courtesy of the Houghton Family and Corning Incorporated

on behalf of the presidential ticket. Specifically, he wanted the ambassador to tour St. Louis and Milwaukee to "keep the so-called
German vote in line." The Republicans viewed Missouri and Wisconsin as vulnerable to the Democratic party because the "wet"
Smith had already made "big inroads" with the Prohibition issue.
The Republican leadership believed Houghton could make a difference with the substantial German–American population by du-
plicating his performance in 1924 against Senator Robert La Follette.
Houghton did not think it wise to abandon, even if only temporarily,
his abbreviated Senate campaign, nor did he believe the national

political situation was analogous to that of 1924. Nevertheless, feeling an obligation to his party and his confident New York handlers, the ambassador agreed to go west for several days. His speeches celebrated Hoover's management of food relief for Germany immediately following the Armistice. He vividly recalled for his audiences the postwar threat to Germany's children, and he hailed the presidential nominee as the "greatest single human force" that had acted to save them.[34]

Houghton finally returned to New York State on October 28. He restoked his campaign in Rochester and returned to Corning before the final push. His candidacy had benefited from many endorsers, including foreign affairs journalist Frank H. Simonds, banker Fred I. Kent, publisher Oswald Garrison Villard, Vice President Dawes, former governor Lowden, and Republican elder statesman Elihu Root, who served as honorary chairman of Houghton's campaign. With the exception of Lowden, who lauded Houghton's understanding of farm problems, the others emphasized his successful diplomatic career and its potential value in the Senate. Villard, a progressive Democrat, published multiple endorsements in *The Nation*, which testified to Houghton's status as an international statesman who recognized that the "worship of tariffs can be extremely dangerous to the world." Villard's editorials were widely reprinted in the New York press, and he also engaged in an active letter-writing campaign among prominent Democrats, including publisher Herbert D. Croly and editor Kirby Page of *The World Tomorrow*. Page responded favorably, telling Villard that he backed Houghton enthusiastically. The ambassador also received support from several large Democratic newspapers, including the *New York World* and the *Syracuse Herald*. Many Democrats, however, failed to understand Villard's fervor for a conservative business candidate who opposed labor organization and collective bargaining at his own glass factories. Villard argued simply that Houghton's progressive approach to international affairs was vastly more important.[35]

During the final week of the campaign, Houghton formally resigned his ambassadorship. This brought forth endorsements from Coolidge and Kellogg, and they were immediately released to the press. "My dear Mr. Houghton," the president's letter read:

> I need not tell you how much I shall feel the loss of your services in that very important post, even though it is to be followed by a continuation of your public life in the Senatorship of the State of

New York. You were our first Ambassador to Germany after the war, where your discretion and ability represented with such fidelity the attitude of our Government, which soon gained for you the entire confidence of that country and did so much to reestablish our friendly relations. Your influence there was of great importance in restoring a spirit of peace throughout Europe. Because of that splendid record, I asked you to take the more burdensome post at London, where your success has been equally marked. The sacrifices you have made in serving your country have been very great. Those of us who are most familiar with them place the highest value on them.

Such praise contrasted with the president's tepid backing of Hoover, a distinction that did not go unnoticed in the New York press.[36]

If the GOP presidential nominee could not depend on Coolidge for active support, he found that he could rely on Houghton. To the great satisfaction of the national ticket, the ambassador dedicated two additional speeches to Hoover's German relief efforts, one at Buffalo and another at New York City in Carnegie Hall. In between, Houghton delivered his last major policy address, which focused on international relations. The ambassador underscored two fundamental conditions of the New Era that made the preservation of peace imperative. Both had resulted from technological progress. First, the revolutions in transportation and communications had "shrunk" the globe to "a mere fraction of its former size" and had integrated and complicated the economies and societies of the world. As a result, any major upheavals in the future, he suggested, would have serious global repercussions. Second, recent developments in weaponry rendered this increased integration even more significant. The awesome power of industrial armaments, he continued, had not only made modern warfare a "profitless" undertaking, but also threatened the ruin of human civilization. To contemplate the destruction of another world war only "staggers the imagination," because the "search for new and more effective methods of destroying lives and property proceeds unwearied." Americans, therefore, needed to recognize these changed conditions and actively promote international agreements such as the Dawes Plan, the Locarno Treaties, and the Kellogg–Briand Pact, as they all were devised to make war less likely. Houghton concluded by expressing his ongoing support for war referendums and arms-control agreements.[37]

Following his final appearance in Buffalo, Houghton returned to Corning. In public, he expressed confidence that he and Hoover would carry New York by a wide margin. Since June, he had predicted that Hoover would win a national landslide over Smith. On election eve, Houghton confided that his own chances for the Senate were probably closer to even. He described his involvement in the local and national campaigns as being "whirled around in a political cyclone" and told a friend that he really could not predict "whether it will land me in the middle of the Atlantic or in the Senate in Washington." Several of the ambassador's longtime supporters believed that party leaders had acted far too confidently regarding Houghton's election and had failed to wage a sufficiently aggressive campaign. In October, Chandler P. Anderson Sr. expressed his fear that the party was "relaxing" when it should be publicizing Houghton's many accomplishments. Party officials responded with assurances of Houghton's election. For his part, the ambassador claimed that he had had little choice but to place his fate in the hands of the "political experts."[38]

Houghton monitored the election results from his hilltop home, "The Knoll." The morning rain heightened the suspense. After 6:30 P.M., the makeshift telegraph hook-up in the billiards room began to spit out dispatches. The Senate returns fluctuated from good to bad. Hoover, however, appeared to be on the road to a major national victory. As midnight approached, an optimistic party official telephoned from New York City, encouraging the candidate to stay awake for the late returns. By 2:15 A.M., with Copeland ahead by 100,000 votes, Houghton retired. According to the next morning's newspapers, Hoover had won the presidency while the ambassador appeared to have lost his Senate bid. With nearly a quarter of the districts still unaccounted for, some hope persisted as Houghton boarded a train for the city. When he arrived there, he learned that he had closed the gap significantly—but not enough to carry the day. More than 4 million people went to the polls; he lost by 50,259 votes. Franklin D. Roosevelt won the governorship by only 25,564 votes.

More surprising than Houghton's defeat was Hoover's victory over Smith in the governor's home state. At best, most politicos expected the commerce secretary to run even with the ambassador. How was it possible that Houghton did not ride on the coattails of Hoover's sudden popularity in New York? At least a few eyebrows were raised when voting records revealed the mystery that Senator Copeland had managed to outperform favorite son Smith in New York City. Had Tammany Hall somehow "arranged" for Houghton's defeat? There was no investigation. A week after the election, the

Houghtons attended a small dinner party at the Vanderbilt mansion in the city. Among the guests were Vice President Dawes and Owen Young. Afterward, Adelaide Houghton noted in her diary that "everyone regrets Alan's defeat more than he and I do."[39]

The ambassador's immediate future was never in doubt. Coolidge wanted him back in London. Houghton lunched at the White House on November 9 and departed five days later aboard the *Leviathan*. By that time, speculation as to the makeup of Hoover's cabinet had already surged. Houghton's name arose immediately as a leading candidate for secretary of state. The ambassador's political handlers in New York, embarrassed by his election defeat, promised to do everything possible to ensure his appointment as secretary. The idea was supported by former Undersecretary Olds, who had recently left the State Department to join the international law firm of Sullivan & Cromwell (just as Allen Dulles had done the year before). Olds was quick to remind Houghton that Kellogg had once lost a bid for the Senate and then became secretary of state after serving as ambassador to Great Britain. "We men of the law," Olds instructed his friend, "have an instinctive respect for the sanctity of precedent." Hoover would not announce his selection until February.[40]

As had happened so often during the previous four years, strained Anglo-American relations greeted the ambassador upon his return to London. Americans were still angry with the British for negotiating a secret arms compromise with France. Suspicions of British naval policy grew when the Foreign Office refused to publish the diplomatic exchanges leading to the agreement. Moreover, the State Department had begun to express frustration with Baldwin's failure to respond to the administration's year-old proposal for a new arbitration treaty. In an Armistice Day speech, Coolidge fanned the flames by attacking the British disarmament policy and by renewing his support for the naval construction bill. An arms race seemed in the offing, and in Britain, Baldwin's opponents in Parliament moved swiftly to blame the Conservative government for souring relations with America.

Houghton adopted a wait-and-see attitude. On November 22, just two days after his return, he appeared as a keynote speaker at the annual Newsvendor Association Dinner. Most of his audience expected a reassuring discourse on the solidity of U.S.–British relations, but he spoke instead on the wonders of the radio as a revolutionary political tool. After the address, Nancy, Lady Astor, the hostess, gently reproached her friend for speaking on the lesser issue of the radio when he, as someone who had "done more for peace than about any living man," should have tackled pressing foreign policy issues. The next day, the Houghtons lunched with the Astors and British playwright George Bernard Shaw. While Shaw proved "the lion of the occasion," the ambassador was visibly upset with his hostess for her mild rebuke at the dinner. "Old Grump," Lady Astor told Mrs. Houghton, "I didn't say a word that wasn't true, damn him; he has done more for peace than almost anyone, and you know it."[41]

The ambassador's reluctance to speak out is easily explained. After nearly four years in London, he had grown all too accustomed to the tension in U.S.–British relations, and he had come to accept that the mere passage of time was often sufficient to extinguish the flare-ups. War between the countries was unimaginable, and he believed that Anglo-American differences over naval arms and the critical issue of belligerent rights would be resolved satisfactorily after the Senate passed a navy construction bill, after Hoover's inauguration in March, and after the British elections in May. "While there is a good deal of bitterness and a good deal of unrest," he wrote to Castle, "I do not believe that at bottom there is any reason to fear a serious difference of opinion between our two peoples. . . . I doubt if an agreement between the two peoples is now possible until we have built our fifteen cruisers or at least built enough of them to show we are in earnest. Then I have no doubt that a new agreement will be possible. That will be one of the big problems for the next administration to solve. It would be idle, it seems to me, to try to solve it now."

This is not to say that Houghton had no opinion on how the Hoover administration could best manage the problems of Anglo-American relations. Drawing lessons from the failed 1927 arms conference and the many inconsequential sessions of the League's preparatory commission, Houghton advocated direct and confidential negotiations between U.S. and British representatives—and the fewer admirals that participated, the better. He staunchly opposed Senator Borah's call for a multilateral conference to codify maritime law and he vigorously supported Baldwin's expressed desire to visit the Hoover White House, where he could "make a really definite effort to thresh out Anglo-American relations."[42]

Not until his last major speech as ambassador, did Houghton attempt to educate public opinion about the complexities of the bilateral relationship. At his farewell dinner at the Pilgrims' Society, he explained that disagreements between the two nations were "wholly natural," because their national interests were not identical. More disputes were on the horizon, he predicted, and the validity of these differences needed to be appreciated and respected. In the broadest sense, however, British and American economic and political interests were "mutually and increasingly dependent," and peaceful conflict resolution was thus becoming paramount to world stability. The ambassador suggested that meaningful arms control, for example, was within reach, and that the two nations should seize upon the Kellogg–Briand Pact as a "fresh start" in the pursuit of a lasting peace.[43]

Although Houghton believed that substantive improvement in U.S.–British relations would have to wait, progress toward a final settlement of Germany's war reparations could not. Throughout 1928, the reparations agent general, Parker Gilbert, had mounted a steady campaign to revise the Dawes Plan. He wanted to finalize the terms of the reparations, terminate Allied intervention in German economic affairs, precipitate an early evacuation of the Rhineland, force Germany to balance its budget, and enhance generally the certainty of reparations payments. Early in the year, Gilbert found in Houghton, his old Berlin mentor, a reliable supporter and confidant. They met several times, and their private correspondence reflects Houghton's ongoing influence with the German government and Gilbert's disdain for the abilities of Ambassador Jacob Schurman, Houghton's replacement in Berlin. In March 1928, Gilbert dispatched his personal secretary to London to brief the ambassador on strategy and deliver a confidential note. In the written message, he confided that any future agreement on reparations "will depend on . . . the German government . . . [which] will depend very much on the advice it gets from America." Gilbert, having little confidence in Schurman or the German government, declared, "What is needed to turn the decision is what you did so effectively five years ago . . . the crisis will come . . . to meet it I am turning to you."[44]

Gilbert also saw a recalcitrant Baldwin government and certain overzealous British and American journalists in London as obstacles to a new reparations agreement. During the spring, he asked for and received Houghton's assistance in curbing the reporters. Shortly afterward, the ambassador engaged in a round of quiet diplomacy with British, German, and French officials in London. Above all, he tried to ferret out the British position. In addition to courting Foreign Office leaders, he began regular dinner sessions with a new friend, Sir Norman Fenwick Warren Fisher, the permanent secretary to the Treasury. By fall, he had impressed upon the diplomatic community the absolute importance of Gilbert's initiative. For example, he instructed Britain's acting foreign secretary, Sir Ronald Lindsay, that until a final settlement is reached, "no real peace could exist in Europe." Before the ambassador had departed London for his ill-fated senatorial campaign, he concluded that the British, although "not keen for a final settlement," would eventually submit since Gilbert had already secured French support.[45]

The ambassador's prediction proved accurate, and Germany and the Allies agreed to organize a new experts' committee to settle the reparations issue permanently. A month after Houghton returned from his failed campaign, Coolidge announced his support for America's unofficial participation on a second reparations commission. With Houghton and Gilbert's hearty approval, the president selected Owen Young as one of two representatives for the United States. Young risked giving the president a "big political shock" by demanding that he be paired with J. P. Morgan Jr. Young reminded Coolidge that he had been through the reparations process once before and declared that he "won't again have the big bankers on the back row looking on and criticizing." Coolidge consented, and he also allowed Morgan partner Thomas Lamont and Houghton's Boston attorney friend Thomas Nelson Perkins to join the delegation as alternates.[46]

The international experts' committee began its work in Paris during early February and appointed Young chairman. About the same time, speculation over Hoover's nominee for secretary of state peaked. Despite continuing encouragement from friends such as Castle, Olds, and Shotwell, Houghton's position as a front-runner had been eclipsed. On February 5 word circulated that Hoover had selected Henry Lewis Stimson, a former secretary of war and the former governor general of the Philippine Islands. Because Houghton had already informed Hoover that he had no desire to remain as ambassador, he began planning for retirement.

During his last two months in London, Houghton actively supported Young's reparations initiatives. Olds encouraged the ambassador to continue his "constructive statesmanship," because "minds like yours, which habitually in times of stress maintain a balanced perspective," were needed to solve the knotty problem. Houghton renewed his regular sessions with Secretary Fisher and continued them until he departed. The envoy had little doubt that Young's committee would reach a satisfactory compromise, but he regretted that it would not be realized during his tenure as America's chief diplomat. "The Reparations question," he reminded friends, "has always been one of my special interests," and "I do wish . . . a satisfactory solution could have been reached before this." Houghton vacated Princess Gate on March 28. Before returning Stateside, the ambassador "took the cure" for several weeks at his favorite spa in Baden-Baden, Germany. Thereafter, at Young's request, he spent a week in Paris sharing his views on the work of the reparations committee. Houghton traveled next to Cherbourg and, on April 27, boarded the *Aquitania* for New York. He had landed at Cherbourg seven years earlier en route to Berlin. With Houghton nearly sixty-six years old, his illustrious diplomatic career had reached an anticlimactic end.[47]

Houghton had spent his final year much as he had the previous six, working to promote active and responsible American leadership in world affairs. His efforts on behalf of the Kellogg-Briand Pact were significant. He considered the antiwar treaty, which eventually included dozens of signatories, a signal achievement toward peace and cooperation. The treaty's immense popularity symbolized a widespread desire to solve postwar conflicts peaceably. More important to Houghton, America's vigorous management of the accord had been broadly supported by the U.S. public, and he hoped that this accomplishment would encourage the nation's further involvement in international politics. He was equally supportive of unofficial American efforts, through Gilbert and Young, to formulate a final settlement of the war reparations imbroglio that had retarded European rehabilitation for nearly a decade. Only weeks after the ambassador had departed France, the framework for the Young Plan, which lowered Germany's obligations and created a new international bank to manage payments and promote trade, had been finalized. It soon superseded the Dawes Plan.

Houghton had proven less than successful in his political attempts to influence the conservative nature of American internationalism. Above all, he hoped that the next president would recognize Europe's vital importance to the United States and, through more active leadership, devise innovative policies to address international problems. He judged that Hoover did not fit this bill. The ambassador attended the 1928 Republican convention with the purpose of preventing Hoover's nomination and uniting the party behind a compromise candidate. But this scheme foundered when no alternative surfaced who could successfully rally the anti-Hoover factions. A few months later, the opportunity arose for Houghton to affect policy through the U.S. Senate. Though he took his senatorial campaign seriously, he and his handlers misjudged the electorate and waged a lackluster and ineffective campaign. Furthermore, Houghton's willingness to suspend his campaign for the benefit of the national ticket was a strategic error. But in doing so, he had ingratiated himself with Hoover and perhaps increased his chances for being named the next secretary of state. Nevertheless, that post was not to be his, and the ambassador retired rather than remain at the London embassy. Dawes, the outgoing U.S. vice president, took his vacant chair at Princess Gate.

Notes

1. Shotwell to Houghton, May 21, 1927, Houghton Papers.

2. Perkins to Houghton, April 25, 1927, and Houghton to Perkins, May 6, 1927, ibid.

3. Houghton, "Harvard Speech," June 23, 1927, ibid.

4. Ibid.

5. "To Put Wars to a Vote," *Literary Digest* 94 (July 16, 1927): 8–9; Charles A. Beard, "Recent Gains in Government," *The World Tomorrow* 10 (November 1927): 438–42; and "Another Vote for Peace," ibid. (August 1927): 324; "Ambassador Houghton Tells Some More Truths," *The Nation* 125 (July 13, 1927): 32; *Congressional Record*, 70th Cong., 1st sess., 1046–48; Houghton, "The Power of the People," *Goodwill: A Review of International Christian Friendship, Life, and Work* 3 (1928): 20–23; Houghton, "War? Let the People Decide!" *Federal Council Bulletin* 10 (September 1927): 9–10; W. Brooke Graves, ed., *Readings in Public Opinion: Its Formation and Control* (New York, 1928).

6. Kellogg to Coolidge, June 27, 1927, and Coolidge to Kellogg, June 29, 1927, *FRUS, 1927*, 2:619–21; Robert H. Ferrell, *Peace in Their Time: The Origins of the Kellogg-Briand Pact* (New Haven, CT, 1952), 264.

7. Paul Claudel to Kellogg, January 5, 1928, *FRUS, 1928*, 1:1–2.

8. Kellogg to Ray Atherton, December 28, 1927, *FRUS, 1927*, 2:628; Howard to Chamberlain, December 30, 1927, *DBFP* 4:480–82.

9. Houghton to Castle, January 31, 1928, and Houghton to Shotwell, February 24, 1928, Houghton Papers.

10. Houghton to Olds, March 1, 1928, Houghton to John H. Finley, March 2, 1928, and Houghton to Isaac Siegel, April 5, 1928, ibid.

11. Chamberlain to Howard, April 26, 1928, FO 371/12790/a2845/1/45, PRO.

12. Houghton to Kellogg, April 27, 1928, NARG59, File 711.4112anti-war/17; ABH Diary, April 25–27, 1928.

13. Kellogg to Houghton, April 30, 1928, NARG59, File 711.4112anti-war/19; ABH Diary, April 28, 1928.

14. Chamberlain to Howard, May 3, 1928, FO 371/12791/a2978/1/45, PRO; Houghton to Kellogg, April 30 and May 3, 1928, NARG59, Files 711.4112anti-war/51, 20, 29.

15. Houghton to Castle, May 15, 1928, Castle Papers.

16. Olds to Houghton, May 4, 1928, Houghton Papers; Houghton to Kellogg, May 7, 1928, NARG59, File 711.4112anti-war/42.

17. Houghton to Castle, May 15, 1928, Castle Papers; Houghton to Kellogg, May 9, 1928, NARG59, File 711.4112anti-war/50.

18. Kellogg to Houghton, May 16, 1928, NARG59, File 711.4112anti-war/72.

19. Houghton to Kellogg, May 25, 1928, *FRUS, 1928*, 1:72–74; Castle Diary, June 4, 1928.

20. Houghton to William C. Boyden, April 17, 1928, and Houghton to John W. Dwight, February 20, 1926, Houghton Papers.

21. Ogden Mills to Houghton, February 7, 1928, ibid.

22. Ferrell, *Presidency of Calvin Coolidge*, 195; Leroy T. Vernon to Houghton, February 23, 1928, Houghton Papers.

23. Houghton to William C. Boyden, April 17, 1928, Houghton Papers.

24. Robert J. Rusnak, "Andrew Mellon, Reluctant Kingmaker," *Presidential Studies Quarterly* 13 (Spring 1983): 269–78; Lowden to Houghton, reprinted in the *Elmira Advertiser* (NY), October 26, 1928.

25. Herbert Hoover, *The Memoirs of Herbert Hoover: The Cabinet and the Presidency, 1920–1933* (New York, 1951), 192; Castle Diary, June 17(?), 1928.

26. *New York Times*, June 17, 1928; Houghton to Ward W. Willets, June 21, 1928, Houghton Papers.

27. Houghton to Oswald G. Villard, June 9, 1928, Houghton Papers.

28. Houghton to Gilbert, September 6, 1928, ibid.

29. Houghton to Henry P. Fletcher, August 30, 1928, ibid.; Castle to Houghton, August 31, 1928, Castle Papers; Houghton to Gilbert, September 5, 1928, and Houghton to Theodore Roosevelt Jr., September 26, 1928, Houghton Papers.

30. *New York Times*, September 28–30, 1928.

31. ABH Diary, October 1, 1928; Houghton to E. E. Norris, October 5, 1928, Houghton Papers.

32. *Elmira Advertiser* (NY), October 15, 1928.

33. Houghton, "Protection, Peace, and Prosperity" (speech), Houghton Papers; *New York Times*, October 22, 1928.

34. *New York Times*, October 23 and 27, 1928.

35. "One Political Event . . . ," *The Nation* 127 (October 10, 1928): 332; "Roosevelt and Houghton," ibid. (October 17, 1927): 389; "To Our Readers . . . ," ibid. (October 31, 1928): 437.

36. Coolidge to Houghton, October 31, 1928, Houghton Papers.

37. Houghton, "Campaign Speeches," ibid.

38. Houghton to Lt. Col. Kenyon A. Joyce, November 3, 1928, Chandler P. Anderson to Houghton, November 3, 1928, and Houghton to Anderson, November 5, 1928, ibid.

39. Adelaide Houghton Diary, November 11, 1928, 235.

40. Olds to Houghton, November 15, 1928, Houghton Papers.

41. Adelaide Houghton Diary, November 22–23, 1928, 236–37.

42. Houghton to Castle, December 17, 1928, Houghton Papers.

43. Houghton, "Pilgrims' Dinner" (speech), March 26, 1929, ibid.

44. Gilbert to Houghton, March 6, 1928, ibid.

45. Houghton to Gilbert, September 6 and 21, 1928, ibid.

46. Adelaide Houghton Diary, March 13, 1929, 263.

47. Olds to Houghton, November 15, 1928, and Houghton to Ogden L. Mills, December 5, 1928, Houghton Papers.

8

Epilogue/Conclusion

Mr. Houghton won universal recognition for his wise knowledge, his tact and his unfailing desire to further the cause of peace and international friendship. His success stands on record as one of the most outstanding in modern diplomatic history.
—Franklin D. Roosevelt, 1930

I have no panacea to offer you. There is none. A durable peace . . . is possible, I am sure, only when the half dozen dominating peoples . . . are prepared to insist on the peaceful settlement of their disputes.
—Alanson B. Houghton, 1932

[Alanson Houghton was] a really great American and one of the wisest and most farsighted statesmen I have ever encountered . . . his influence was always used to promote cooperation and forbearance between the nations. Unfortunately, forces of dissolution were developing which no enlightened diplomacy could check.
—Oswald Garrison Villard, 1941

Ambassador Houghton returned to the United States in May 1929, and his diplomatic service was formally celebrated the next year at a grand dinner at the Hotel Commodore in Manhattan. Among the speakers extolling his accomplishments were the German, French, and Italian ambassadors and the British general counsel. F. W. von Prittwitz, the German envoy, declared that Houghton played a crucial role in "the history of Germany's reconstruction" and "his name will, therefore, always stand foremost in our memory." James W. Gerard, the American ambassador who had been recalled from Germany in

1917, also spoke. He called Houghton's successive achievements in Berlin and London "unexampled in the history of U.S. diplomacy." Dinner organizers included in the printed program and distributed to reporters copies of laudatory telegrams sent by American and European dignitaries, including President Hoover, former president Coolidge, former secretary of state Hughes, Governor Franklin D. Roosevelt, Dwight Morrow, Charles Dawes, General John J. Pershing, Sir Austen Chamberlain, Lord Robert Cecil, and Reichsbank president Hjalmar Schacht. The *New York Times* approved of the affair, concluding that Houghton "was deservedly praised for the high order of his diplomatic work in Berlin and London."[1]

In retirement, Houghton and his wife enjoyed full and active lives. Their living arrangements assumed a pattern, with the ambassador's personal routine including walking, golf, reading, and yachting. During the winter, the Houghtons lived in Washington, DC, in a thirty-room mansion they had built on Embassy Row (later to become the Iranian Embassy), and they frequently visited posh resorts in Virginia, Georgia, and Florida. For one month each spring, they traveled to Baden-Baden and took the cure at Dr. Dengler's sanatorium. During summer and early fall, they relocated to "The Meadows," their sixteen-acre estate on the Massachusetts coast near Buzzards Bay. They returned to Corning several times a year and occasionally went to such exotic places as Hawaii and the West Indies.

Retirement allowed Houghton to devote more attention to religious and educational endeavors. The ambassador had always supported the Episcopal Church, and he again served as a delegate to several General Conventions. He took special interest in the operations and beautification of the National Cathedral in Washington, DC, donating more than $100,000 to it (equivalent to $1.3 million in 2003). As he had before the war, Houghton continued to act as a benefactor of Harvard and as a trustee of Hobart College and St. Stephen's College (now Bard College); and, beginning in 1930, he served one term as president of the Academy of Political Science and became a director of the newly formed, nonpartisan Brookings Institution. Few records of Houghton's involvement with Brookings survive, but economist Harold Moulton, then its president, remarked that Houghton possessed "a greater understanding and deeper appreciation" of his work than any other trustee. The ambassador's "counsel on the Institution's policies and programs was always clear, penetrating, and constructive and was often a decisive influence."[2]

No educational institution dominated the ambassador's thinking more than the new Institute for Advanced Study in Princeton, New Jersey. Houghton was the first chairman of the board of trustees at the institute, which was directed by Abraham Flexner, a renowned education critic. Years earlier, Houghton and Flexner had become fast friends after meeting at the American embassy in Berlin. Flexner's new research institute was "a paradise for scholars," who, while highly paid, were given no responsibilities beyond their pursuit of personal research interests. When the institute opened in 1933, its elite faculty included mathematician Oswald Veblen and the eminent physicist Albert Einstein, who spent the rest of his career there. Houghton served as board president from 1933 until 1941, and during that time oversaw the institute's dramatic expansion, including the creation of its School of Economics and Politics.[3]

Business and economics remained central to Houghton's life throughout the 1930s, especially with the onset of the Great Depression. He served as director of Metropolitan Life Insurance Company and several New York banks, including Paul M. Warburg's International Acceptance Bank. From 1931 to 1933 the ambassador presided over the National Industrial Conference Board (now The Conference Board), a nonpartisan group that organized business forums to discuss pressing economic issues. Naturally, the operation of Corning Glass Works remained a foremost concern for Houghton, who was its controlling shareholder and executive committee chairman. His son, Amory, became president of the family firm in 1930, and the thirty-one-year-old relied heavily upon his father for encouragement and strategic decision-making. The glassworks had been remarkably successful while Houghton was engaged in public service, reporting a net income of $4.7 million in 1929 alone. During the early years of the depression, the company saw sales, profits, and employment fall considerably. Nevertheless, the tenacious Houghtons persevered by underwriting consumer market research programs and product and process research and development, and by expanding through licensing, acquisitions, and joint ventures.

Their commitment to scientific research contributed to the firm's 1935 creation of the 200-inch, 20-ton telescopic reflector for the Mount Palomar Observatory in California. In 1936, Corning acquired Macbeth–Evans, a large Pennsylvania manufacturer of opaque glassware and lamp glass. During the next two years, the firm established two successful joint-venture companies, Pittsburgh–Corning

Alanson B. Houghton with his son Amory, who would become U.S. ambassador to France during the Eisenhower administration. *Courtesy of the Houghton Family and Corning Incorporated*

and Owens–Corning, which manufactured glass blocks and fiber-glass, respectively. By 1937, the economic depression had ended for Corning, as the firm rehired most of its laid-off workers and reported record annual sales along with nearly $3 million in prof-its. In 1940, Alanson gave his son 2,500 shares of company stock valued at $100,000 (approximately $1.3 million in 2003): "I do this because I am proud of the manner you have carried on the family tradition at the Glass Works and assumed the responsibility for the family property. . . . I feel very confident that your achievements in the coming years will bring me even greater satisfaction."[4]

Throughout retirement, Houghton never lost his passion for international affairs, and he happily assumed the role of elder states- man for both the Republican party and the nonaligned American peace movement. He maintained regular contact with GOP stal- warts and Capitol Hill power brokers and conferred with officials at the White House and State Department. He joined the Council on Foreign Relations, was elected to the governing board of the Carnegie Endowment for International Peace and served as its trea- surer for ten years, and chaired the Committee on International Jus- tice and Goodwill for the Federal Council of Churches.

Houghton took full advantage of the numerous speaking requests that came to him from various religious, business, educational, and peace organizations. Shortly after his return from Europe in 1929, the ambassador embarked on a lecture tour for the Foreign Policy Association. He also gave a series of Commencement addresses, receiving honorary doctorates from Syracuse University, Hobart College, the University of Rochester, the University of Wisconsin– Madison, and the Carnegie Institute of Technology (now Carnegie Mellon University). His speeches attracted press attention, and his broad involvement and frequent pronouncements on foreign affairs led the *New York Sun* to dub him America's "diplomat at large."[5]

Houghton's foreign policy views in the 1930s remained consis- tent with the core beliefs he had held as an official diplomat. He believed that the United States had an obligation to lead the world economy and to promote the peaceful resolution of international conflicts. This leadership required close communication and coop- eration among officials in Washington, London, and Berlin, but it could not defer to prearranged military commitments. In economic matters, Houghton continued to emphasize America's relative wealth and the need for the United States to stimulate international trade and investment. He lobbied for the cancellation of both war debts and reparations, and in light of the ongoing depression, he began calling for a substantial reduction in U.S. tariffs, which had been increased with the 1930 Smoot–Hawley Tariff Act. In July 1931, Houghton met with Hoover at the White House to discuss interna- tional debt relief. Houghton left the meeting disappointed, believ- ing that "the net result of the President's proposal will be a wholly inadequate measure of relief." Soon after, Hoover initiated a one- year moratorium on intergovernmental obligations. By 1935, nearly all of the debtor nations had defaulted outright.

Alanson B. Houghton. *Courtesy of the Houghton Family and Corning Incorporated*

On the issue of world peace, Houghton urged the great industrial powers to build upon the successes of the 1920s, most notably
the establishment of the World Court, the Washington Disarmament Conference, the Locarno Treaties, and the Kellogg-Briand Pact.
He clung to his belief that a second world war would prove far
more devastating than the first, given the increasing power of modern weaponry and the integration of the world economy. As one
means for enhancing American leadership and promoting interna-

tional conciliation, Houghton led a national campaign for U.S. entry into the World Court. In speeches, some broadcast via radio, he assailed opponents of the court for believing "that America should hold herself aloof and apart from other nations and live in a sort of splendid isolationism. . . . No, ladies and gentlemen," he stated, "the time has passed, if indeed it ever existed, when we can safely think of America in terms of comparative isolation."[6]

Consistent with his willingness to use U.S. economic power as a foreign policy lever, Houghton sought to supplement and fortify the Kellogg–Briand Pact. He called for a new multilateral treaty that would impose severe economic sanctions on belligerents. To further check the outbreak of war, he continued his populist drives for the war referendum and arms control. The movement in the United States to amend the Constitution by adding a war referendum culminated in 1938, when a House resolution supporting the measure was narrowly defeated, 209 to 188. Meanwhile, the Anglo-American deadlock over arms control was finally broken at the 1930 London Naval Conference, which resulted in a tripartite treaty with Japan. More comprehensive success was anticipated at the upcoming World Disarmament Conference. In November 1931, Houghton, as the representative of the Carnegie Foundation, the Federal Council of Churches, and other U.S. peace groups, traveled to Paris for an unofficial preliminary conference on arms control. The trip was a debacle as French opponents of disarmament disrupted the proceedings being chaired by Edouard Herriot, the former French prime minister. According to news reports, the riotous demonstrations climaxed just minutes before Houghton was to make the keynote address, which he was never able to deliver. This calamity signaled the ultimate fate of all subsequent disarmament conferences of the 1930s.

Two months before Houghton's Paris trip, the Japanese army moved to seize control of Manchuria from China. The aggression was a clear violation of the Washington Conference treaties and the Kellogg–Briand Pact. Houghton urged multilateral economic sanctions against Japan and viewed the League of Nations as the best vehicle for organizing a boycott. Along with prominent American supporters of the League, he signed two open letters encouraging the Hoover administration to coordinate the U.S. reaction with the League's governing council. Hoover criticized Japanese belligerency and consulted with the League; however, the president feared that sanctions might lead to war and settled instead for a policy of not recognizing Japan's conquest. To Houghton's chagrin,

Britain, France, and members of the League did little more than Washington had.

The issue of territorial aggression emerged again in 1935, when Italy invaded Ethiopia. Houghton advocated U.S. economic sanctions consistent with those being imposed by the League. President Roosevelt, guided by recently passed neutrality legislation, implemented an arms embargo on Italy and Ethiopia, but he did not impose an economic boycott, which weakened the effectiveness of the League's action and contributed to French and British appeasement. Houghton assailed the timidity of the U.S. policy in a speech at Philadelphia. He argued that Italy was clearly the aggressor and applauded the League's collective aim to end the conflict and lessen the chance of the war's spreading elsewhere: "No people knows better than we that war anywhere on the earth's surface must sooner or later affect us. . . . A war, once started, may drag into its fiery orbit those who at the beginning seemed far beyond its reach." He cautioned that American foreign policy could not rest solely on the principle of neutrality. "Let us not forget," he warned, "that neutrality does not give us isolation. Isolation we cannot have. It is impossible. And if neutrality . . . involves the right to sell to whoever will buy, bear in mind it does not take us out of the [war] picture. It definitely puts us in. And it puts us in today, not on the side of nations which are striving to safeguard peace but on the side of the nation [Italy] which has broken it."[7]

By the time of Houghton's speech in November 1935, six years into his retirement, Italy's future Fascist ally, Germany, had undergone a comprehensive revolution. The ambassador's annual pilgrimages to Dr. Dengler's health spa in Baden-Baden allowed him an intimate view of the dramatic changes in Germany. In the spring of 1932, with the Nazis becoming increasingly powerful, Houghton reported to his American friends that economic conditions were dismal and unsettling, but that the wisest leaders in Germany still realized that Hitler and the Nazis were incapable of governing the country. Within the next eighteen months, Hitler was named chancellor. He withdrew Germany from the League of Nations and oversaw passage of the Enabling Laws granting him dictatorial powers. Houghton stood "appalled at the situation," and he continued to lament the United States and the Allies' failure in the 1920s to work more cooperatively with the pioneering democratic leaders such as Ebert, Rathenau, Cuno, and Stresemann. Nevertheless, by June 1933, Houghton was surprised by the "high spirits" that seemed to pervade much of German society despite the loss of many civil liberties. "A definite revolution has taken place," he wrote to his close friend, Nicholas Murray Butler, then president of Columbia University. "There is no such thing as freedom of speech . . . there is no freedom of the press . . . the present government stands frankly on force and will use it unhesitatingly . . . to crush any effort to unseat it."

No record survives of Houghton's reflections for the following year, but he did visit the State Department in June 1934 and briefed Secretary of State Cordell Hull on his travels. By the spring of 1935, with most nations still reeling from the depression, Germany's economic revival and political stability amazed and intrigued Houghton. He informed the *New York Times* that economic conditions, especially the level of employment, were surprisingly favorable and that the majority of people appeared to be "enthusiastic" about Hitler's leadership, which had reversed their industrial depression and restored "their self-respect." When asked about the prospect for military conflict in Europe, he answered optimistically and naively. He did not think that Hitler wanted war. Two years later, when he returned from a remilitarizing Germany, he predicted that a war, if it came, would not arrive sooner than 1941.[8]

By the time of Houghton's visit to Germany in 1935, Hitler had completely consolidated his domestic power, and he soon began to maneuver outward. During the next two years, Germany signed a naval accord with Britain, militarized the Rhineland, proclaimed the Rome–Berlin Axis, and aided the Fascist revolution in Spain. In 1938, Hitler and the German army marched into Austria, where they received a warm welcome from much of the German-speaking population. Despite mild protests from France, Britain, and Soviet Russia, Germany's annexation of Austria, the Anschluss, was largely unopposed. Shortly afterward, at the infamous Munich Conference, France, Britain, and Italy condoned Germany's further annexation of the German-speaking portion of Czechoslovakia, the Sudetenland.

Houghton continued to be impressed by Germany's revival, which he had always thought inevitable, and by the apparent contentment of its population. He did regret the treatment of German Jews, which he described as "severe and wholly objectionable from every tolerant or decent point of view." Houghton had many German and American Jewish friends, including Walther Rathenau, financier Paul Warburg, former New York congressman Isaac Siegel, and Abraham Flexner, one of his confidants in retirement. But in awe of Germany's phoenixlike recovery, Houghton convinced himself that the overt acts of anti-Semitism would be short-lived, serving

as interim tactics to bolster Hitler's control of the government.
Moreover, he and many of his American associates, such as Nicholas Murray Butler, the cowinner of the 1931 Nobel Peace Prize,
elected not to criticize the Nazis' heavy hand, because a few Jewish friends had convinced them that "public protest would be most
undesirable" and would only intensify anti-Semitic attacks.
Houghton stubbornly maintained this rationalization throughout
the 1930s, despite Germany's routine and increasingly severe per-
secution of the Jews. By 1939, he publicly admitted that the Nazis
had amassed "a disgusting and disheartening record," but clung
to his belief that vocal opposition to the anti-Semitism would only
make the plight of German Jews "infinitely worse." Thus, instead
of protesting, he chose to give money to Jewish relief organizations,
encouraged his friends to do likewise, and helped some Jewish refugees secure employment in the United States.[9]

Like the American, British, French, and Italian governments,
Houghton supported the policy of appeasing Germany's rearmament and its peaceful expansion into Austria and the Sudetenland.
The ambassador, along with many in the United States and Britain,
had considered the terms of the Versailles Treaty irrationally punitive, especially given the postwar emergence of German democracy. Therefore, Germany's rebound to Great Power status in the
1930s was acceptable, provided that it did not include aggressive
expansion into non–German-speaking regions. Any lofty idea that
Germany's drive to overturn the Versailles Treaty had ended at the
Munich Conference came crashing down in March 1939, when
Hitler invaded Prague and occupied all of Czechoslovakia. Two
weeks after the invasion, Houghton gave a speech in Washington
that recounted, not always unsympathetically, Germany's history
from the Armistice to the Ruhr crisis to the end of democracy to
the Czech invasion. He did describe the complete occupation of
Czechoslovakia as "an act of sheer force" distinct from "taking into
the Reich Germans and German territory separated from her by
the post-war treaties." Germany and Europe's immediate future,
he believed, depended on Berlin's approach to Poland: "If Hitler
presses on to ever new and more formidable acts of aggression,
and unites the whole world against him, sooner or later, as a matter of course, Germany may collapse, and, in the doing, drag all
Europe down with her in a sea of blood." Houghton, who was distraught over Hitler's deceptions at Munich, still did not believe
that the dictator would risk everything he and Germany had gained
by invading Poland. He did not yet think Hitler "a madman"; in

fact, he perceived him as uniquely shrewd and calculating, effectively balancing caution and boldness in his foreign policies. Still, he acknowledged the possibility that Hitler "may fall a victim to the Napoleonic complex, and like a madman press on to destruction."[10]

Exactly five months later, on September 1, 1939, Germany invaded Poland and ignited World War II. The onset of the war broke Houghton's political spirit, as he and the other foreign policy architects of the New Era had failed to keep the peace. An old State Department friend, William Castle, described his former colleague as "a very sad man." Houghton supported President Roosevelt's

Alanson's portrait, hanging in the background, watches over his son's family in 1964. Amory, his son (seated center), had five children: Amo (far left), who has occupied his grandfather's New York congressional seat since 1986; Laura (standing third from left); the Rev. Alanson B. Houghton II (standing fourth from left); Elizabeth (seated far right); James (standing far right), who is currently CEO of Corning Incorporated. *Courtesy of the Houghton Family and Corning Incorporated*

general program for increased defense spending and even offered his yacht, "the good ship Lochinvar," to the U.S. Navy. But he, like most Americans, also sympathized with the 1940 Democratic platform plank that stated: "We will not participate in foreign wars, and we will not send our army, naval or air forces to fight in foreign lands outside of the Americas except in case of attack." Houghton, who had spent the previous two decades looking outward, contemplating world affairs, became increasingly introspective. "Human leadership has apparently broken down," he wrote to a friend. He began collecting and reading books on Quakerism hoping to draw inspiration from "the Friends spirit." Distraught and disillusioned, he did not like to think about war. In June 1941, nearly seventy-eight years old, he admitted to an interviewer that the United States ultimately "must fight to prevent [Britain's] defeat because [the ideological] values at stake we do not want to see endangered." The key "problem" of the future, as in the past, he stated, was whether the "three great nations"—the United States, Britain, and Germany—could "live together peaceably in the world."[11]

During the summer of 1941, Houghton worked with Jonathan Mitchell of the Institute for Advanced Study to prepare his lengthy diplomatic diary for publication. Much editing had been completed by the time of Houghton's sudden death from a heart attack on September 16. Mitchell enlisted the aid of other members of the institute to work on the manuscript. Frank Aydelotte, its new director and former president of Swarthmore College, assured Adelaide Houghton that, when published, the diary "will be received by scholars with the greatest interest and will become a source book for this important period of history." With the Houghton family's permission, Mitchell submitted a draft of the diary to the prominent Macmillan publishing house. Two months after America's entry into the war, he received a reply from H. S. Latham, a Macmillan vice president, who stated that there were "very difficult publishing problems." First, there was need of further editing. More significant was that "the tone of this diary is not altogether in harmony with today's events, for Houghton, with some reason, saw the Germany of 1922–25 as a victim." Latham continued, "We all recognize the truth of many of Houghton's comments and observations favorable to Germany of that day, but these will not be very popular reading in this country. . . . On the other hand, perhaps this is one reason why the diary is especially important now—this element of controversy in many passages written twenty years ago. As we face the possibility of a new war settlement, perhaps this has something to contribute." Yet, in the end, Latham rejected the project, and the diary was never published. The diary and the ambassador's voluminous papers were boxed and stored, and before long, Alanson B. Houghton faded from public memory. To this day, the most prominent ambassador of the New Era remains a distant historical figure, recognized by only a few scholars.[12]

No American official of the 1920s was more actively engaged in European political affairs than Alanson Houghton, and no ambassador wielded more influence. His diplomatic authority stemmed principally from two sources. As an envoy of the United States, he commanded respect by representing one of the globe's two dominant industrial powers. His exceptionally high personal standing in Germany was also decisive. The ambassador's close ties to German politicians and business leaders derived from his respect for and familiarity with German society and from his earnest commitments to promoting peace and restoring Western European prosperity.

During his three years in Berlin, Houghton had demonstrated an ability to shape certain American and German foreign policies. Besides helping to prolong the U.S. occupation of the Rhineland, he assumed a decisive role in devising and negotiating a war claims agreement that improved U.S.–German relations and won him the confidence of both governments. Washington's appreciation for the envoy as a leading German and European expert grew dramatically when his vivid forecasts of Germany's economic and political destabilization materialized. Of all his diplomatic activities, perhaps most important were his positive contributions to the Dawes Plan and the related London agreements, especially his ability to champion their acceptance in Germany. Houghton's veto of Dwight Morrow's candidacy for reparations agent general and the ambassador's direct role in the 1924 presidential election provided further evidence of his mounting influence. Speaking to students of the State Department's Foreign Service School in 1926, William Castle testified: "Mr. Houghton is a man of a very broad viewpoint. . . . We used to think he was very pro-German. . . . But, as [former] Secretary Hughes said later, if it had not been for Houghton's extreme friendliness with Germany we would have been quite hopeless."[13]

Houghton's accomplishments in Berlin led to his move to London as ambassador to the Court of St. James's. Because of his special standing with the German and American governments, he worked effectively in London as an honest broker between Germany and the Allies. In that self-appointed capacity, he played a valuable supporting role in the negotiation of the Locarno security treaties. Moreover, he was instrumental in the management of the turbulent Anglo-American relationship, and he warrants recognition for his persistent efforts to settle bilateral conflicts such as the war claims and crude rubber controversies. During his four years in London, Houghton also served Washington as a chief policy adviser on arms control, and he helped to facilitate Europe's acceptance of the Kellogg–Briand Peace Pact. Although he clearly blundered at his March 1926 press conference in Washington, the ambassador deserved his reputation as an exceptional diplomat.

Houghton's desire for American leadership on the world stage propelled his active diplomacy. After the Great War, he concluded that peace and prosperity depended upon cooperation among the leading industrial nations, especially the two predominant powers—the United States and Great Britain—and the inevitably resurgent Germany. For Houghton, America's participation in the war and its emergence as a first-rank power required that Washington be engaged in world affairs. The U.S. Senate's refusal to ratify the Treaty of Versailles and join the League of Nations did not diminish America's responsibilities as a Great Power.

Influenced by his privileged upbringing and worldly education and by his business career and congressional experience, Houghton advocated a policy approach that blended America's three competing brands of internationalism—the collective progressivism espoused by Woodrow Wilson, the unilateral progressivism touted by Republican senators William Borah and Robert La Follette, and the unilateral conservatism championed by the Harding and Coolidge administrations. Wilson generally believed that America's strategic and economic interests reached worldwide and could best be served by establishing a new global order, one based on a democratic orientation, arms control, regional and collective security, and economic expansion through freer trade and investment. The Republican party's ascendancy in the New Era thwarted the Wilsonian approach and largely restored official policy to its tradition of unilateral action in world affairs. Although favoring multilateral disarmament, the conservative internationalists who succeeded Wilson in the White House and the Republican conservatives and progressives in the Senate tended to define the nation's vital interests more conventionally and thus more narrowly, limiting them essentially to the Western Hemisphere. The Republicans eschewed participation in regional or collective security agreements in favor of unilateral political and military action. They preferred, moreover, to foster international growth in commerce and investment through "Open Door" market access and through equal-tariff treatment instead of blanket low-duty trade. Although both wings of the GOP supported unilateralism, Republican progressives such as Borah and La Follette differentiated their approach by articulating an overtly moralistic policy that broadly opposed militarism, imperialism, and big-business capitalism.

Houghton found aspects of the Republican and Wilsonian approaches to internationalism wanting, and his conception of America's postwar vital interests defined his foreign policy outlook. He considered the Republican approaches short-sighted in failing to account for fundamental shifts in the global balance of power. Its rise as a dominant financial and industrial force required the United States to assume increased responsibility for international peace and prosperity. In the New Era, he believed that Western Europe, not just the Western Hemisphere, fell within the realm of vital U.S. economic interests, and thus long-term stability depended on consistent international collaboration, especially among officials in Washington, London, and Berlin.

Although the ambassador recognized the need to alter America's traditionally conservative foreign policy, he considered Wilsonianism too drastic a shift. He opposed Wilson's plan for a military guarantee of French security, believing that a separate alliance would only bring about the formation of German counteralliances and the renewal of prewar power politics. He also feared that the punishing nature of the Versailles Treaty would stimulate a German revenge movement, and he ultimately concluded that League of Nations membership would jeopardize American sovereignty and freedom of military action. Furthermore, fearing that cheap labor and depreciated currencies abroad would undercut domestic agriculture and manufacturing during the 1920s, he objected to Wilson's desire for wholesale reductions in U.S. tariffs.

Houghton offered, instead, a policy alternative that drew from progressive and conservative approaches to postwar internationalism. He agreed with Wilson that America's prosperity depended upon Western Europe's rehabilitation and that the United States must assume more active leadership in solving international economic and political problems. To promote recovery, he advocated the cancellation of war debts, moderation in war claims, a substantial reduction in reparations, and the acceptance of European raw material monopolies. Though opposed to any radical adjustment of U.S. tariffs, he favored a fairer and more flexible duty schedule and the widespread application of the most-favored-nations principle.

At the same time, Houghton agreed with the Republican administrations that Europe's failure to recover economically would not automatically risk U.S. military security. Consequently, he supported

American political involvement in Europe short of any strategic alliance or collective security arrangement. His advocacy of a U.S. Army presence in Germany came less from a willingness to build a serious military deterrence, and more from a desire to demonstrate America's new role as a conciliator in the Old World. To help foster peace and security, the ambassador recommended that the principal powers, including the United States, execute a nonaggression pact and adopt the war referendum. Moreover, he endorsed multilateral arms control, arbitration agreements, and Great Britain's guarantee of the French and Belgian borders with Germany.

Houghton's approach to diplomacy mirrored his prewar business practice of taking the initiative, of abandoning traditional methods, and of making immediate sacrifices for long-term gains. As America's leading diplomat, he worked tirelessly to activate comparable U.S. leadership and promote compromise among the Great Powers. He often felt hindered by Republican leaders who, being more accountable to domestic economic and political priorities, refused to employ the nation's economic might and moral authority aggressively to achieve its objective of bringing peace and stability to the international community. The failure of the GOP's conservative internationalism was strikingly evident during the months before the January 1923 Ruhr crisis, when Houghton pleaded for the application of American economic power against France for refusing to accept a renegotiation of reparations. The Ruhr crisis was perhaps the most momentous world event of the 1920s, contributing to the ultimate destruction of Germany's first democratic government and the rise of Adolf Hitler. Only the United States possessed the means to prevent the French invasion of Germany's industrial heartland and the catastrophic hyperinflation that followed. The ruinous effects of the Ruhr crisis permanently weakened the Weimar Republic and strengthened radical political parties, including the Nazis. According to Gerald Feldman, the leading historian of the hyperinflation, "The direct contribution of the inflation to National Socialism and its success is difficult to measure, but the existence of such direct linkages is undeniable." Feldman adds, "Surely, the German inflation is one important reason why so many Germans defaulted not only on democracy but also on civilization itself."[14]

The German government's "passive resistance" to French aggression—a military defense was infeasible and nonresistance was politically untenable—contributed greatly to the hyperinflation. Historians have rightly criticized Germany and France for their roles in the disastrous Ruhr crisis, but too few have rebuked the United States for its intransigence. Instead, American historians, wanting to debunk the notion of U.S. isolationism in the 1920s, have routinely commended Secretary of State Hughes for his much-overdue and ineffectual December 1922 speech calling for a bankers' conference. In 1922 and during the first half of 1923, Hughes and Coolidge insisted that the United States would not intervene in the all-important reparations question because the country had no "direct" interest in the matter. They were content to let Germany's democracy and economy slide into the abyss. And yet, as the 1924 presidential election approached, America's financial claims resulting from the Great War and from the subsequent occupation of Germany suddenly constituted for the Coolidge administration a "direct" U.S. interest in the settlement of reparations. This politically motivated reversal led not only to unofficial representation on the Dawes committees but also to official government participation at the related London Conference.

Although Houghton embraced Washington's belated intervention in European politics, he believed that the Harding and Coolidge administrations had generally failed to exercise prudent and farsighted leadership and he criticized their conservative policies as inadequate for solving postwar problems. Houghton's foreign policy perspectives and his criticisms of the Republican administrations were often enlightened, but some of his recommendations were politically impractical, even fatuous. Broadly speaking, Houghton rightly understood that the United States needed to sacrifice wealth to stimulate economic recovery and to lessen international animosities. He never challenged the legitimacy of British or French imperialism, and he accepted foreign raw material monopolies and favored moderation in war claims. More important, he viewed America's forgiveness of the billions of dollars in war debts as the lynchpin mechanism for improving economic and strategic affairs. The Republican administrations and a majority in Congress, although willing to grant favorable repayment terms to the Europeans, never supported his plan to use debt forgiveness as a stimulus to economic growth and the promotion of security through multilateral arms control and nonaggression treaties. Houghton's advocacy of the war referendum as a check on international aggression, though reflective of popular opinion in the New Era, was supremely idealistic and wrongheaded.

At its core, Houghton's foreign policy approach called on Washington to accept new responsibilities in world affairs by using its economic power to promote compromise and prosperity. Clearly, the United States did not fulfill those duties satisfactorily in the 1920s, and central to that failure was diffident and parochial presidential leadership. Houghton's policy of engagement and sacrifice demanded an assertive executive, one willing to use the "bully pulpit" and manage a presumptuous Senate. Instead, Harding and Coolidge, and their secretaries of state, paid extraordinary deference to the vocal and oft-divided Congress. To be sure, even with assertive presidential leadership, Houghton's vision of swapping the war debts for security agreements and reparations reductions would have been a difficult political sell. Without bold executive action, Houghton's policies were completely unrealizable. Certainly, Houghton's diplomatic experience demonstrates both the limits of one individual's influence in world affairs and the centrality of domestic politics in the history of American foreign policy.

American historians continue to give the Republicans of the 1920s considerable credit for understanding the limits of national power. GOP leaders should be criticized for not maximizing the limits of that power. Houghton's criticism of Republican policy helps to illustrate why the United States failed to establish a stable world order in the 1920s. Above all, policymakers and most Americans failed to recognize that the scope of the country's vital economic interests had expanded to include Western Europe. As a result of their shared miscalculation, the Republicans lacked the will to intervene more fully in Europe, to lever the country's tremendous power, and to make the economic sacrifices necessary to bolster the international system. By failing to provide more active leadership and share the burdens of postwar reconstruction, the Republicans squandered critical opportunities to prevent, or mitigate, the misfortunes of the 1930s that resulted in a second world war.

Does this suggest that scholars should view U.S. foreign relations during the 1920s as isolationist? No—at least not in sweeping terms. Historians from Charles Beard to Mira Wilkins, Emily Rosenberg, and Frank Costigliola have demonstrated convincingly that America's economic activity and cultural influence abroad expanded dramatically during the postwar decade. Moreover, the Harding and Coolidge administrations were actively involved in maintaining stability in Latin America and aggressively pursued multilateral arms control agreements. The Republicans considered success on both of these issues essential to safeguarding and enhancing vital American interests. On the other hand, there were isolationist tendencies. Republicans failed to join the League of Nations and the World Court, and because of the refusal to elevate the priority of European stability to new heights, their most active involvement in the Old World (beyond arms control), namely, the Dawes Plan and Kellogg-Briand Pact, came slowly and reluctantly, and with severe limitations.

As a result of this dichotomy, many historians have adopted Joan Hoff-Wilson's dated catchphrase, "independent internationalism," to describe the Republican approach to world affairs in the 1920s. At best, this label works as a simplistic description. Admittedly, it is superior to the misnomer of "isolationism," but the phrase is historically inadequate and misleading. Scholars should emphasize the conservative and circumscribed nature of official Republican internationalism that Ambassador Houghton so frequently castigated.[15]

Notes

1. *New York Times*, February 7 and 9, 1930.

2. Moulton to Adelaide Houghton, October 23, 1941, Houghton Papers.

3. *Institute for Advanced Study Bulletin*, no. 2, Institute for Advanced Study Archives, Princeton, NJ (hereafter cited as IAS Archives).

4. Alanson Houghton to Amory Houghton, June 13, 1940, Houghton Papers.

5. *New York Sun*, November 12, 1931.

6. Houghton to Amory Houghton, July 2, 1931, Houghton Papers; Houghton, "The Permanent Court of International Justice" (speech), January 11, 1931, ibid.

7. Houghton, "St. Andrew's Day Dinner" (speech), November 30, 1935, ibid.

8. Houghton to Abraham Flexner, April 8, 1933, IAS Archives; Houghton to Nicholas Murray Butler, June 1, 1933, Carnegie Endowment Archives, Columbia University, New York; *New York Times*, May 10, 1935, and May 21, 1937.

9. Houghton to Nicholas Murray Butler, June 1, 1933, Carnegie Endowment Archives; Houghton, "Literary Society—Post-war Germany" (speech), April 1, 1939, Houghton Papers.

10. Houghton, "Literary Society" (speech), April 1, 1939, Houghton Papers.

11. Castle Diary, May 30, 1940; Houghton to Amory Houghton, June 7, 1941, Houghton Papers; Kirk H. Porter and Donald B. Johnson, eds., *National Party Platforms, 1840–1972* (Urbana, IL, 1973), 382; Houghton to Flexner, March 28, 1940, IAS Archives; Mitchell interview, June 4, 1941, Houghton Papers.

12. Aydelotte to Adelaide Houghton, October 14, 1941, IAS Archives; Latham to Mitchell, February 16, 1942, Oswald Garrison Villard Papers, Houghton Library, Harvard University.

13. Castle speech to Foreign Service School, March 20, 1926, NARG59 (Stack Area) 250/46/08/05-06, Box 5.

14. Gerald D. Feldman, *The Great Disorder: Politics, Economics, and Society in the German Inflation, 1914–1924* (New York, 1997), 854, 858.

15. Joan Hoff-Wilson, *American Business and Foreign Policy* (Lexington, KY, 1971). The use of Hoff-Wilson's "independent internationalism" is especially prevalent in textbook surveys of U.S. foreign relations; see Howard Jones, *Crucible of Power: A History of Foreign Relations from 1897* (Wilmington, DE, 2001), 112; Thomas G. Paterson et al., *American Foreign Relations: A History since 1895* (Boston, 2000, 5th ed.), 113; and Walter LaFeber, *The American Age: United States Foreign Policy at Home and Abroad since 1750* (New York, 1989), 318. Even Robert D. Schulzinger's *U.S. Diplomacy since 1900* (New York, 2002, 5th ed.) emphasizes America's "independent internationalism" and "independent foreign policy," despite his titling the 1920s chapter "The Triumph of Conservative Internationalism," 125–45.

Bibliographical Essay

For scholars interested in Alanson B. Houghton, there is a rich historical record. The single most important source of information is his manuscript collection at the Corning Incorporated archives in Corning, New York. These papers, still controlled by the Houghton family, are especially helpful for Houghton's ambassadorial years. The extensive collection includes personal, business, and diplomatic correspondence, political and diplomatic speeches, his ambassadorial diary, newspaper clippings, and State Department telegrams. Other document collections containing significant information on Houghton are the General Records of the State Department, Record Group 59, National Archives, College Park, Maryland; the General Records of the British Foreign Office, Record Group 371, Public Records Office, London–Kew Gardens; the William R. Castle Papers in the Herbert Hoover Presidential Library–Museum, West Branch, Iowa; the Frank O. Lowden Papers in the University of Chicago Library; and the Oswald G. Villard Papers in the Houghton Library at Harvard. (Alanson's nephew, Arthur A. Houghton Jr., was the benefactor of the Houghton Library, which opened in 1942.)

Other helpful document collections include the Economic-Reparations Records in the Political Archive of the German Foreign Ministry, Bonn, Germany; the Joseph C. Grew Papers and the William Phillips Papers in the Houghton Library at Harvard; the Warren G. Harding Papers at the Ohio Historical Society, Columbus, Ohio; the William Borah Papers, the Calvin Coolidge Papers, the Charles Evans Hughes Papers, and the Chandler P. Anderson Papers at the Library of Congress in Washington, DC; the Fred I. Kent Papers at the Princeton University Library; the Owen D. Young Papers at the Owen D. Young Library, St. Lawrence University, Canton, New York; the Houghton Papers at the Institute for Advanced Study Library, Princeton, New Jersey; the Houghton file, the James T. Shotwall file, and the Nicholas Murray Butler file in the Carnegie Endowment for International Peace Records at Columbia University, New York; the Frank B. Kellogg Papers at the Minnesota

Historical Society, St. Paul, Minnesota; and the Herbert Hoover Papers and the Hugh R. Wilson Papers at the Hoover Presidential Library.

Newspapers, periodicals, memoirs, and published government records also provide key information on Houghton's business, political, and diplomatic activities. The best sources for Houghton's two congressional terms are reports from his two House committees, including the Committee on Ways and Means, *Hearings on Internal-Revenue Revision*, 67th Congress, 1st session, 1921; *Hearings on American Valuation*, 67th Congress, 1st session, 1921; the Committee on Foreign Affairs, *Hearings on Diplomatic and Consular Appropriations Bill*, 66th Congress, 2d session, 1920; *Hearings on Disarmament*, 66th Congress, 3d session, 1921; and *Hearings on Conditions in Russia*, 66th Congress, 3d session, 1921. Helpful for understanding his ambassadorial work are the related volumes of *Akten Der Reichskanzlei, Weimarer Republik* (Boppard on the Rhine, 1968–1977); *Documents on British Foreign Policy, 1919–1939* (London, 1966–1977); and *Papers Relating to the Foreign Relations of the United States, 1920–1929* (Washington, DC, 1934–1949). Insightful memoirs include Henry T. Allen, *My Rhineland Journal* (Boston, 1923); Allen, *The Rhineland Occupation* (Indianapolis, 1927); Viscount Edgar Vincent D'Abernon, *The Diary of an Ambassador* (Garden City, New York, 1929–1931); Charles G. Dawes, *Notes as Vice President, 1928–29* (Boston, 1935); Dawes, *A Journal of Reparations* (London, 1939); Robert Murphy, *Diplomat among Warriors* (New York, 1964); and George Santayana, *Persons and Places* (New York, 1944–1953). Among the many newspapers and periodicals covering Houghton's activities are the *Corning Evening Leader* (New York), the *Elmira-Star Gazette* (New York), the *Elmira Advertiser*, the *Philadelphia Public Ledger*, the *New York Times*, the *New York World*, the *St. Louis Post-Dispatch*, the *New York Journal-American*, the *Washington Star*, the *Baltimore Sun*, the London *Times*, *The New Republic*, *The Independent*, *Time*, and *The Nation*.

Feature newspaper articles on Houghton the diplomat include James B. Morrow, "A Business Man Ambassador," *Nation's Business* 10 (June 1922): 18–19; "A Business Man As Ambassador to Germany," *Current Opinion* 2 (August 1922): 193–95; Horace Green, "An Unloquacious Ambassador: Alanson B. Houghton, Who Practices Diplomatic Silence in Berlin," *New York Times Magazine* (November 4, 1923): 10; Frank H. Simonds, "After Locarno—A New Era," *American Review of Reviews* 72 (December 1925): 593–605; Frederick L. Collins, "Abroad with Our Ambassadors II—The Ablest

American in Europe," *Woman's Home Companion* 5 (January 1926): 15, 60; Collins, "Under the High Hats," *Collier's, The National Weekly* 77 (March 13, 1926): 8–9, 41; and T.R.Y., "He Snips the Red Tape from Diplomacy," *New York Times*, August 14, 1927.

The Houghton family has published books and articles beneficial to historians. John W. Houghton, Alanson's distant cousin, prepared a detailed family record through 1911, *The Houghton Genealogy: The Descendants of Ralph and John Houghton of Lancaster, Massachusetts* (New York, 1912). Alanson's nephew, Arthur A. Houghton Jr., wrote a delightful, anecdotal family history, *Remembrances* (Queenstown, MD, 1986). Alanson's wife's diary was published as *The London Years: The Diary of Adelaide Wellington Houghton, 1925–1929* (New York, 1963). Alanson's own publications include multiple articles in the *Harvard Monthly* (1886); *Seven Tables: Illustrating in Some Points the Extent of Governmental Interference in Great Britain and the United States* (London, 1888); "Italian Finances from 1860–1884," *Quarterly Journal of Economics* (January 1889 and April 1889): 233–58, 373–402; "Travel, Study, and Play in Europe," *Christian Science Monitor*, April 30, 1925; "War? Let the People Decide!" *Federal Council Bulletin* 10 (September 1927): 9–10; "The Power of the People," *Goodwill: A Review of International Christian Friendship, Life, and Work* 3 (1928): 20–23; "The Causes of Anglo-American Differences: III—An American Plea for Understanding," *Current History* 30 (May 1929): 203–5; "The Permanent Court of International Justice," *Commission on International Justice and Goodwill* (New York, 1931); "Germany on the Brink," *The Nation* (July 1, 1931): 7–8; "Address by the Honorable Alanson B. Houghton," *International Conciliation Special Bulletin* (December 1931): 21–24; "Disarmament and Depression," *The Nation* (December 23, 1931): 695.

Until recently, historians knew little of Houghton's business career at Corning Glass Works. There are two informative dissertations available: Regina L. Blaszczyk, "Imagining Consumers: Manufacturing and Markets in Ceramic and Glass, 1865–1965," Ph.D. diss., University of Delaware, 1995; and Jeffrey J. Matthews, "The Pursuit of Progress: Alanson B. Houghton, Corning Glass Works, and America as a World Power, 1863–1941," Ph.D. diss., University of Kentucky, 2000. The Houghton family and officials at Corning Incorporated recently oversaw and underwrote the publication of two high-quality company histories: Davis Dyer and Daniel Gross, *The Generations of Corning: The Life and Times of a Global Corporation* (Oxford, 2001); and Margaret B. W. Graham and Alec T. Shuldiner, *Corning and the Craft of Innovation* (Oxford, 2001). My review of the

Dyer and Gross volume can be found in *Technology and Culture* 43 (April 2002): 445–46.

The secondary literature analyzing American foreign policy in the 1920s is voluminous, and Houghton's diplomatic and political activity is commonly minimized or overlooked entirely. This occurred in large part because Houghton was not the subject of a biographer, he never published his ambassadorial diary, and his descendents limited access to his personal papers, which were not organized by archivists until the 1980s. In the historical literature where Houghton does appear, the focus is almost exclusively on his Berlin experience. Nevertheless, there are some important assessments of the ambassador's diplomacy. German historians, who were the first to write extensively on U.S.–German relations during the 1920s, were also the first to recognize the ambassador's considerable influence. See Dieter Bruno Gescher, *Die Vereinigten Staaten von Nordamerika und die Reparationen, 1920–1924: Eine Untersuchung der Reparationsfrage auf der Grundlage amerikanischer Akten* (Bonn, 1956); Robert Gottwald, *Die deutsch–amerikanischen Beziehungen in der Ära Stresemann* (Berlin, 1965); and Werner Link, *Die amerikanische Stabilisierungspolitik* (Düsseldorf, 1970). A more recent German perspective is taken by Manfred Berg, *Gustav Stresemann und die Vereinigten Staaten von Amerika: Weltwirtschaftliche Verflechtung und Revisionspolitik, 1907–1929* (Baden-Baden, 1990). The one American scholar ahead of his German peers was William McHenry Franklin, who interviewed Houghton several times for his Tufts University doctoral dissertation, "The Origins of the Locarno Conference," 1941.

Other instructive secondary works analyzing aspects of Houghton's diplomacy are: F. G. Stambrook, " 'Resourceful in Expedients'— Some Examples of Ambassadorial Policy Making in the Inter-War Period," *Canadian Historical Association's Historical Papers* (1973): 301–20; Ernest C. Bolt Jr., *Ballots before Bullets: The War Referendum Approach to Peace in America, 1914–1941* (Charlottesville, VA, 1977); Sander A. Diamond, "Ein Amerikaner In Berlin Aus Den Papieren Des Botschafters Alanson B. Houghton, 1922–1925," *Vierteljahrshefte Für Zeitgeschichte* 27 (July 1979): 431–70; Diamond, *Herr Hitler: Amerikas Diplomaten, Washington, und der Untergang Weimars* (Düsseldorf, 1985); Hermann J. Rupieper, "Alanson B. Houghton: An American Ambassador in Germany, 1922–25," *International History Review* 1 (October 1979): 490–508; Rupieper, *The Cuno Government and Reparations, 1922–23: Politics and Economics* (The Hague, 1979); Frank Costigliola, "The Politics of Financial Stabilization:

American Reconstruction Policy in Europe, 1924–30," Ph.D. diss., Cornell University, 1973; Costigliola, "The United States and the Reconstruction of Germany in the 1920s," *Business History Review* 50 (Winter 1976): 477–502; Costigliola, *Awkward Dominion: American Political, Economic, and Cultural Relations with Europe, 1919–1933* (Ithaca, NY, 1984); Kenneth Paul Jones, "Discord and Collaboration: Choosing an Agent General for Reparations," *Diplomatic History* 1 (Spring 1977); Jones, "Alanson B. Houghton and the Ruhr Crisis: The Diplomacy of Power and Morality," in *U.S. Diplomats in Europe, 1919–1941,* ed. Kenneth Paul Jones (Santa Barbara, CA, 1981), 24–39. The most recent Houghton scholarship is Jeffrey J. Matthews' "The Businessman Diplomat: A. B. Houghton, A Case Study," *Business and Economic History* 28 (Winter 1999): 137–44; and his "Industrialist Turned Diplomat: The 1926 Houghton Controversy and the Limits of U.S. Policy toward Europe," *Mid-America: An Historical Review* 83 (Winter 2001): 5–38.

There are a great many biographies (although some are outdated) of the major actors in American foreign policy during the 1920s. For Harding, see Eugene P. Trani and David L. Wilson, *The Presidency of Warren G. Harding* (Lawrence, KS, 1977); Robert K. Murray, *The Harding Era: Warren G. Harding and His Administration* (Minneapolis, MN, 1969); Francis Russell, *The Shadow of Blooming Grove: Warren G. Harding in His Times* (New York, 1968); and Andrew Sinclair, *The Available Man: The Life behind the Masks of Warren Gamaliel Harding* (New York, 1965). For Hughes, see, David J. Danelski and Joseph S. Tulchin, eds. *The Autobiographical Notes of Charles Evans Hughes* (Cambridge, MA, 1973); Betty Glad, *Charles Evans Hughes and the Illusions of Innocence: A Study in American Diplomacy* (Urbana, IL, 1966); Dexter Perkins, *Charles Evans Hughes and American Democratic Statesmanship* (Boston, 1956); and Merlo J. Pusey, *Charles Evans Hughes* (New York, 1951). For Coolidge, see Robert H. Ferrell, *The Presidency of Calvin Coolidge* (Lawrence, KS, 1998); Robert Sobel, *Coolidge: An America Enigma* (Washington, DC, 1998); Donald R. McCoy, *Calvin Coolidge: The Quiet President* (New York, 1967); and Claude M. Fuess, *Calvin Coolidge: The Man from Vermont* (Hamden, CT, 1939). For Kellogg, see Robert H. Ferrell, *Frank B. Kellogg and Henry Stimson* (New York, 1963); L. Ethan Ellis, *Frank B. Kellogg and American Foreign Relations, 1925–1929* (New Brunswick, NJ, 1961); and David Bryn-Jones, *Frank B. Kellogg: A Biography* (New York, 1937). For Hoover, see Martin L. Fausold, *The Presidency of Herbert C. Hoover* (Lawrence, KS, 1985); Richard Norton Smith, *An Uncommon Man: The Triumph of Herbert Hoover* (New York,

1984); David Burner, *Herbert Hoover* (New York, 1978); and Joan Hoff-Wilson, *Herbert Hoover: Forgotten Progressive* (Boston, 1975). For Dawes, see Bascom N. Timmons, *Portrait of an American: Charles G. Dawes* (New York, 1953).

For senators influential in setting the 1920s U.S. foreign policy, see Nancy C. Unger, *Fighting Bob La Follette: The Righteous Reformer* (Chapel Hill, NC, 2000); Karen A. J. Miller, *Populist Nationalism: Republican Insurgency and American Foreign Policy Making, 1918–1925* (Westport, CT, 1999); Robert D. Johnson, *The Peace Progressives and American Foreign Relations* (Cambridge, MA, 1995); Michael Weatherson and Hal W. Bochin, *Hiram Johnson: Political Revivalist* (Lanham, MD, 1995); Richard C. Lower, *A Bloc of One: The Political Career of Hiram W. Johnson* (Stanford, CA, 1993); William C. Widenor, *Henry Cabot Lodge and the Search for American Foreign Policy* (Los Angeles, 1980); Robert J. Maddox, *William E. Borah and American Foreign Policy* (Baton Rouge, LA, 1969); Wayne Cole, *Senator Gerald P. Nye and American Foreign Relations* (Minneapolis, 1962); and John Vinson, *William E. Borah and the Outlawry of War* (Athens, GA, 1957).

For information on several of Houghton's confidants and other New Era diplomats, see Thomas Neville Bonner, *Iconoclast: Abraham Flexner and a Life of Learning* (Baltimore, 2002); Alfred L. Castle, *Diplomatic Realism: William R. Castle, Jr., and American Foreign Policy, 1919–1953* (Honolulu, 1998); Josephine Young Case and Everett Needham Case, *Owen D. Young and the American Enterprise: A Biography* (Boston, 1982); Harold Josephson, *James T. Shotwell and the Rise of Internationalism in America* (Rutherford, NJ, 1974); William T. Hutchinson, *Lowden of Illinois: The Life of Frank O. Lowden* (Chicago, 1957); Kenneth Paul Jones, ed., *U.S. Diplomats in Europe, 1919–1941* (Santa Barbara, CA, 1981); and Gordon A. Craig and Felix Gilbert, eds., *The Diplomats, 1919–1939* (Princeton, 1953, 1994).

An advantageous starting point for studying 1920s American foreign policy is Brian McKercher's "Reaching for the Brass Ring: The Recent Historiography of Interwar American Foreign Relations," in *Paths to Power: The Historiography of American Foreign Relations to 1941*, ed. Michael J. Hogan (Cambridge, 2000), 176–223. Other historiographic overviews include Jon Jacobson, "Is There a New International History of the 1920s?" *American Historical Review* 88 (1983): 617–45; John Braeman, "The New Left and American Foreign Policy during the Age of Normalcy: A Re-examination," *Business History Review* 57 (Spring 1983): 73–104; Braeman, "Power and Diplomacy: The 1920's Reappraised," *Review of Politics* 44 (July 1982): 342–69; Braeman, "American Foreign Policy in the Age of

Normalcy: Three Historiographical Traditions," *Amerikastudien/ American Studies* 26 (November 1981): 125–58; Ernest C. Bolt Jr., "Isolation, Expansion and Peace: American Foreign Policy between the Wars," in *American Foreign Relations, A Historiographical Review*, ed. Gerald K. Haines and J. Samuel Walker (Westport, CT, 1981), 133–57; and Robert James Maddox, "Another Look at the Legend of Isolationism in the 1920's," *Mid-America: An Historical Review* 53 (January 1971): 35–43.

For the conventional interpretation of the 1920s as a broadly isolationist decade, see Samuel Flagg Bemis, *A Diplomatic History, 1900–1950* (New York, 1950), and George Kennan, *American Diplomacy, 1900–1950* (Chicago, 1951). For William Appleman Williams, who challenged that view in light of American economic expansionism, see "The Legend of Isolationism in the 1920s," *Science and Society* 18 (Winter 1954): 1–20; Williams, "A Note on United States Foreign Policy in Europe in the 1920s," *Science and Society* 22 (Winter 1958): 1–20; and Williams, *The Tragedy of American Diplomacy* (Cleveland, 1959, 1962, 1972, 1984). Other so-called New Left historians supported Williams; see Carl P. Parrini, *Heir to Empire: United States Economic Diplomacy, 1916–1923* (Pittsburgh, 1969); Robert Freeman Smith, *The United States and Revolutionary Nationalism in Mexico, 1916–1932* (Chicago, 1972); and Lloyd C. Gardner, Walter F. LaFeber, and Thomas J. McCormick, *Creation of the American Empire: U.S. Diplomatic History* (Chicago, 1973, 1976).

Many other scholars publishing before 1970 noted America's attempts to avoid multilateral political commitments, but also recognized its continued involvement in world affairs. These scholars were less inclined to see Republican foreign policy as a blueprint for economic imperialism; see Herbert Feis, *The Diplomacy of the Dollar: First Era, 1919–1932* (Baltimore, 1950, 1965); Robert H. Ferrell, *Peace in Their Time: The Origins of the Kellogg-Briand Pact* (New Haven, 1952, 1968); Ferrell, *American Diplomacy, A History* (New York, 1959, 1975); Robert E. Osgood, *Ideals and Self-Interest in American Foreign Relations: The Great Transformation of the Twentieth Century* (Chicago, 1953); Foster Rhea Dulles, *America's Rise to World Power, 1898–1954* (New York, 1955, 1963); Selig Adler, *The Isolationist Impulse: Its Twentieth-Century Reaction* (New York, 1957, 1966); Adler, *The Uncertain Giant, 1921–1941: American Foreign Policy between the Wars* (New York, 1965); John D. Hicks, *Republican Ascendancy, 1921–1933* (New York, 1960, 1963); Joseph Brandes, *Herbert Hoover and Economic Diplomacy: Department of Commerce Policy, 1921–1928* (Pittsburgh, 1962, 1975); Akira Iriye, *After Imperialism: The Search for a*

New Order in the Far East, 1921–1931 (Cambridge, MA, 1965); and L. Ethan Ellis, *Republican Foreign Policy, 1921–1933* (New Brunswick, NJ, 1968).

Building on these older works and benefiting from new archival material, Joan Hoff-Wilson, Michael J. Hogan, Frank Costigliola, and Melvyn P. Leffler wrote classic monographs on 1920s U.S. foreign policy. Hoff-Wilson's *American Business and Foreign Policy* (Lexington, KY, 1971) uncovered the business community's widely divergent interests in foreign affairs, and she argued convincingly that New Left scholars had exaggerated the degree of foreign policy coordination between government and business leaders. Her lasting characterization of U.S. foreign policy as "independent internationalism" owed much to the scholarship of preceding historians, especially the work of Selig Adler. Hogan's *Informal Entente: The Private Structure of the Cooperation in Anglo-American Economic Diplomacy, 1918–1928* (Columbia, MO, 1977, 1991) again emphasized the degree of cooperation between business and government and developed fully the concept and practice of corporatism in American foreign relations (an idea suggested by W. A. Williams decades earlier). Ellis W. Hawley's *The Great War and the Search for Modern Order: A History of the American People and Their Institutions, 1917–1933* (New York, 1979), and Emily Rosenberg's *Spreading the American Dream: American Economic and Cultural Expansion, 1890–1945* (New York, 1982) applied this same "associationalist" framework but much more broadly. Costigliola's *Awkward Dominion: American Political, Economic, and Cultural Relations with Europe, 1919–1933* (Ithaca, NY, 1984) emphasized the "flawed genius" of Republican foreign policy, which attempted to promote world peace and increase American economic and cultural influence abroad, but without assuming international political responsibilities. Melvyn P. Leffler's work demonstrates the keenest understanding of 1920s American foreign policy. His scholarship focuses on the complex influence of domestic imperatives and the narrow conceptions of national interests that weakened Republican attempts to contribute to the postwar peace. He also provides the most penetrating assessment of Hoover's strident nationalism. See Leffler, *The Elusive Quest: America's Pursuit of European Stability and French Security, 1919–1933* (Chapel Hill, NC, 1979), and his other works: "Herbert Hoover, The 'New Era,' and American Foreign Policy, 1921–29," in *Herbert Hoover as Secretary of Commerce: Studies in New Era Thought and Practice*, ed. Ellis W. Hawley (Iowa City, 1981), 148–79; "1921–

1932: Expansionist Impulses and Domestic Constraints," in *Economics and World Power: An Assessment of American Diplomacy since 1789*, ed. William H. Becker and Samuel F. Wells Jr. (New York, 1984), 225–75; "American Policy Making and European Stability, 1921–1933," *Pacific Historical Review* 46 (May 1977): 207–28; "Political Isolationism, Economic Expansionism, or Diplomatic Realism: American Policy toward Western Europe, 1921–1933," *Perspectives in American History* 59 (December 1972): 585–601; and "The Origins of Republican War Debt Policy, 1921–1923: A Case Study in the Applicability of the Open Door Interpretation," *Journal of American History* 59 (December 1972): 585–601.

More recent scholarship focusing on U.S. foreign policy in the 1920s includes that of Margot Louria, *Triumph and Downfall: America's Pursuit of Peace and Prosperity, 1921–1933* (Westport, CT, 2001); Benjamin D. Rhodes, *United States Foreign Policy in the Interwar Period, 1918–1941: The Golden Age of American Diplomatic and Military Complacency* (Westport, CT, 2001); Emily S. Rosenberg, *Financial Missionaries to the World: The Politics and Culture of Dollar Diplomacy, 1900–1930* (Cambridge, MA, 1999); Akira Iriye, *The Globalizing of America, 1913–1945* (Cambridge, MA, 1993); and Warren I. Cohen, *Empire without Tears: American Foreign Relations, 1921–1933* (New York, 1987). Louria's book often veers on hagiography in its depiction of Republican leaders, especially of Hughes, and it lacks an appreciation for the formidable literature on 1920s U.S. and international diplomacy. In contrast, Rhodes offers a more nuanced reading of U.S. foreign policy and of the historiography. He is on the mark with his critical portrayal of Republican policy and its shifts between complacency and pragmatism. Rosenberg's detailed monograph is a sophisticated analysis of the extensive international activities of American private bankers and financial experts. It adheres to the Williams school of U.S. financial imperialism and the corporatist theme of business–government cooperation. Iriye and Cohen successfully synthesize much of the literature on the 1920s. Cohen, however, overstates the extent of the Republican commitment to solving world political problems, and Iriye, like Rosenberg, makes the all-too-common mistake of understating the role of official diplomats. In his recent survey of twentieth-century U.S. foreign policy, Frank Ninkovich tends to overstate the "warming" of U.S.–Latin American relations in the 1920s and he gives Hoover far too much credit for understanding the "indispensability" of Europe to American interests, but his general conclusion on the 1920s is sound—the Republicans practiced an anemic political policy of "uncommitted internationalism" in conjunction with a disabling, "halfhearted" economic internationalism. See Ninkovich, *The Wilsonian Century: U.S. Foreign Policy since 1900* (Chicago, 1999).

For studies of the American Foreign Service and the foreign policy establishment, see Priscilla Roberts, " 'All the Right People': The Historiography of the American Foreign Policy Establishment," *Journal of American Studies* 26 (December 1992): 409–34; Roberts, "The Anglo-American Theme: American Visions of an Atlantic Alliance, 1914–1933," *Diplomatic History* 21 (Summer 1997): 333–64; Michael Wala, *The Council on Foreign Relations and American Foreign Policy in the Early Cold War* (Providence, RI, 1994); Robert Schulzinger, *The Making of the Diplomatic Mind: The Training, Outlook, and Style of the United States Foreign Service Officers, 1908–1931* (Middletown, CT, 1975); Schulzinger, *The Wise Men of Foreign Affairs: The History of the Council on Foreign Relations* (New York, 1984); Martin Weil, *A Pretty Good Club: The Founding Fathers of the United States U.S. Foreign Service* (New York, 1978); Waldo H. Heinrichs, *American Ambassador: Joseph C. Grew and the Development of the United States Diplomatic Tradition* (Boston, 1966, 1986); and Richard Hume Werking, *The Master Architects: Building the United States Foreign Service, 1890–1913* (Lexington, KY, 1977).

For American business and cultural expansion in the 1920s, see Rosenberg's *Financial Missionaries to the World* and *Spreading the American Dream*; Iriye's *The Globalizing of America, 1913–1945*; Costigliola's *Awkward Dominion*; and Mira Wilkins, *The Maturing of Multinational Enterprise: American Business Abroad from 1914 to 1970* (Cambridge, MA, 1974).

For studies of American isolationism, relations with the League of Nations and the World Court, and the peace movement, see Warren F. Kuehl and Lynne K. Dunn, *Keeping the Covenant: American Internationalists and League of Nations, 1920–1939* (Kent, OH, 1997); Hariot H. Alonso, *The Women's Peace Union and the Outlawry of War* (Knoxville, TN, 1989, 1997); Justus D. Doenecke and John E. Wilz, *From Isolation to War, 1931–1940* (Arlington Heights, IL, 1991); Michael Dunne, *The United States and the World Court* (London, 1988); Thomas Guinsburg, *The Pursuit of Isolationism in the United States Senate from Versailles to Pearl Harbor* (New York, 1982); Charles DeBenedetti, *Origins of the Modern American Peace Movement, 1915–1929* (Millwood, NY, 1978); and Selig Adler, *The Isolationist Impulse: Its Twentieth-Century Reaction* (New York, 1957, 1966).

For analyses of interwar disarmament conferences, see Carolyn J. Kitching, *Britain and the Problem of International Disarmament, 1919–34* (London, 1999); Phillips Payson O'Brien, *British and American Naval Power: Politics and Policy, 1900–1936* (Westport, CT, 1998); Richard W. Fanning, *Peace and Disarmament: Naval Rivalry and Arms Control, 1922–1933* (Lexington, KY, 1995); Emily O. Goldman, *Sunken Treaties: Naval Arms Control between the Wars* (University Park, PA, 1994); B. J. C. McKercher, ed., *Arms Limitation and Disarmament, 1899–1939: Restraints on War* (New York, 1992); and Christopher Hall, *Britain, America, and Arms Control, 1921–37* (New York, 1987).

For interwar European diplomacy, see Sally Marks, *The Ebbing of European Ascendancy: An International History of the World, 1914–1945* (London, 2002); Marks, *The Illusion of Peace: International Relations in Europe, 1918–1933* (London, 1976, 2003), and Charles S. Maier, *Recasting Bourgeois Europe: Stabilization in France, Germany, and Italy in the Decade after World War I* (Princeton, 1975, 1988). Marks's work on the 1920s is unsurpassed in quality and breadth of scope. For more on France, see Stephen A. Schuker, *The End of French Predominance in Europe: The Financial Crisis of 1924 and the Adoption of the Dawes Plan* (Chapel Hill, NC, 1976); P. M. H. Bell, *France and Britain, 1900–1940: Entente and Estrangement* (London, 1996); and A. Adamthwaite, *Grandeur and Misery: France's Bid for Power in Europe, 1914–1940* (London, 1995). On German politics and diplomacy, see Jonathan Wright, *Gustav Stresemann: Weimar's Greatest Statesman* (Oxford, England, 2002); Gerald D. Feldman, *The Great Disorder: Politics, Economics, and Society in the German Inflation, 1914–1924* (New York, 1997); V. R. Berghahn, *Modern Germany: Society, Economy, and Politics in the Twentieth Century* (Cambridge, 1987); William C. McNeil, *American Money and the Weimar Republic: Economics and Politics on the Eve of the Great Depression* (New York, 1986); Stephen A. Schuker, *American "Reparations" to Germany, 1919–33* (Princeton, 1988); Manfred Jonas, *The United States and Germany: A Diplomatic History* (Ithaca, NY, 1984); Peter H. Buckingham, *International Normalcy: The Open Door Peace with the Former Central Powers, 1921–1929* (Wilmington, DE, 1983); Hans W. Gatzke, *Germany and the United States: A "Special Relationship"?* (Cambridge, MA, 1980); Gatzke, *Stresemann and the Rearmament of Germany* (Baltimore, 1954, 1969); Robert P. Grathwol, *Stresemann and the DNVP: Reconciliation or Revenge in German Foreign Policy, 1924–1928* (Lawrence, KS, 1980); Keith L. Nelson, *Victors Divided: America and the Allies in Germany, 1918–1923* (Berkeley, 1975); Jon Jacobson, *Locarno Diplomacy:*

Germany and the West, 1925–1929 (Princeton, 1972); and Peter Berg, *Deutschland und Amerika, 1918–1929: Über das deutsche Amerikabild der zwanziger Jahre* (Lübeck and Hamburg, 1963).

For understanding British diplomacy and U.S.-British relations, I relied heavily on Brian J. C. McKercher, *Transition of Power: Britain's Loss of Global Pre-eminence to the United States, 1930–1945* (Cambridge, 1999); McKercher and L. Aronsen, eds., *The North Atlantic Triangle in a Changing World: Anglo-American–Canadian Relations, 1902–1956* (Toronto, 1996); McKercher, ed., *Arms Limitation and Disarmament, 1899–1939: Restraints on War* (New York, 1992); McKercher, ed., *Anglo-American Relations in the 1920s: The Struggle for Supremacy* (London, 1991); McKercher, *Esme Howard: A Diplomatic Biography* (Cambridge, 1989); McKercher, *The Second Baldwin Government and the United States, 1924–1929: Attitudes and Diplomacy* (Cambridge, 1984); and McKercher and D. J. Moss, eds., *Shadow and Substance in British Foreign Policy, 1895–1939: Memorial Essays Honouring C. J. Lowe* (Edmonton, Can., 1984). Also see John E. Moser, *Twisting the Lion's Tail: American Anglophobia between the World Wars* (New York, 1999); Richard S. Grayson, *Austen Chamberlain and the Commitment to Europe: British Foreign Policy, 1924–1929* (London, 1997); and Hogan, *Informal Entente.*

For studies of U.S. relations with Soviet Russia, Asia, and Latin America, I relied upon Melvyn P. Leffler, *The Specter of Communism: The United States and the Origins of the Cold War, 1917–1953* (New York, 1994); Jon Jacobson, *When the Soviet Union Entered World Politics* (Berkeley, 1994); Christine A. White, *British and American Commercial Relations with Soviet Russia, 1918–1924* (Chapel Hill, NC, 1992); Akira Iriye, *The Origins of the Second World War in Asia and the Pacific* (London, 1987); Iriye, *Across the Pacific: An Inner History of American–East Asian Relations* (New York, 1967); Iriye, *After Imperialism: The Search for a New Order in the Far East, 1921–1931* (Cambridge, MA, 1965); Kyle Longley, *In the Eagle's Shadow: The United States and Latin America* (Wheeling, IL, 2002); David F. Schmitz, *Thank God They're on Our Side: The United States and Right-Wing Dictatorships, 1921–1965* (Chapel Hill, NC, 1999); and Walter LaFeber, *Inevitable Revolutions: The United States in Central America* (New York, 1983, 1993).

Index